# DROPOUTS FROM SCHOOL

SUNY Series
# FRONTIERS IN EDUCATION
*Philip G. Altbach, Editor*

The Frontiers in Education Series features and draws upon a range of disciplines and approaches in the analysis of educational issues and concerns, helping to reinterpret established fields of scholarship in education by encouraging the latest synthesis and research.

Other books in this series include:

*Dropouts from School*

Issues, Dilemmas, and Solutions

Edited by Lois Weis, Eleanor Farrar
and Hugh G. Petrie

*State University of New York Press*

*Published by*
*State University of New York Press, Albany*

Printed in the United States of America

For information, address State University of New York
Press, State University Plaza, Albany, NY 12246

Library of Congress Cataloging-in-Publication Data

Dropouts from school.

   (SUNY series, frontiers in education)
   Bibliography: p.
   Includes index.
   1. High school dropouts—United States.   2. Socially
handicapped youth—Education (Secondary)—United States.
3. Minorities—Education (Secondary)—United States.
I. Weis, Lois.   II. Farrar, Eleanor.   III. Petrie,
Hugh G.   IV. Series.
LC146.6.D76   1989   373.12'913'0973   88-34932
ISBN 0-7914-0108-1
ISBN 0-7914-0109-X (pbk.)

10 9 8 7 6 5 4 3 2 1

# Contents

# Acknowledgments

Numerous people provided assistance as this volume took shape. Sharon Hladczuk and Sandra Mitchell copyedited the manuscripts, and Carol Norris and Marilyn Faulise provided much-needed secretarial assistance. Our sincere thanks to all those who encouraged and enabled us to bring this volume to press.

# Introduction

## LOIS WEIS, ELEANOR FARRAR, AND HUGH G. PETRIE

Within the past several years, school dropouts has emerged once again as a significant issue.* Although the primary focus in American education is currently excellence, it has become increasingly clear that a large number of students do not make it through school at all. A relatively high proportion of these students are racial and linguistic minorities who reside in our central cities, although dropping out is a rural and suburban problem as well. Increasingly, policy makers, practitioners, and scholars have become aware that these youth cannot be ignored, that they have their own distinctive set of educational problems which cannot be addressed simply by intensifying cries for excellence.

The concern for dropouts is based on some hard realities. It has been estimated that the nation loses about $77 billion dollars annually because of school dropouts—$3 billion in crime prevention, $3 billion in welfare and unemployment, and $71 billion in lost tax revenue.[1] Behind the recent push for dropout prevention programs is the fact that it may make better economic sense to put money into prevention and retraining programs to keep youth in school rather than deal with the heavy economic and social consequences later. There is also an unstated sense in the debates on school dropouts that American society, given its largely egalitarian ideology, cannot be divided into such obviously unequal sectors which reflect racial and class divisions.

The national dropout rate has been reported to be between 25 and 28 percent, although figures of 50 and 70 percent for blacks and Hispanics, respectively, are often cited.[2] The present concern about school dropouts stems from one reaction to the excellence reports of the early

---

*Some of the ideas for this introduction were drawn from a working document on at-risk students prepared by Jeanne Weiler and Eleanor Farrar, SUNY Buffalo, June 1987.

1980s. These reports centered on the quality of education and demand-
ed a renewed emphasis on raising standards. An underlying assumption of the reports was that our economy is failing because our schools
are failing and that we must renew our efforts toward quality education
if America is to retain its competitive edge.[3]

The excellence reports have been criticized in a number of places,
and it is not our intention to repeat that criticism here.[4] What must be
pointed out, however, is that the reports generated a counterdiscussion
of the possible effects of raising standards on those already at risk of
dropping out of school.[5] It is this issue that we will explore here.

The literature on school dropouts is varied, and there has been surprisingly little research done on the subject to date. A major concern
which has come to characterize the literature is the lack of an agreed-
upon definition for the term *dropout*. The Bureau of the Census has
defined a dropout as "any person who is not enrolled in school or who
is not a high school graduate or the equivalent." As Anthony Cipollone
points out, however, the problem with this definition is that it leaves too
much room for different interpretations.[6] For example, some school
districts count transfer students as dropouts, but others do not. There is,
as has been pointed out by Floyd Hammack, intense political pressure
to keep the school-leaving rate down, and this pressure can affect the
data.[7] For example, schools may deliberately miscode students who
have left by saying that they have transferred to private schools, when
the school may not actually know where the students have gone. Some
states also limit dropouts to those above the sixteen-year-old legal
school-leaving age, thereby ignoring younger students in the calculation of dropouts, whereas others do not.

George Morrow has pointed out that the term *dropout* has been applied to a variety of cases. These include pushouts (undesirable
students), the disaffected (students no longer wishing to remain),
educational mortalities (those who fail), capable dropouts (those whose
background socialization does not agree with school demands), and
stopouts (those who drop out and return to school within the same
year).[8] Because the term is so ill-defined and potentially includes any or
all of the above, it is difficult to monitor the population we now call
dropouts and conduct systematic research on the subject. Not only does
the imprecise use of the term tend to impede systematic research and
comparison across states and districts, but, perhaps even more importantly, it tends to keep the debate about dropouts on definition and
measurement rather than on other more important issues.

## THE "CAUSES" OF DROPPING OUT

We do know, however, that students from certain social backgrounds are prone to dropping out. Students from lower social economic backgrounds, with lower levels of self-esteem and poorer grades, are more likely to drop out than other students. During the 1960s and 1970s, research tended to focus on student characteristics which correlated with lack of success in finishing high school. The assumption of such research was that it is the entering students who themselves are responsible for dropping out rather than the institution of schooling or aspects of the broader society which must be held accountable for the problem. Placing the blame on the students themselves, or the families from which they come, was consistent with the general research of this time period. James Coleman, for example, argues that it is the characteristics of the entering students which best predicted success or failure in school, and the well-known Moynihan Report located the blame for the failure of the poor in the black family structure.[9] A focus on student background characteristics was, therefore, consistent with other research of the period.

As Gary Wehlage points out in this volume, the research has now begun to move from a simple description of the background characteristics associated with dropping out to explanations of what it is about these characteristics that causes dropping out and how these characteristics interact with schooling to produce dropouts.[10] Along these lines, there is evidence that certain school-based practices are correlated with dropout rates. It has been suggested that tracking, overcrowded classrooms, mislabeling of a high proportion of minority youth as having needs for special education, and high expulsion rates have an independent impact on the rate of dropout.[11] Such factors, of course, tend to be correlated with poor academic achievement to begin with, but the argument here is that these factors exert an independent effect on the dropout rate. High expulsion rates, for example, appear to cause higher-than-average dropout rates if one holds all other factors constant in the analysis.

We are, however, at the point of needing more systematic analysis of exactly how school dropouts are produced. Although we know now that certain background and school-based variables are related to dropout rates, we know very little about the way in which background characteristics interact with school variables to produce dropouts. In other words, do certain groups of students in combination with certain school-based practices exhibit higher or lower dropout rates than other groups? Do black and Hispanic youth drop out for similar reasons? Do they respond to similar dropout prevention programs? Do the same programs work for working-class white students as work for racial and linguistic minorities? We do not, in fact, have answers to these critically important questions. Although the research on dropouts has shifted from a focus on individuals' characteristics to the institutional characteristics of schools and, to some extent, how they interact, we still do not know much about why youth drop out.[12] Given a lack of research as to why students drop out of school, it is not terribly surprising that we do not yet know much about how to design programs which intervene in the dropout problem. This is not to say that there is no information on why youth drop out, but rather to suggest that such information is limited in scope and often based on the responses of youth to items on survey instruments.[13] Given the complexity of the dropout problem, it just may be that a multiple choice survey might not be the best way to gauge the true reasons for why young people drop out of school.

## ADDRESSING THE PROBLEM

There has been little research to date on providing school-based programs for youth at risk.[14] High-quality program evaluations are few in number, and it would be difficult to replicate successful programs in other settings even if such programs were tested and disseminated through the literature. Numerous questions exist regarding "what works" with dropouts. Should we focus on alternative teaching methods, class size, or curricular offerings? Should programs be preventive, vocational, re-entry, or employment based? The literature has little definitive to say, in fact, about these issues. Dale Mann has suggested that only complex solutions will be able to address the complexity of dropping out. He suggests that schools need, first and foremost, to ameliorate school failure and lack of basic skills. Teachers must care, and coalitions must be built between business and schools, to provide jobs for youth upon high school completion. Early school leaving and the causes of such leaving involve everyone—schools, youth employment agencies, parents, community organizations, business and industry, and, of course, youth themselves.

Despite a clear lack of research on what works, certain programs do appear to exert positive effects on the dropout rate. It has been suggested that programs aimed specifically at clearly defined categories of potential dropouts are successful. It appears that potential dropouts can experience success if placed in special programs designed to meet their needs and those aimed primarily at vocational training. The idea is that a "school within a school" is the most productive use of resources if the dropout rate is to be lowered.

Although there is, as noted above, *some* literature on the subject of dropouts, we still know relatively little about the subject. We do not know why, from the students' own perspective, dropping out may appear to be a viable option. We also do not know the extent to which an economy that denies jobs to so many at this point in time relates to the dropout problem. This is obviously exacerbated by the relatively high proportion of minorities in current society who are without steady work in the legitimate sector of the economy. Whether we would have fewer minority dropouts if the economy were more and equally responsive to the variety of groups in the society is a key issue, one which may make the dropout problem more of a structural and economic one rather than purely an educational one.

We also do not know enough about the educational aspects of school dropouts. We know very little about the actual effects of teachers and a variety of teaching practices, for example, on the creation of the problem and we know very little about the actual cultures which students create in school which may lead to dropping out. There is a difference, obviously, between being pushed out of school and choosing to drop out of school. The extent to which student and teacher cultures are related to either or both of these notions needs to be examined carefully. The ways in which these cultures are constructed and work for blacks, Hispanics, and whites, both male and female, also need to be assessed. There is also a sense in which the dropout problem is being discussed only in terms of inner-city youth. In addition, the literature tends to assume that when girls drop out, they do so largely because of pregnancy.

This volume addresses these issues head on. Alan DeYoung points out that the dropout problem is not confined to urban youth at all, but that there is a comparable problem among rural youth. R. Patrick Solomon suggests that many minorities do, in fact, stay in school, particularly when social class is controlled for in the analysis. He also suggests, however, that another form of dropping out occurs among minority youth, even among those who do stay in school. Many black youth, particularly males, drop out into a sports subculture, thus not doing very well in school in strictly academic terms, even though they stay. Michelle Fine and Nancie Zane provide the first sustained look at female dropouts. It is commonly assumed that girls drop out because of pregnancy. It does appear, however, that over 60 percent of girls drop out for reasons other than pregnancy. By focusing on pregnancy as the *only* cause of female dropouts, we ignore the possibly wide range of conditions and factors which may affect females in school, a point which Fine and Zane take up. We also end up envisioning females in terms of biological reproduction rather than production in the broader sense. Needless to say, this is not the most progressive way of conceptualizing females in the late 1980s. Defining female dropouts in this way only contributes to the problem.

In the second section of this book we look inside schools. There has been, as noted above, extremely little work in this all-important area. Here we examine a number of within-school factors in the creation of dropouts. Charles Payne argues that teachers do indeed play a role in the dropout problem. Eleanor Farrar and Robert Hampel conceptualize the issue of school dropouts in unusually broad terms and examine the delivery of social services to students. They ask about the formal and informal delivery of social services to at-risk youth in schools. Amelia Kreitzer, George Madaus, and Walt Haney explore the issue of minimum competency testing and dropouts. There are those who argue that the key to preventing dropouts (and upgrading schooling in general) is minimum competency testing. The authors argue that such testing serves a largely symbolic function and that there is no hard evidence that testing lowers the rate of dropouts. In point of fact, they suggest that there is some evidence that suggests the opposite. Fred Newmann explores the issue of student alienation from schools and offers guidelines for reducing alienation, which, he suggests, is a key component of the dropout problem.

The two essays in the last section of this volume raise a different type of question. Both John Ogbu and Michael Apple suggest that the dropout problem is being conceived too simplistically. Ogbu suggests that the current focus on dropouts is too limiting and that the behavior of castelike minorities, in particular, is complex and cannot be understood by reference to the dropout issue as currently conceptualized. He offers an alternative way of understanding the problem of low academic performance which tends to characterize a relatively high proportion of involuntary minority youth. Michael Apple argues that the issue of school dropouts must be seen as originating in the structure of the American economy, which denies so much to so many. This means that, in the long run, school-based solutions to the problem will fail to address in a major way the issue of school dropouts.

The essays in this book attempt to raise new questions about school dropouts. We do not attempt to have the last word here. Rather we attempt to push the discussion forward in ways not currently considered. We attempt to take a more holistic look at the problem than is traditionally done. We believe that this volume forces us to consider a variety of research traditions in attempting to understand the dropout problem. From the classroom and teacher effectiveness research we need a better understanding of how different instructional practices contribute to or alleviate the dropout problem. From the school effectiveness research, we need a better grasp of how school organization and practices affect dropouts. We also need to look far more closely at the sociocultural matrices which intersect in schools. What cultures do students bring to school? How do these interact with teacher cultures? What are the cultures of schools as organizations? What place do schools occupy within the larger society? How do other social institutions impact on schools? Families? Communities? Social agencies? What is the role of political economy in posing the problems of dropouts? And, finally, how can we bring this wide variety of research traditions to bear on our thinking about the dropout issue? The challenge is great. The stakes are enormous.

## NOTES

1. Henry Levin, "Accelerated Schools for Disadvantaged Students," *Educational Leadership,* 44, No. 6 (March 1987): 19–21.

2. Dale Mann, "Action on Dropouts," *Educational Leadership* (September 1985): 16–17; and New York State African American Institute of the State of New York, "Dropping Out of School in New York State: The Invisible People of Color," a report of the Task Force on the New York State Dropout Problem, 1986.

3. See, for example, National Commission on Excellence in Education, *A Nation at Risk: The Imperative for Educational Reform* (Washington, D.C.: U.S. Government Printing Office, 1983).

4. For a critical set of perspectives on the reports, see Philip Altbach, Gail Kelly, and Lois Weis, *Excellence in Education: Perspectives on Policy and Practice* (Buffalo, N.Y.: Prometheus, 1985).

5. Gary Natriello, A. Pallas, and Edward McDill, "Taking Stock: Reviewing Our Research Agenda on the Causes and Consequences of Dropping Out," *Teachers College Record,* 87, No. 3 (Spring 1986): 430–40.

6. Anthony Cipollone, *Research Program and Policy Trends in Dropout Prevention,* Connecticut Department of Education, 1986.

7. Floyd Hammack, "Large School Systems Dropout Reports: An Analysis of Definitions, Procedures and Findings," *Teachers College Record,* 87, No. 3 (Spring 1986): 324–41.

8. George Morrow, "Standardizing Practice with Analysis of School Dropouts," *Teachers College Record,* 87, No. 3 (Spring 1986): 342–55.

9. James Coleman et al., *Equality of Educational Opportunity* (Washington, D.C.: U.S. Government Printing Office, 1966), and Daniel P. Moynihan, *The Negro Family, The Case for National Action* (Washington, D.C.: U.S. Department of Labor, 1965).

10. See also Gary Wehlage and Robert Rutter, "Dropping Out: How Much Do Schools Contribute to the Problem?" *Teachers College Record,* 87, No. 3 (Spring 1986): 374–93.

11. See, for example, M. W. Edelman and H. Howe, *Barriers to Excellence: Our Children at Risk* (Boston: National Coalition of Advocates for Students, 1984).

12. Michelle Fine has, however, begun this discussion in earnest. See Michelle Fine, "Why Urban Adolescents Drop Into and Out of Public High School," *Teachers College Record,* 87, No. 3 (Spring 1983): 393–409.

13. Data from the High School and Beyond study provide an example here. This is not to criticize the data per se, but rather to suggest that such data do not encourage us to unravel the complexity of the problem.

14. Dale Mann, "Can We Help Dropouts: Thinking About the Undoable," *Teachers College Record,* 87, No. 3 (Spring 1986): 307–23.

GARY G. WEHLAGE

## Chapter 1

# Dropping Out:
# Can Schools Be Expected to Prevent It?*

### INTRODUCTION

American educators as well as the public have been ambivalent throughout the twentieth century about what, if anything, can be done about the "early school leaver," or dropout. Is there anything the *school* can do to retain the would-be dropout? Ambivalence has been expressed by competing arguments, with one side claiming that schools can change their ways and thereby reduce the number of dropouts, and the other side claiming that not much can be done because the dropout is either willfully negligent or socially deficient. Recently, Chester Finn, assistant secretary of education, presented a variation of the latter argument when he asserted that it is unlikely any school-based strategies for retaining the potential dropout will have their intended effect.[1] The reason is that dropouts come disproportionately from the underclass of our society. Finn points out that nearly every study shows that dropping out is correlated with low socioeconomic class, minority status, low test scores and grades, and dissatisfaction with school. Finn states, "Along

*This paper was prepared at the National Center on Effective Secondary Schools, School of Education, University of Wisconsin-Madison, which is supported in part by a grant from the Office of Educational Research and Improvement (Grant No. G-008690007). Any opinions, findings, and conclusion or recommendations expressed in this publication are those of the author and do not necessarily reflect the views of this agency or the U.S. Department of Education.

1

with hapless demographics and lagging educational achievement, dropouts have a third set of characteristics: misbehavior of various sorts." (pp. 14–15).

The point of Finn's argument is that, to the extent that dropping out of school is caused by social factors originating beyond school, "the symptom is not likely to be eradicated by school-based remedies. Insofar as it [dropping out] is a manifestation of linked social pathologies and inherited characteristics, it is more like 'going on welfare' or 'committing a crime' than like the commonplace problems of school effectiveness that are susceptible to alteration within the framework of education policy and practice." (p. 15) Here we have the quintessential argument against holding the schools responsible for their dropouts or offering interventions designed to retain them. The problem exists not because of deficiencies in the schools but rather because of deficiencies in individuals and families.

This chapter examines the issue of whether we can expect schools to be more effective in preventing students from dropping out. It begins with a brief review of several national studies of dropouts. The observation is made that most studies have focused on identifying the personal and social characteristics of students that correlate with dropping out rather than on asking if school practices affect the dropout rate. The analysis then shifts to an overview of new evidence that Catholic schools have a substantially better record than public and other private schools in retaining at-risk students. Data on the relative effectiveness of Catholic schools are presented along with the conclusion that certain school characteristics may be important variables affecting the retention of those at risk of dropping out. Finally, a theory is presented that offers a partial explanation of why some schools, including Catholic, are more effective. This theory views students and schools as interacting to establish school membership for individuals. This interaction involves reciprocal relations between the student and adults that act either to strengthen or weaken student bonds to the school.

## MAINSTREAM RESEARCH ON DROPOUTS

As the national graduation rate from high school approached 75 percent in the mid-1960s, those students who dropped out came to be seen as deviants. The success schools had with most students made it relatively easy to construe those who dropped out as the problem, not school practices. Apparently, collective reasoning went something like this: If the majority of youth can succeed in school to the point of graduation, the school must be an effective institution. Dropouts are aberrant individuals who are deviant, dysfunctional, or deficient because of personal, family, or community characteristics.

Mainstream research on dropouts parallels this commonsense construction of the situation. The pattern among researchers was to examine a sample of dropouts in terms of the personal and social characteriestics they have in common. This approach, although not without its legitimacy, has the effect of suggesting that the characteristics are the cause of dropping out. By focusing exclusively on personal and social characteristics shared by dropouts, this research makes it appear that dropouts are deviant, deficient, or negligent with regard to school. This focus contributes to a pathological view of these youth and deflects attention from the school itself.

The most dramatic example of research labeling dropouts in this way was done by Cervantes.[2] His book appeared at the very time that graduation rates reached their zenith. Through a series of case studies, Cervantes developed a social-psychological portait of the dropout. He claimed to have discovered a "variant breed of teen-agers." (p. 5) They were a social problem who were "clumsily dysfunctional in the computer-precise, machine-oriented, communication-saturated society." (p. 196) He supported the notion that dropouts would become an "outlaw pack" who could not be absorbed into society.

From his case study data, Cervantes arrived at a list of bipolar characteristics that distinguish the dropout from the graduate. His list of characteristics pairing dropout against graduate includes the following:

Instinctoid / Holistic
Radical / Conservative
Class-bound / Upwardly mobile
Proletarian / Capitalistic
Affectless / Affectionate
Hyperactive / Alert
Leisure and thrill oriented / Occupation and goal oriented
Sexually exploiting / Monogamous
Double standard / Single standard
Pawn of environment / Master of environment

Viewed from a contemporary perspective, Cervantes' value-laden and fanciful characteristics suggest a naivete that must make sociologists wince. His description would seem humorous except that it reflects a persistent definition of the problem that continues down to the present. As then, we see in Finn's contemporary argument a construction of the problem claiming that the dropout is deficient or comes from a deficient home and background.

Subsequent studies of the dropout were more subtle in their descriptions and selections of categories than Cervantes'. Nevertheless, there is a chain of studies that share the view that the basic research question is: What are the personal, family, and social class characteristics of those who drop out? This chain continues with Combs and Cooley, who used Project TALENT data on 440,000 ninth graders.[3] Following this was a major work by Bachman, Green, and Wirtanen, who used the Youth in Transition data on 2,000 boys.[4] More recently, Rumberger analyzed the National Longitudinal Survey of Youth Labor Market Experience.[5] Finally, the most recent national data base is High School and Beyond (HS&B), a longitudinal study of a national sample of 1980 sophomores. These data have produced a number of analyses touching on the dropout (for example, see Peng.)[6] Each of these studies focuses primarily on the student characteristics associated with dropping out.

Although the various data bases and analyses differ in certain respects, mainstream research has tended to confirm a persistent set of findings about dropouts. It is the characteristics of *students,* along with their families and cultural backgrounds, that are correlated with dropping out. Whatever the differences in their findings, the major studies do *not* question the policies and practices of schools. These studies have not lent themselves to asking if some schools are more effective in retaining the potential dropout. Thus, research has not encouraged inquiry into the possibility that schools themselves may be part of the problem. Instead, it appears from the research that school as an institution is healthy, rational, and performing appropriately for students, except for a few deviants who are incapable of succeeding.

## CATHOLIC SCHOOLS:
## AN EMPIRICAL CASE OF EFFECTIVENESS

Coleman and Hoffer, in their analysis of HS&B data, focused on Catholic schools and their students.[7] This study opens the door to understanding the relationship between school characteristics and dropping out. Empirical evidence is provided to show that, in fact, some schools are more effective with students who are at risk of dropping out.

Their construction of the dropout problem, although limited in important ways, lends support to the view that some schools are able to respond more effectively to those at risk of dropping out.

The work of Coleman and Hoffer provides particularly important
evidence on the issue of effective schools by comparing Catholic high
schools with other private and public schools. To preview their findings, Coleman and Hoffer show that Catholic schools are markedly
more effective than public or other private schools in retaining to
graduation, not only poor and minority youth, but also other students
who come from what they define as "families with deficiencies" and
students who had academic and disciplinary problems that typically
make them at risk of dropping out.

Coleman and Hoffer found that Catholic schools were substantially more successful with black and Hispanic students than either the
public or other private schools (see Table 1.1). Using data on socioeconomic status (SES), low SES being one of the traditionally strong
correlates of dropping out, they found that Catholic schools did much
better with low-SES students than did the public schools. Catholic
schools also did better than other private schools, except with those
from the lowest of the four SES quartiles (see Table 1.2). Of course, a

Table 1.1
Dropout Percentages by Race/Ethnicity and School Sector

| Race/ethnicity | Public | Catholic | Other private |
| --- | --- | --- | --- |
| White | 13.1 | 2.6 | 10.8 |
| Black | 17.2 | 4.6 | 14.4 |
| Hispanic | 19.1 | 9.3 | 22.9 |

Table 1.2
Dropout Percentages by SES and School Sector

| SES quartile | Public | Catholic | Other private |
| --- | --- | --- | --- |
| 1 low | 22.3 | 14.9 | 7.2 |
| 2 | 13.2 | 3.3 | 15.8 |
| 3 | 10.7 | 0.2 | 14.3 |
| 4 high | 7.1 | 1.7 | 8.9 |

question can still be raised regarding family background differences that exist when a conscious choice is made to send children to a Catholic school. Regardless of class, income, race, and other variables, such a choice may indicate a commitment to education otherwise absent in families.

There are other family background factors that have been correlated with high dropout rates. Most notably, these include single-parent homes. An important question concerns the relative success exhibited by Catholic schools with students from these disadvantaged family situations. For example, are Catholic schools successful in retaining children from homes in which there has been a divorce? It might be claimed, of course, that the favorable differences shown by Catholic schools with respect to dropout rates are due to the advantage of greater stability in students' homes regardless of race, ethnicity, or income. It is important to pursue this issue before claiming that Catholic schools are more successful than other schools with at-risk youth.

Coleman and Hoffer devised two indicators for what they term "family deficiency." One, "structural deficiency," refers to single-parent households and working mothers. Their assumption, that such homes are deficient, is open to question; nevertheless, they include as disadvantaged homes those in which the mother is head of the house or in which the mother works outside the home. The other indicator, "functional deficiency," refers to low involvement of parents with their children. This deficiency is evidenced by a lack of shared activities and an absence of verbal communication between parents and children. The assumption by Coleman and Hoffer is that in such families the knowledge, experience, and value orientations associated with middle-class status are not transferred to their children. Some characteristics that distinguish middle-class homes, and have a powerful effect on school performance and expectations toward obtaining higher education, may be missed in these families. More generally, "functionally deficient" families are thought by Coleman and Hoffer to fail to transfer to children the "social capital" that parents have acquired.

The analysis by Coleman and Hoffer is that Catholic schools are especially effective with families exhibiting "functional and structural deficiencies" (see Table 1.3). It is worth quoting their interpretation of the above results. "The Catholic sector benefits are especially great for students from families with deficiencies, whether structural, functional, or combined. The relation of dropout to deficient families is small or absent in Catholic schools, which show very low dropout rates for students from all types of families. In contrast, the public sector and the

Table 1.3
Dropout Percentages for Students from Families with Varying Degrees of
Functional and Structural Deficiencies

| Deficiencies | Public | Catholic | Other private |
|---|---|---|---|
| None | 6.8 | 2.7 | 9.5 |
| 1 | 11.8 | 3.1 | 5.1 |
| 2 | 18.5 | 4.6 | 13.4 |
| 3 or 4 | 24.3 | 4.1 | 40.2 |

Table 1.4
Dropout Rates by Sector for Students with Scholastic or Disciplinary Problems

| School problem | Public | Catholic | Other private |
|---|---|---|---|
| Grades below C | 37.0 | 22.6 | 35.3 |
| Discipline problems | 28.0 | 13.1 | 27.1 |
| Probation | 32.7 | 13.3 | 34.8 |
| 5 or more absences | 33.2 | 13.3 | 40.3 |

other private sector show strong relationships of dropout to family deficiencies, whether structural, functional, or combined." (p. 129)

Coleman and Hoffer also discovered that Catholic schools were markedly more effective in retaining to graduation those students who had school problems, that is, who had academic or disciplinary difficulties. This is important because one of the main assumptions of this paper is that schools often exacerbate the dropout problem by discouraging many students who have academic and disciplinary problems. Analysis of data on students who had academic and behavioral problems indicates that Catholic schools do better with these students than other schools (see Table 1.4). These findings indicate that the dropout rates for students with academic and behavior problems is very similar in the public and other private schools. The Catholic schools, on the other hand, have significantly lower dropout rates than either.

The evidence is clear and dramatic. Coleman and Hoffer use four categories to elaborate the concept of the at-risk student—minority, poor, "deficient families," and school problems. The results of their analysis produce a clear empirical case for the effectiveness of Catholic schools. In other words, the Catholic school "rescues students at risk of failure." The data argue directly against the claim often heard that Catholic schools can eliminate their problem students by pushing them into the public schools. Apparently quite the opposite happens. Catholic schools retain their at-risk students to a greater degree than public schools. If there is a "push-out" phenomenon, it is in the public sector, where schools continue to receive financial support regardless of their ineffectiveness with at-risk youth. Catholic schools, whether for moral or economic reasons, or both, succeed in retaining students in danger of dropping out.

It may be the case that Catholic youth who are defined as at risk of dropping out because they fall into the generally accepted categories of poor, minority, "deficient homes," and school problems actually differ in some unspecified but important way from their non-Catholic public school counterparts. However, even if this is true, it is our hypothesis that there is something different about the way Catholic schools interact with at-risk youth. What the operational characteristics of this difference are and why they exist are yet to be fully explained, but it is our assumption that many of the qualities that make Catholic schools relatively more effective with respect to lower dropout rates can be reproduced in the public sector.

## SCHOOL MEMBERSHIP THEORY:
## A LOOK "INSIDE"

Coleman and Hoffer theorize that the difference between Catholic and other schools arises *outside* the school and is a product of what they call "functional communities." By this they mean two things. First, there is a value consistency among the parents of the children who attend Catholic schools. Second, and this is crucial to their argument, value consistency in such communities is generated and sustained through a degree of functional social interaction. This interaction is between parents of children in the school system and is cross-generational: that is, it occurs between parents and students. It reinforces values about schooling for children, parents, teachers, and the school itself. Face-to-face interaction among adults and children is the key to generating and sustaining functional communities.

Although this "functional community" theory may have some validity, at best it offers only a partial explanation for Catholic school effectiveness. The theory is inadequate because it is based on a methodology that treats the school as a "black box." The "black box" methodology uses a set of quantified inputs and outputs, but not much is revealed about what happens in between the two sets of variables; that is, it does not look inside the school. The input-output model treats communities, students, and families as the input. Dropouts and achievement data are the output. In between is the "black box" of the research model—the school building where daily activities of students and teachers take place. It is a "black box" because almost nothing is revealed about the day-to-day events occurring inside the school. On the basis of an extensive body of ethnographic data that now exists on the importance of the culture of schools, it would seem that any explanation for the differential success of schools that ignores the internal workings of the institution is almost certainly inadequate. A theory of school effects ought to include factors that arise outside the institution and those that occur as a result of the culture and social relations produced inside.

We suspect that Catholic schools have a culture and ethos that are, in some ways, different from those of the public schools because of the doctrines and ideology of Catholicism. The school culture is partly a product of basic tenets of the church. For example, these schools tend to operate on the belief that one should love God and love others as oneself, that it is important to care about others. Studies of Catholic schools confirm that such principles are acted upon.[8] They are communicated to students in religion classes, masses, school bulletins, and various school events and have an effect on peer group relations. Teacher behavior is different also. Teachers see a need to monitor student behavior closely. The differences in Catholic school culture are seen, in part, by the extra effort put forth by faculty and the responsibility they assume for the success of young people. Faculty see their role as broader than providing instruction in a subject matter area. They are concerned with the character of each student as well as how much a student knows. A number of teachers report that they consider their work as a ministry and their role as one of shaping young adults.[9] Catholic schools include among their obligations to students the creation of a "safety net" to protect young people. All who enter the school are worthy of attention and concern. This culture, it is suspected, makes an important impact on Catholic school students who are at risk of dropping out.

Research at the National Center on Effective Secondary Schools on at-risk students discloses a parallel factor in the public sector that is described as "school membership".[10] A yearlong study of fourteen schools designed for at-risk students gathered data through observation, interviews, and testing. Also collected were a variety of demographic and outcome measures about the effectiveness of these schools. The fourteen were selected after a national search for schools that had established a track record of success with at-risk students. One of the major conclusions of the study is that social relations in these fourteen schools are different from those that occur in most conventional public schools. The difference in social relations is due primarily to the concern by adults to help students who have failed and become alienated to overcome a set of impediments to school membership. The complete claim, based on the study of the schools, is somewhat more complex than is implied by the concept of school membership. It is that any school is likely to be successful with at-risk students to the extent that the culture of the school promotes two things: (1) academic engagement, and (2) school membership. Both of these factors are important in reducing the number of students who drop out.

Briefly, academic engagement is defined as students putting forth mental effort to achieve the knowledge and skills generally associated with the outcomes of formal schooling. There are at least three problems preventing such engagement within traditional public schools. First, academic learning is not structured to be extrinsically rewarding; except for a few who compete for college entrance, there is no payoff for working at academic achievement. Second, the learning process is too restricted, rewarding only a narrow range of intellectual competence that people can develop and display. Again, except for a few, this makes it uninviting to become engaged in academic work as it is currently defined by schools. Third, educators are obsessed with the "coverage" of vast amounts of subject matter to the point that school knowledge becomes superficial and prevents many individuals from gaining a sense of competence and intrinsic reward from learning. Only through "in-depth" experiences can this be avoided. Schools cannot expect much academic engagement, particularly from at-risk students, until these three problems have been addressed.[11]

School membership, the focus of discussion in this chapter, is more than simple technical enrollment in a school. It means that students have established a social bond between themselves, the adults in the school, and the norms governing the institution. Membership is achieved when students are attached, committed, and involved in the activities of the institution, as well as believe in the institution. It has legitimacy, and their involvement in it will be rewarded. Membership for students is established through a reciprocal relationship between them and the adults who represent the institution. In defining and describing school membership, there is a need to capture the social relations between students and the school that exist in both the formal and informal life of the institution.

School membership requires the student and the school to establish a reciprocal relationship based on an exchange of commitments. The theory hypothesizes that school membership is promoted by the following adult practices: (1) actively creating positive and respectful relations between adults and students; (2) communicating concern about and providing direct help to individuals with their personal problems; (3) providing active help in meeting institutional standards of success and competence; and (4) helping students identify a place in society based on a link between self, school, and one's future.

In exchange for this energetic and active commitment from the institution, students are to provide their own commitment. This includes the following: (1) behaviors that are positive and respectful toward adults and peers; and (2) academic engagement, or a level of mental and physical effort in school tasks that makes their own achievement likely and makes the commitment of adults rewarding.

Reciprocal relations imply an exchange of commitments and supporting behaviors. These commitments also imply corresponding beliefs about the legitimacy and efficacy of both the institution and the student. If the school believes, for example, that the student is incompetent to engage in institutional activities and reach institutional goals, the commitment by the school will be weak or nonexistent. If the student believes that the activities and goals of the school are inappropriate for him or her, then the commitment of the student will be weak. In either case, school membership is impaired.

In the following section, the theory of school membership will be developed more thoroughly and will be applied to our research findings about at-risk students and the experiences they had in the fourteen schools.

## SCHOOL MEMBERSHIP AND DROPPING OUT

The theory of school membership helps interpret and explain much of the data about social relations gathered during the study of schools designed to prevent dropping out. Each school was an intervention for junior or senior high students who either had been dropouts or were considered at risk of dropping out. The theory of school membership borrows from the work of Vincent Tinto, who examined the "college dropout."[12] There are significant parallels between the "early departure" from college that Tinto describes and the dropping out of secondary schools that we describe. School membership as a theory is a partial, but helpful, way of explaining why students drop out and, on the other hand, why some schools are relatively more effective in retaining those at risk of dropping out.

Tinto developed his theory through an analysis of empirical studies of early college leavers. In describing the roots of early departure from college, he uses two sets of concepts, one referring to the individual student and the other to the institution. The individual roots of college departure are found partly in the strength of a person's "intention and commitment" to acquire a college education. These dispositions are brought to college by the student. They are, however, strengthened or weakened during the college experience, primarily by the student's interaction with the institution. According to Tinto, voluntary departure from college is due much more to institutional experiences after a student arrives than to prior experiences, preparation, and the strength of individual dispositions. This is an extremely important claim because it suggests that the institution of college is an active agent encouraging or discouraging students' continuation. We strongly endorse this claim as it applies to at-risk high school students based on evidence from our study.

Tinto finds that the institutional roots of departure from college lie in the quality of interactions the student has with the institution. The terms used by Tinto to describe this quality of institutional experience are *adjustment, difficulty, incongruence,* and *isolation.* We find this conceptual framework useful because it describes important dimensions of school membership and subsumes much of our data on at-risk students. When these concepts are assembled as a theory of school membership, explanations of both dropping out and school effectiveness are possible. In the next few paragraphs, each of the component concepts of school membership developed by Tinto is applied to the data from the fourteen schools.

*Adjustment* is a major requirement if students are to acquire school membership. It is most apparent when students move from middle or junior high school into the high school. This transition point is a source of both academic failure and alienation from the institution. Students are asked to meet new standards and expectations. In addition, a different social milieu exists in the typical high school. Our research found that high school teachers deliberately create a social distance between themselves and students. This is considered essential by many teachers to help students to "grow up" and become more "independent and responsible," and yet this social distance is a major source of strain for students. Many students need a more personal and supportive relationship with adults than high school typically provides.

A number of the schools studied recognized the adjustment problem and devised specific and regular strategies for dealing with it. One example of how the problem of adjustment is acted upon comes from the Wayne Enrichment Center (WEC), located in Indianapolis. WEC uses "family" meetings each week to deal with problems of adjustment throughout the year. The first meeting at the beginning of the school year is devoted to the essential task of learning names; teachers and students are all expected to know each person's name. Some "family" meetings are devoted to solving peer group problems, such as conflicts between individuals. Others are held to clarify and remind students of the "ABCs of WEC." "A" stands for attendance; the attendance rules are spelled out and reiterated from time to time. If a student is to be absent for any reason, he or she must call the school *before* the fact. "B" stands for behavior. All students must sign an agreement upon admission to the school that they will abide by the school's code of conduct. "C" stands for credit. Almost all of the students are credit deficient. The teachers then provide an explicit set of strategies and guidelines that will assist students toward their goal of graduation by helping them accumulate the appropriate credits. The students understand that unless specified work is completed each semester, they will be dropped from the school. These mechanisms are examples of the way schools actively sought to help students adjust. It was, in part, through this help in adjusting that students came to be members of the school.

*Difficulty* with academic matters is a useful and commonsense way of explaining one cause of academic failure. Although it was found that literal inability to do the work was a relatively rare characteristic of at-risk students, both more time and more intensive tutoring were required for many. For some, the difficulty issue is more correctly described as "difficulty in sustaining interest and effort." Students complained that teachers made learning "dull, boring and stupid." The common format students complained most about was the ubiquitous "lecture-discussion" based on reading assignments. They found it difficult to know what teachers wanted and where they were going with the subject.

Many of the successful interventions designed for dropout prevention respond to the difficulty issue by using special courses and pedagogy in an effort to keep students on track in accumulating credits for graduation. These include individualized learning packets and cooperative learning. The intent is to provide a clearer sense of progress toward stated goals. One of the most frequently used strategies is breaking courses into shorter units. A semester, or even a quarter, is often too long for students to keep their bearings, and if personal or family problems arise that distract them, an entire semester's credit for one or more courses can be lost.

To counter this problem, Sierra Mountain High in Grass Valley, California, instituted the "5-1-5" schedule, which breaks the semester into three 5-week units, each followed by a week of vacation. Although students eventually accumulate the same total time, these shorter units are seen as more manageable by students in that they can keep their eye on the goals and requirements of courses. Another school, Orr Community Academy in Chicago, has students focus on "two majors at a time." Each semester student time is focused on only two of the four traditional core subjects—math, science, English, social studies. The two majors strategy has the effect of doubling the amount of time on those subjects taken and avoids the problem of competing demands from two additional courses.

These examples suggest a degree of institutional responsiveness to the students in an effort to deal with the difficulty issue. Schools assumed that many of the students who had failed courses in traditional high schools could be successful if accommodations were made. These accommodations were aimed primarily at the problem of sustaining student effort rather than at changing the content of courses. These institutional responses contributed to student perceptions that they could demonstrate academic achievement. And school membership was possible once students could demonstrate academic achievement and competence.

*Incongruence* is a more ambiguous term than *adjustment* or *difficulty.* However, we find that it captures an important dimension of our data about at-risk students. Applied to schools, it is concerned with the cultural match between the student and the institution. The quality of the match is reflected in answers to several questions that students implicitly ask about how well they fit into the school: What kind of person am I? Where did I come from? Where am I going in the future? How does this school fit with answers to these questions?

Incongruence between students and a school applies to all who identify themselves as out of the mainstream in some way. We found that many of the students interviewed saw themselves as "outsiders." Some were "punkers," others liked "heavy metal," and still others were simply social outcasts because of physical or personality characteristics. In some instances race and ethnicity made students "outsiders." In general, however, to the extent that school represents mainstream middle-class culture, the problem of incongruence is most universally associated with youth from lower-social-class backgrounds. Fitting into the middle-class value structure of a school is a major issue for many young people.

Most schools, mainstream or otherwise, tend to acquire their own character. They come to stand for or represent something in the eyes of students. This raises questions for the individual student about the kind of person a school represents. Implicitly students make a judgment about whether or not they will "fit in" based on their views of who attends the school. Is there a respected peer group that one can join? In addition, students make a judgment about what kind of student is valued at a school by the adults in control. Does one have to a "jock" or a "brain" to be respected by teachers?

One example of how a school tries to create congruence is found in the Media Academy at Fremont High School in Oakland, California. This is an inner-city school serving poor black and Hispanic youth. At the Media Academy students "major" in print and electronic media for three years. While they take the normal core courses, Media Academy students concentrate their electives in a program that emphasizes writing, speaking, radio and television, and the production of two newspapers. This curriculum is designed to help these students perceive a relationship between themselves, academics, and the world outside.

Prior to enrollment, many students indicate little interest in higher education. Their knowledge of career opportunities is limited. Since these students often have restricted experiences, an objective of the program is to introduce them to the world of media and a set of opportunities for future work and education that otherwise would escape their attention. Through a network of contacts with professionals in the field, students are introduced to a wide array of media work. Over thirty professionals have opened their businesses and themselves to the Media Academy. A number of these people are black or Hispanic.

Students visit the production facilities of newspapers, radio, and television. They receive class instruction from reporters and cartoonists. They apply their newly learned skills in the production of both their school paper and a locally distributed Spanish/English language paper. They produce public service announcements on radio and television.

The Media Academy is an example of how the apparent incongruence between school and poor black and Hispanic youth has been reshaped into congruence. For the most part, these young people saw little connection between school and who they were and where they were going. Now, for example, being able to write well is part of the image many of these students associate with themselves. The Media Academy has created a context in which reading, writing, speaking, and thinking critically about issues make sense. This effort by the school is an example of the way in which institutional commitment to students through a particular program can help create a sense of congruence. The school actively accommodates students without weakening the central task of the school—teaching academics. In turn, this accommodation creates a more congruent match between students and the school and allows them to become members of the school.

*Isolation* refers to both academic and social experiences. Socially students can be isolated from other students, but our concern is isolation from adults. A central tenet of school membership theory is the need to have frequent and high-quality interaction between students and adults. This is particularly important as other institutions that formerly provided valuable adult-adolescent contact—family, church, voluntary organizations—decline in their influence.

Tinto found that in explaining college departure, isolation was one of the most powerful predictors. Of great importance to student persistance in college is the amount and warmth of faculty-student interaction outside the classroom. This finding contributes to his claim that what happens after a student enters a college is far more important than what occurred before. Our findings from studying the various special programs for at-risk students are similar. Teachers found a variety of ways to break down the barriers between themselves and students. One of the most frequent comments made by students to us can be paraphrased in this way: "This school is better because the teachers here care about me." This caring attitude is revealed in different ways, but it almost always communicates active interest on the part of adults in the welfare of students.

Alcott Alternative Junior High in Wichita, Kansas, has a staff that recognizes that one of their first responsibilities is to reach out to students and prevent them from remaining isolated. The students come to Alcott as a last resort after failing in one of the regular junior highs. Most of these students come with serious home and personal problems as well as academic failure. Doug is a typical example. His parents are divorced, and he is living with his mother during the week and his father on weekends. He came to Alcott extremely shy and was described by the principal as a "school phobic." He attended another junior high for a while, but in his own words, "I just didn't fit in." In contrast, Alcott has provided a place where he has made friends with both peers and teachers. Through the help of a teacher who took an interest in him, Doug became involved with flying through the Explorer Scouts. He is now a "flying buff." He spends weekends with a group that is dismantling and reconstructing an old plane under the guidance of a man who restores antiques. These associations and activities, according to him, were inconceivable when he entered the school two years earlier.

Isolation is countered when adults show explicit interest about either academic or personal matters. This interest is an expression of support and contributes to the general belief that individuals are important and worthy of adult attention. The interest by adults is sometimes a form of counseling and mentoring. Teachers, for example, make conversation with particular students in an effort to coach them, helping them think through some of the choices that lie ahead. This attention is important in breaking down the isolation from adults that many adolescents experience. In many cases, a student's own family is unable to help solve a problem, or worse, the family is part of the problem. Most youth are unable to use social services when the need arises. In such instances the adults in a school are the most likely source of advice and counsel. Close contact with caring, supportive adults is crucial to helping students avoid isolation as they face a host of day-to-day decisions. This close adult supervision through expressions of interest contributes to a student's sense of membership in a school.

## CONCLUSION

This chapter began with a question: Can schools be expected to prevent dropping out? In offering an affirmative answer, two kinds of evidence were provided. The first kind of evidence is empirical. There is convincing evidence that one type of school—Catholic— is persistently more effective than either public or other private schools in preventing at-risk students from dropping out. The second kind of evidence is both theoretical and empirical. A theory of school membership offers a partial explanation for dropping out and school effectiveness. It implies a set of actions by educators that facilitate the social bonding of students to school. Educators can take the initiative by actively seeking to establish reciprocal relations with students. The school can be active in developing strategies to deal with the problems of adjustment, difficulty, incongruence, and isolation on which many students stumble.

Having said this, there still remains the problem of creating the conditions in schools that foster the kind of active role by educators described in this chapter. The schools in the study were selected in part because they had already created different structures and environments for students and teachers. These differences were significant in allowing teachers to reach out to students. The problem of creating the structural conditions that will permit educators in public schools to engage young people in academics and help them become members of the school is another story.

## NOTES

1. C. Finn, "The high school dropout puzzle," *Public Interest* (Spring 1987): 3–22.

2. L. Cervantes, *The dropout: Causes and cures.* (Ann Arbor: University of Michigan Press, 1965).

3. J. Combs and W. Cooley, "Dropouts in high school and after high school," *American Educational Research Journal,* 5(3) (1968):343–63.

4. J. G. Bachman, S. Green, and I. D. Wirtanen, *Dropping out—problem or symptom?* (Ann Arbor, Michigan: Institute for Social Research, 1971).

5. R. Rumberger, "Dropping out of high school: The influence of race, sex and family background," *American Educational Research Journal,* 20(2) (1983): 199–220.

6. S. Peng, *High school dropouts: Descriptive information from High School and Beyond* (Washington, D.C.: National Center for Educational Statistics, 1983).

7. J. Coleman and T. Hoffer, *Public and private high schools: The impact of communities.* (New York: Basic Books, 1987).

8. N. Lesko, *Symbolizing society: Stories, rites, and structure in a Catholic high school* (New York: Falmer, 1988).

9. A. Bryk et al., *Effective Catholic schools: An exploration* (Washington, D.C.: National Center for Research in Total Catholic Education, 1984).

10. Gary G. Wehlage, R. A. Rutter, G. A. Smith, N. L. Lesko, and R. Fernandez, *The way back to school: A study of programs for at-risk youth* (tentative title), (Madison: University of Wisconsin-Madison, National Center on Effective Secondary Schools, forthcoming).

11. For a more detailed discussion of "academic engagement," see Wehlage, *Engagement, Not Remediation or Higher Standards* in ed. J. Lakebrink, *Children at Risk* (Springfield, Illinois: Charles C. Thomas, 1989).

12. V. Tinto, *Leaving college: Rethinking the causes and cures of student attrition* (Chicago: University of Chicago Press, 1987).

# Part I

## *Who Are the Dropouts?*
## *The Topic Reconsidered*

Chapter 2

# Bein' Wrapped Too Tight: When Low-Income Women Drop Out of High School

*Field Note from a public comprehensive high school class. Sociology, October.*

*Teacher, white woman to class of black and Latino students:* Matina Horner had an idea that females weren't so happy about success. [She writes on board: Young women capable of success in careers are more fearful of success than capable men—90 percent of men are happy about John's success, 33 percent of women showed no fear about Anna's future.] Lots of times when women go into corporations women are trained to compete because they do hold back. Let's see if you have fear of success. What if you and your bother were equally brilliant and wanted to go to college and your mother had enough money to send only one? Who should go?

*Deirdre, black female student:* This is actually the case now. My brother is in college and we are struggling and hopefully I'll be able to go but I don't know. We're making it but it's hard.

*Teacher:* Anybody feel it should be the man 'cause he should earn a living?

No hands.

*Hazel, black female, youngest of seventeen:* Maybe . . . a little.

*Teacher:* Hazel?

*Suzanne:* Hazel just wants to talk.

*Hazel:* It is more for a man to do that sort of. When we get older we should both work, but he should get educated more.

*Patty:* When we get older we should both work, but he should be educated more. After all, if a man don't get educated it's more likely he'll be out on the street corner, and there's nothing sorrier than seeing a black man on the corner with nothing to do.

*Teacher:* You know many women raise kids alone.

*Hazel:* I know.

*Deirdre:* It's true. Some guys should go away to college 'cause they not wrapped too tight. They say, "If I can't go to college I'm going to do something crazy." They wack [crazy]. They get sick, go to jail, get into drugs.

*Hazel:* I like to see men be so nice and do things for me!

*Michael:* I should go!

*Deirdre:* Girls and women, we can take care of ourselves better, we're wrapped tight.

This essay explores the prices that low-income adolescent women, dropouts and students, pay for being wrapped tight.

Public schools are marbled by social class, race and ethnicity, and gender. Yet they are laminated in denial, represented as if race, class, and gender neutral. This essay takes as its project a single cut into the lives and educations of low-income students, a cut into the dimension of gender. We offer a perspective on the ways in which the material circumstances, the consciousness, and the bodies of low-income adolescent women are undermined by their public schools, the very institutions which promise them better. We examine critically the extremely high dropout rates for young women in urban areas.[1]

The story unfolds by reviewing first the evidence on the incidence and consequences of dropping out for young women, then by examining how the structures and practices of public urban education place low-income women "at particular risk," and finally by exploring possibility—what could be. We track the ways in which schools disorder the practice of female adolescence by rendering the material conditions of their lives and relationships irrelevant to public schooling; by neglecting the split subjectivities by which they make sense of a world held together by the sweat, passion, and oppression of low-income women; and by splitting their bodies and sexualities along an artificailly constructed dimension of victimization and desire.

The arguments offered derive from two independent and blended data sources. The first involves an intensive ethnographic investigation of a public comprehensive high school in New York City in which Michelle Fine spent an academic year attending both classes and administrative offices, tracking archivally the 1978 cohort of 1,430 ninth graders through to graduation or discharge, interviewing approximately forty recent and fifteen long-term high school dropouts, and analyzing materials, biographies, short stories, and displays hung in the public spaces of this high school.[2] The second data base derives from focused group interviews conducted by Nancie Zane, in which eighty young women were interviewed about their experiences as students, dropouts, teen mothers, and/or pregnant teens. The adolescents interviewed in the ethnography were predominantly black and Latina and from low-income homes in Harlem, New York. The young women who constituted the focus groups were also low income but were black, Latina, and white and from Philadelphia, Pennsylvania.[3]

## THE DROPOUT SCENE:
## A METHOD FOR A GENDERED ANALYSIS

Approximately 25 percent of fifth-grade students will not, in all likelihood, graduate from high school.[4] In urban areas nearly 50 or 60 percent of adolescents leave high school prior to graduation with neither degree nor diploma.[5] Although nationally many dropouts return to school for a standard degree or a graduate equivalency diploma (G.E.D.) within a few years, in urban areas this is true for 43 percent of young men and only 25 percent of young women.[6]

If the incidence of dropping out is approximately equivalent for young men and women, the economic consequences are markedly more severe for young women, particularly for young women of color. White males with and without diplomas are in far better economic shape in this society than are black females with and without diplomas. Among U.S. adults aged twenty-two to thirty-four, only 15 percent of white male dropouts live below the poverty line, compared with 28 percent of white females, 37 percent of black males, and 62 percent of black female dropouts.[7] Among high school graduates, 8 percent of white males live in poverty, compared with 11 percent of white females, 16 percent of black males, and 31 percent of black females.[8] A high school diploma does not convert the opportunities for a black woman into those of a white man. Whether dropout or graduate, black women are two to three times more likely to live in poverty than white women, and four times more likely than white men.

The positive effects of a diploma are nonetheless compelling *within* demographic groups. Black female graduates are half as likely to live in poverty (31 percent) as are black female dropouts (62 percent). They are substantially less likely to work inside a private household (20 percent vs. 52 percent) and more than twice as likely to hold a white-collar position (60 percent vs. 25 percent). The absence of a diploma for women within race and ethnic and class lines can be economically devastating.

## THE "CAUSES" OF DROPPING OUT

National data confirm that social class is the most reliable predictor of dropping out for females and males.[9] Although, in the aggregate, native American adolescents are more likely to drop out than Latino adolescents, followed by blacks and then whites, once we control for social class we see that among low-income adolescents, *white students* are relatively more likely to drop out of high school than Latinos, who are more likely to than blacks. Social class operates, however, as a substantially more protective buffer against dropping out for white students than for students of color. Upper-income white students are 29 percent as likely to drop out as low-income white students, whereas upper-income black students are 82 percent as likely as low-income blacks to drop out.

Once gender is introduced into the analysis, the patterns grow even more complicated. Black males report the highest rates of dropping out nationally, with white females reporting the lowest. And among Latinos gender differences slip to be relatively inconsequential. In urban areas, however, we find that white males and females drop out at equivalent rates (15.7 percent and 15.3 percent, respectively); black females drop out far less often than black males (16.6 percent and 24.4 percent respectively); and Latina females drop out with far greater frequency than Latino males (26.2 percent and 20.2 percent, respectively). The social assaults associated with being low-income black and male in urban culture, and the responsibilities of being low-income Latina and female "effectively" operate, for probably very different and relatively unexplored reasons, to facilitate early exit from high school.[10]

These incidence data suggest that in the aggregate young women are *not* at greater numeric "risk" of dropping out of high school than young men. Their patterns diverge some, but, except for urban Latinas,

they depart in smaller proportions than young men do. Yet as we disen-
tangle their reasons for leaving and the consequences of their leaving,
we are compelled to move beyond simple biology and discharge rates to
acknowledge that the politics of being female, low income, and of color
in contemporary public schools denies these women full participation
inside public schooling in part on the basis of their gender. They are
neglected, dismissed, and relegated to positions of substantial educational, economic, and social "risk."

## DOWN THE UP STAIRCASE:
## WHAT THEY SAY ABOUT WHY THEY LEAVE

We turn now to how young women explain their early departure
from high school, and we segregate the data into family concerns,
school experiences, and "being female."

### *Family Concerns*

When we examine specifically what young women say about dropping out, we learn that females drop out primarily in response to family
concerns. As Naomi noted, "Sometimes when you're the oldest child,
you have a lot of responsibilities. Your mother's out working and you
have to take care of the house and be a mother to the other kids. You
can't operate in school when you got so much else on your mind." An
analysis of a national sample of high school dropouts reports that 5
percent of male dropouts compared with 37 percent of female dropouts
select "family-related problems" as the reason they left high school.[11]
Eight percent of the young women had to help support a family, 31 percent said they left to marry, and 23 percent reported a pregnancy as the
reason they dropped out.[12] Janice Earle, Virginia Roach, and Katherine
Fraser, in a rich synthesis of available evidence on female dropouts,
report that young women are systematically more likely than young
men to drop out when they reside in low-income households, when
they live with multiple siblings, when their mothers are high school
dropouts, and when their fathers work in low-wage positions.[13] Family
complexity strains adolescent females and interrupts their educational
careers far more dramatically than is true for young men.

## The Experience of Schooling

In addition to family matters, young women drop out of high school for the same reason that young men do. They don't like school. A full 31 percent of the female respondents to the High School and Beyond data set indicated that they "did not like school." Thirty percent reported "poor grades."[14] Data from the Comprehensive High School (CHS) and the focus groups offer us some clues as to when young women decide that they don't like school, and when their dislike swells sufficiently to flee. Two primary issues emerge: in-grade retention and the impersonality of large, overcrowded, comprehensive high schools.

*In-Grade Retention.* Being "held back," "left down," or retained in grade bears devastating academic consequences for young women. National data confirm that retention in grade doubles the likelihood of dropping out for males and females.[15] Evidence from CHS indicates that retention is particularly problematic for young women. After being retained, females leave school even earlier than male dropouts, losing additional years of education.[16] And female dropouts from CHS *described* far more negative effects than males after having been retained in grade. Of all those interviewed who had been retained, a full 92 percent of the female dropouts, compared with only 22 percent of the males, spontaneously related their decision to drop out to having been retained in grade: "It felt real bad. First I felt so tall compared to them little ones, and then my brother was in the class, and so finally I just left. Embarrassed and not working I felt so stupid."[17]

Our analysis suggests that young women *read* and *express* retention decisions as an institutional message of their personal inadequacy. When educators indicate that they need to be retained or that they deserve to fail a class, they internalize these decisions as signifiers of their own incompetence.[18] Although these young women at CHS who had been retained were as likely to drop out as retained young men, they were *far more likely* to leave school prior to age eighteen, and four times more likely to express a relationship between being retained and eventually dropping out.

*Relationships with Educators.* Many young women linked their dissatisfaction with school to inadequate relationships with teachers and counselors.[19] Their sense of self, their experiences of belonging in the classroom, and their interest in course content were strongly related to the presence and quality of these relationships. Although such relationships with teachers may be crucial for the success of students of either gender, in the case of female students the problem is, again, described by them as more undermining of their desire to connect and be known.[20]

This problem of forming relationships with educators is confounded by the class-stratified distribution of human resources inside public schools. In the poorer schools of Philadelphia some guidance counselors report frustration with caseloads of up to one thousand students, each of whom needs personal attention. Not surprisingly, some of the young women we interviewed reported that they had never met with a counselor, much less developed a personal relationship with one. Others said they met with their counselors as infrequently as once a year—for fifteen minutes. The exception seemed to be the female student who had a problem that captured the attention of some adult in the school system, who notified a counselor. Even then, however, couselors were often too overwhelmed to provide more than cursory service.

One young Latina woman softly noted, "Nobody called me. All they know is that it's one less student. One less student to worry about. They don't care."

## On Being Female

Finally, quantitative evidence substantiates what many of us have feared about the female gender role. Young women who most loyally subscribe to traditional views of gender roles are more likely to drop out of high school. The Hispanic Policy Development Project analyzed the national High School and Beyond data set specifically for low-income respondents and found that young women who as sophomores expected to be married and/or have a child by age nineteen were more likely to not graduate than those who said they did not expect to marry and/or have a child by nineteen.[21] Sophomores who were nongraduates were 400 percent more likely than those who did graduate to anticipate being a mother by age nineteen, and 200 percent more likely to expect to be a wife.[22]

Ekstrom et al. analyzed attitudinal data from High School and Beyond and generated conclusions which reinforced these findings. Of the High School and Beyond respondents, young women who ultimately dropped out were more likely to agree that "most women are happiest when making a home" and "it is usually better if the man is the achiever and the woman takes care of the home."[23]

What then do we know about why young women drop out? Relative to young men, they are more vulnerable to fluctuations in socioeconomic level and family strain; more likely to leave school if family problems emerge, including but not limited to pregnancy and child care needs; more stereotyped by gender role than their peers; more painfully affected by in-grade retention and poor grades; and more likely to feel alienated in large, urban high schools. Our next question is, with what consequence?

## THE CONSEQUENCES:
## EDUCATIONAL, ECONOMIC, AND SOCIAL

Compared to young men, young women who have dropped out of urban high schools are substantially less likely to return to school for a degree or a G.E.D., and more likely to live in poverty. Relying on High School and Beyond data analyses provided by Kolstad and Ownings,[24] we see that the percentage of dropouts who graduated within two years of when they would have (if they had remained in high school) is substantially higher for Latino (34 percent) and black males (39 percent) and for urban males (43 percent) than for females (Latina 26 percent; black 26 percent; urban 25 percent).[25]

Although the economic value of a G.E.D. remains contested, the available evidence indicates that financial benefits do accrue to recipients of a G.E.D., at least compared with those who have neither high school diploma nor G.E.D.[26] The combined information on rates of return, passage of the G.E.D. examination, and the poverty of low-income female dropouts document the relative finality and costs of dropping out of high school for urban adolescent females.

If the G.E.D. data tell us what female dropouts are *not* doing, moving our analysis to the classrooms of proprietary schools informs us about what they *are* doing. Low-income female high school dropouts are apparently more vulnerable to the promises and often unethical practices of private proprietary schools than are males. Evidence collected on and by these schools, including institutes for cosmetologists, computer technicians, business skills, beauticians, and trade schools, indicates that enrollment is disproportionately female, black and Latina, low income, urban, and failed.

The New York State Education Department in 1985 released a report which found proprietary schools to be in violation of entry requirements, involved in questionable recruitment practices, reporting high dropout rates, and failing to offer instructional programs approved by the State Department of Education. The report concludes: "An indepth analysis of six schools revealed that more than 70% of TAP [Tuition Assistance Plan] recipients failed to complete their program of study, nearly 60% failed to complete more than half; nearly 30% received no more than one TAP award before withdrawing. Business schools, it was found, generate more revenue when students fail to pursue their programs than when they complete them."[27] A report from the state of Pennsylvania more recently revealed another troubling aspect of the proliferation of these private schools which thrive on public monies. This report finds that "Black first year students in proprietary schools more than tripled between 1976 and 1984," and in 1984 "22 percent of all black first year students enrolled in postsecondary institutions were in proprietary schools compared with just 7% in 1976."[28]

To the extent that many of these schools report dropout rates in excess of 70 percent and that the students who attend, who drop out, and who ultimately default on state loans are disproportionately low-income women, we conclude that female dropouts are not only attracted to but rendered extremely vulnerable by these institutions.

*Sharon, a seventeen-year-old dropout:* They paid me for everybody in the projects that I could get to sign up for the—business institute, and then go down there. I think they get money if people who up a coupla times, and I get money too.

Sharon was paid to knock on doors in the projects and recruit friends, neighbors, and kin to this business institute. Apparently a semester's worth of state-financed tuition was available if a student showed up a minimum of three times. Michell Fine hired an assisant, Sherry Rose, to go undercover to a number of such facilities and to represent herself as a dropout eager for training.

*Sherry:* They do seduce you. The man said, he was a black man, so they try to get us to trust him, he said if I gave him $20 he would save a spot for me, and then I could tell my mother that I already gave them $20 so she would be more likely to let me enroll. If I were really desperate and wanted to believe him, I would have done it.

At a public school luncheon recently Fine sat next to the mother of a second-grade boy at a Philadelphia public elementary school. When Fine mentioned her work, the mother proceeded to talk about another consequence of her involvement with proprietary schools:

> *Ms. Marcus:* I went to one and dropped out, they weren't really teaching me anything. But I owe money on the loan, so now when I want to go to Community College I can't get the funds. I have to pay full tuition out of my own pocket and can't afford to go full time to college 'cause they ripped me off.

The cumulative consequences of dropping out and enrolling in what are represented as fabulous opportunities for education, fame, and fortune only exacerbate young women's biographies of academic failure and economic troubles.

Graduation as a credential and graduation as a signifier of education are both disrupted by early departure from high school, and disrupted disproportionately for young women. It has been documented, for example, that the skill loss associated with dropping out is greater for females than for males, for blacks than for whites. In the areas of language development, including vocabulary, reading, and writing, women's skills (compared with men's) and blacks' skills (compared with whites') deteriorate substantially when they leave school early.[29]

It is perhaps redundant to conclude with the obvious. Those who are likely to confront the greatest obstacles in the economy are those who suffer the most for having dropped out of high school. The consequences for these young women should be sufficiently compelling to provoke us to rethink the ease with which low-income women are "allowed" to leave high school and are pushed out. That a full 49 percent of families headed by female high school dropouts live in poverty makes it obvious that we can do no less.[30]


## THE MARBLING OF RACE, CLASS, AND GENDER
## AND THE DENIAL: AN ANALYSIS

Public schools represent themselves as gender, race and ethnicity, and class neutral: that is, in the 1980s, all children and adolescents are legally entitled to universal and compulsory access to public education. A history of legislation and litigation guarantees equal access, and yet a history and currency of unequal outcomes persists unchallenged, and indeed buttressed by contemporary reform movements.

The first third of this essay elaborated the ways in which gender entwines with race, ethnicity, and social class to render substantially different educational and economic outcomes for young, low-income women and men. In this second section we offer an analysis which suggests that public schools are structured in ways that systematically undermine the material conditions of low-income women's lives, derogate their experiences and ways of viewing the world around them, and artificially split their bodies and sexualities into dichotomous positions of desire and victimization. Materially and ideologically, public schools are organized in ways that render low-income young women "at risk" and that deny their collusion in this process.

### Undermining the Material Conditions of Young Women's Lives

*Patricia:* I just can't concentrate in school, thinkin' about my mother gettin' beat up last night. He scares me too but I just don't understand why she stays.

*Marina:* Just can't do it all. I've got a baby and I have to work. School will just have to wait for now.

*Ms. Porter, a teacher, to Michelle Fine:* I spoke with Sylvia and I wondered if you would talk to her. She is having some problems. She can't come to school because her boyfriend waits for her every morning and fights with her. He threatens her. Sylvia said she wants to move out for a while but her relatives live in the Bronx. Maybe you could talk with her. There are no brothers, so I know she is troubled. I taught her last year when I am sure she wasn't going with anyone and she is much changed now.

Low-income adolescent women are involved in caring for themselves as well as their kin, and they are vulnerable. Nested inside relationships of care, responsibility, and sometimes violence, their lives are woven with others'.[31] We found this to be the case for Latina, black, and white women whom we interviewed. And what we learned was not that they resented these responsibilities nor considered them excessive, but that the material and relational conditions of their lives were experienced as demanding, primarily because their schools imposed an artificial split between "public" and "private" issues.[32]

Public schools posit separate spheres:[33] that is, they presume that what goes on *in* school—the "public"—should be separated from what

goes on *out* of school—the "private." But by so doing, public schools actually preserve the hegemony of private interests such as AT&T,
Shearson-Lehman investors, Ford Foundation, Shell Oil and endless
textbook publishers inside these schools. They may sponsor mentor
programs, part-time employment opportunities, guest speakers, and/or
"adopt-a-school." At the same time, the interests of family, community
advocates, health care, and family planning are constructed as private—beyond the limits of the typical low-income public high school.[34]
The consequences of this artificial, but enforced, position are many for
low-income adolescent women. First, low-income families and communities are rendered extraneous if not a nuisance to the workings of
the school. Parent disempowerment, a telling moment of race, class,
and gender alienation, bears serious consequence for enhancing the
likelihood of adolescent dropout.[35] Second, issues that young women
experience as "private" and "personal"—even if they affect large numbers of adolescents across social classes and racial and ethnic groups—
are reserved for discussion inside counselors' offices, rather than in
classrooms. That domestic violence was a secret not to be discussed in
social studies, English, or science, but only in the protected offices of
school psychologists or guidance counselors (who are available in a 500
to 1 ratio to students) marks a betrayal of these young women's lives.
And third, that schools have determined "private" lives to be beyond
their work means that young women who traverse the public-private
boundary must typically make a choice. That is what happened to
Portia:

> *Portia:* I have to drop out to care for my grandmother.
> *Michelle Fine:* Do you want me to see what I can do for you to stay in
> school?
> *Portia:* No, I've got to go.

Moved by this interaction, Fine repeated the story to a social worker
friend from the suburbs. She questioned Fine, and the story: "Why
wasn't a social worker called in?" And so Fine asked the guidance counselor why a social worker wasn't brought in, and was greeted with a
familiar smile indicating her naivete: "Michelle, all 3,200 of these kids
require a social worker. Anyway, if Portia is concerned about her future
she needs not to get so involved in her family but worry about herself."
Portia's responsibility at home was translated into a lack of motivation
at school.

Enacting responsibilities they do not experience as inherently incompatible, female students are often forced to sacrifice their own educations and aspirations in the service of others. Inside their lives the needs of self and others are braided together. Inside their schools these needs are posited as incompatible. With families, boyfriends, girlfriends, and school all competing for top priority, these young women feel the emotional toll of being pulled in all directions. Perhaps this is why national and local data so consistently reveal that social class, family strain, and number of siblings predict so well female dropout rates.

## DEROGATING THE SPLIT SUBJECTIVITIES OF LOW-INCOME ADOLESCENT FEMALES

Feminist philosopher Sandra Harding writes that "unitary consciousness" poses an obstacle to learning, that women engage split consciousness in both their understandings and analyses of the world around them.[36] What has historically been read as woman contradicting herself, Harding reframes as woman, from a position of disempowerment, viewing a world from both inside and from the margins. Low-income women of color, at the intersection of class, race, and gender oppression, embody the most dramatic space from which social critique and commentary can be generated and hurled.[37]

Through the stories and words of these low-income adolescent women, the richness of their contradictions, complexities, and concerns flourish. Whether discussing gender, welfare, violence, retention policies, racism, social class, or the questionable value of a high school diploma, their social stance—that which has been allocated to them and that which has been created by them—blossoms with a split consciousness.[38]

It is precisely the contradiction, complexity, and concern which informs their thinking that is given little room inside those spaces called public school classrooms—"at risk" or not. We eavesdrop again on a discussion in history class:

> In early Spring, a social studies teacher structured an in-class debate on Bernard Goetz, New York City's "subway vigilante." She invited "Those students who agree with Goetz sit on one side of the room, and those who think he was wrong sit on the other side." To the

large residual group who remained mid-room, the teacher remarked,
"Don't be lazy. You have to make a decision. Like at work, you can't be
passive." A few wandered over to the "pro-Goetz" side. About six
remained in the center. Somewhat angry, the teacher continued, "OK,
first we'll hear the pro-Goetz side and then the anti-Goetz side. Those
of you who have no opinions, who haven't even thought about the
issue, you won't get to talk unless we have time."

Deirdre, a black senior, bright and always quick to raise contradictions otherwise obscured, advocated the legitimacy of the middle group. "It's not that I have no opinions. I don't like Goetz shootin'
up people who look like my brother, but I don't like feelin' unsafe in
the projects or in my neighborhood either. I got lots of opinions. I ain't
bein' quiet cause I can't decide if he's right or wrong. I'm talkin."

Deirdre's comment legitimated for herself and others the right to
hold complex, perhaps even contradictory, positions on a complex,
even contradictory, situation. Such legitimacy was rarely granted inside
classrooms—with clear and important exceptions, including activist
faculty and those paraprofessionals who lived in Central Harlem with
the kids, who understood and respected much about their lives.

Among the chorus of voices heard within this high school lay little
room for Antonio Gramsci's contradictory consciousness[39] or Sandra
Harding's split subjectivities.[40] Artificial dichotomies were institutionalized as if natural: right and wrong answers; appropriate and
inappropriate behaviors; moral and immoral people; dumb and smart
students; responsible and irresponsible parents; public and private
issues. Contradiction and ambivalence were experienced often, expressed rarely, and for the most part forced underground.

Low-income black, Latina, and white adolescents—male and
female—live in a world that is clearly not organized around their needs.
Given the political spaces that they occupy and create, their social
analyses offer the complexity of split consciousness, social critique, and
devastating commentary. What may appear to be contradictory in their
thoughts must be reframed as the complexities of social views voiced
from the position of one upon whom social institutions, programs, and
policies are imposed (and withheld), rather than by whom or for whom
these projects are designed. The reflections of these young women, for
whom the knots of relationships further complicate and enhance their
ways of viewing, merge their experiences, critiques, and longings for
what could be.

*Michelle Fine:* What do you think of welfare?
*Lavanda:* It's terrible. Makes you feel bad standing' on line, and embarrassed like you're no good. Them girls on welfare are lazy...
*Michelle Fine:* Then you think welfare programs should be cut?
*Lavanda:* No way. We need it when we are sick, or can't work, or somethin' like that. Just makes you feel so bad...

Lavanda offers to welfare what Deirdre, in the opening quotation, offered to gender—an analysis filled with the seeming contradiction between what is [It makes you feel so bad...] and what should be [We need it...]. What would be misread as a contradiction is revealed, upon probing, as a full and knotty analysis of policy at variance with practice. If a contradiction lies inside this conversation, it lies in the fact that welfare policies are advertised to "help," designed to "discourage," and implemented in ways that "humiliate." This is not a case of faulty reasoning by young women.[41]

The extent to which these social policies and ideologies, which most dramatically affect young women, are preserved and protected by a hegemonic public school curriculum speaks to the second form of miseducation for low-income adolescent females. Not only are their material circumstances undermined, but their ways of viewing the world are systematically subordinated to "right answers." Social ideologies and arrangements which ultimately do them in—racism, sexism, the strutures of advanced capitalism, domestic and community violence, beliefs in a meritocracy—survive comfortably inside public school classrooms, unchallenged and unanalyzed. Take, for instance, the traditions of the female gender role, romance, marriage, and babymaking:

*Michelle Fine:* Where will you be in five years?
*Millie:* I plan to be rich, get me a condominium and put my name on the least [sic.] so I can throw him out when I need to.
*Ilana:* I'm still in love with Simon, but I'm seeing Jose. He's OK, but he said, "Will you be my girl?" I hate that. It feels like they own you. Like I say to my girlfriend, "What's wrong, you look terrible." And she said, "I'm married."
*Mr. Perry to Michelle Fine, about Elisa, in the attendance office:* Don't worry. She's dropping out, but it's a good case. She's fifteen, pregnant but getting married. She'll go for a G.E.D.

No one told Elisa that teen pregnancy compounded by marriage is more likely to result in divorce, domestic violence, a second child, and a disrupted education than teen pregnancy alone.[42] No one reminded her that she was disrupting her education. Marriage somehow "legitimated" the activity.

In the first section of this essay we learned that young women who hold traditional notions of what it means to be a woman, a mother, or a wife are most likely to abort their own educations prematurely. Public schools uncritically protect and defend the social conventions of marriage, heterosexuality, motherhood, and work (usually in that order). The fact that young women and men have questions, doubts, and concerns and have witnessed the contradictions is basically off limits inside public schools—except in the unusual classroom of the unusual educator who knows that what she or he knows, what the text and curriculum teaches, and what the students think derive from very different political spaces and deserve equal time inside a process of educating.

> *September 12. Classroom discussion of values. Six of twelve rate "health" as the value of first importance. That's obviously what is important when you don't have access to primary health care.*
> *Teacher:* What is your first choice?
> *Willie:* I picked freedom 'cause you need freedom to do what you got to do, on your own, no rules.
> *Alicia:* That ain't never gonna be. Somebody always giving you a paycheck or an apartment or your mother or your kid. You ain't never free.
> *Teacher:* Anybody choose love?
> *Five girls raise their hands.*
> *Michelle Fine:* Why did the girls choose love and the boys didn't?
> *LeShan:* 'Cause girls are mushier.
> *Yolanda:* Girls admit it.
> *Willie:* Anybody say they don't cry, lying. Especially if somebody hits you . . . but sometimes guys don't say it.
> *Yolanda:* That's different. If something pain you in your heart, would you come here and cry in school?
> *Willie:* I would cry and talk to somedy out there. You don't know my business and so you can't help.

Females appear to express emotions more easily, and indeed it is suspected by many that they experience them for self and others more easily as well. This scene, combined with the evidence on the negative impact of retention—in which males and females appear to be *equally* affected but females admit the pain of retention *400 percent* more often than males do—suggests that young women may "make public" emotional needs and desires which affect low-income adolescents, male and female.

As we have suggested throughout the paper, the consequences of holding female students back include a diminished sense of self-worth and increased feelings of failure, both linked to the decision to drop out. Although one might not expect students who feel victimized by such policies to support their continued practice, a majority of the young women whom we interviewed expressed both their pain and their endorsement of those policies. As we unravel these young women's responses, their positions—as victims, critics, and supporters of a policy which undermines them—appear more obvious.

Many of the women we interviewed located the failure to learn the grade-appropriate material within themselves. Others identified a lack of skilled, caring teachers and a prevalence of overcrowded, underresourced classrooms in their formula of culpability. Regardless of blame, most of these women nevertheless believed that students should not be allowed to pass on to the next grade level if they lack basic information and skills that serve as the basis for future learning. One young black woman commented, "You have to know certain things before you go on. You have to learn how to read and write and do basic math or you're going to be sitting in the next grade and realize you don't understand anything that's going on. That's a sure set-up for failure." They also believed, however, that students should be held back only after they have had access to specialized instruction and/or high-quality tutoring—opportunities infrequently offered to lower-class students.

Some acknowledged that being held back was often experienced as punishment and increased students' dropout rate. At the same time, they believed that being passed on without learning anything was a disservice to the students themselves. Crystal, a black teen mother, told a story about her mother, who had gone through twelve years of school and was essentially illiterate. Although described as a talented seamstress, her mother would concel her illiteracy at work by taking the instructions that her customers left her to her sister or her daughter to read. Crystal commented: "And that was a crime! She should have been held back at some point and taught to read. If she had, she could have been a successful businesswoman."

Several women suggested that promoting students prematurely into the next grade contributed to the facade that students and teachers were engaged in some kind of educational process. Rather than taking responsibility for their contribution to the problem of students' illiteracy, teachers were passing students on, thereby deferring and even compounding the problem. Thus, the female students' response to holding failing students back was less a desire to support a practice that damages students' self-concept, and more an acknowledgement of the dilemma for students who are not being educated.

If low-income adolescent females carry all the richness of contradiction and are willing to express it, they may suffer for their insights. Public school settings typically privilege singular and linear views of the way things are—particularly in "low-track" or "remedial" classrooms. They silence evolving responses and groom for success those who obscure, deny, and contain the contradictions. Indeed, in an analysis comparing the social ideologies of low-income high school graduates and dropouts, Michelle Fine found that high school graduates—academic successes—are much more likely than dropouts to *dismiss* the pain and suffering they see on the streets; to *imagine* that they will have better lives; to *mimic* social ideologies which promise the correspondence of education and success; and to believe it. Dropouts in general do not so easily dismiss, mimic, or act as if they believe. And the young women among them speak out. Perhaps their appeal lies in the raw willingness to tell. But their academic vulnerability lies inside public institutions committed to protecting the secrets of race, class, and gender privilege, which these young women give away.

## POSITIONING THE BODIES OF ADOLESCENT WOMEN AS VICTIMS

If the material conditions of their lives are neglected, and their split subjectivities dismissed, then so too are the bodies and sexualities of adolescent women sabotaged inside public schools. This argument, developed more fully in the *Harvard Educational Review*,[43] suggests that while the contexts of low-income adolescent lives, their minds, and their ways of viewing are rendered irrelevant if not disruptive to public schooling, young women's bodies and sexualities are experienced as dangerous, threatening, and in need of containment. "If the body is seen as endangered by uncontrollable forces, then presumably this is a society or social group which fears change—change which is perceived simultaneously as powerful and beyond its control."[44] The public discussion typically isolates this "problem" as if it were only inside the adolescent uterus. Within public schools, however, it becomes clear that the more primitive obsession lies with the female student's body, her sexuality, and ultimately her ways of acting upon the world autonomously. As class and race oppression historically blend with societal sexual anxieties, the low-income black or Latina woman is rendered the particularly threatening social icon.[45] Although healthy male sexuality also receives less than adequate attention in the public school curriculum, the explicit positioning of the adolescent-female-body-as-victim deserves comment for its intended, and its unintended, consequences.

In the *Harvard Education Review* article, Michelle Fine writes about the pervasive ambivalence which organizes social ideologies of female sexuality.[46] Inside these ideologies the image of the female sexual *victim* (object) has been fully split from the image of the female sexual *subject*. Severing pleasure from danger, and sexual victimization from agency, this simple splitting denies the huge abyss and complexity (which is only begining to be scrutinized) that organizes, obscures, defines, and deforms what it means to be female and sexual.[47] In this context, the female adolescent has been posed as the sexual innocent or object. Trained to "Say No" in school, she rehearses strategies for fighting off the male heterosexual pursuer and learns about the risks of pregnancy, disease, loss of reputation, self-esteem, and the tax burdens she imposes on her communities, in the event that she takes the leap from heterosexual innocent to subject.

Our dispute is not with individual sex educators who typically have to juggle diverse religious, political, and eduational interests. Our problem lies with the more general ideological positioning (within and without schools) of adolescent female bodies as primarily the site of sexual victimization, with no analysis of desire. In the absence of an education which grants females the possibility of imagining themselves to be subjects of sexuality—to determine if, when, how, under what circumstances, with whom or without whom—then young women are indeed being trained to be *victims,* that is, objects. To the extent that the active moments in their bodies are silenced by schools and a society terrified of the female sexual subject, young women are taught only how to respond to heterosexual male questions—Yes or No—not their own; only to respond, not act; only to defend and not create for themselves a sexual subjectivity which blends an assessment of coercion, desire, pain, pleasure, risk, and danger.

Evidence from school-based health clinics (SBHCs) implemented onsite suggests that the provision of contraception and abortion information appears sufficient to reduce not only the rate of teen births but also to increase the use of contraception and to postpone the onset of heterosexual intercourse.[48] Perhaps because these clinics recognize the possibilities for victimization and for pleasure, they empower young women to be responsible as participants *or not* in heterosexual relations. These young women may then be in a position to explore their needs, desires, and limits for themselves—rather than sitting at the mercy of boyfriends, peers, or strangers.

To the extent that family planning and sex education classes remain silent about adolescent female sexuality as pleasure, they educate to only half of young women's experiences, severing from their bodies the pleasures—actual, imagined, fabricated, and mystified—particularly as long as they remain undiscussed.

## CONCLUDING THOUGHTS ON ANALYSIS

Young women, black, Latina, and white, promised us in our interviews and our observations that they very much wanted a good life, if not for themselves, then for their babies: "It's too late for me, I'm seventeen. But for my baby, Catholic schools and a house in New Jersey." On the streets, searching for employment opportunites that were once available to dropouts but which are little more than an urban memory shadowed in the abandoned buildings of urban factories and warehouses, dropouts face few options. The G.E.D. is tough to pass (the New York State pass rate for 1984 was 46 percent) and will only get tougher as "standards" are improved. Proprietary schools are swelling in enrollments with no discernible improvement in their dropout rates, placement rates, or *appropriate* training procedures. Even the military, a dream held by many low-income women, holds the quite ambiguous promise for perhaps some vocational training at the expense of race and gender discrimination and the waiving of one's civil rights.[49]

Title IX assures us that young women are entitled to a public education that does not discriminate against them on the basis of sex. If we move beyond sex as a biological category and place gender into its social and political context, we see that, among low-income adolescents, being female means caring for relatives and neighbors (not only after 3:00); thinking about the world in contradictory, creative, sometimes self-defeating and sometimes self-enhancing ways, and about social ideologies that require disruption; and having a body that is changing, moving, transforming, and being transformed.

For these same young women, attending public high school typically means learning to dismiss the material complexities and relationships which enrich and entangle their lives; ignoring the rich split consciousness with which they see the world and engaging instead in a single, linear view of mobility, progress, and justice; and practicing to protect (or not) their bodies from "invasion." These three meanings of public schools, unacknowledged and essential to institutional coherence, place low-income young women in positions of academic, economic, and social jeopardy. To presume any different is to reproduce the ideology which believes that those public institutions we call "public schools" are gender, race and ethnicity, and class neutral. Instead we must realize that those institutions serve in ways that could empower but that currently, more typically, betray those young women who most believe, who most need, and who most suffer from the absence of a high school degree.

## ON POSSIBILITY:
## PREVENTING AND RETRIEVING FEMALE DROPOUTS

For public schools to prevent the loss of low-income female students and retrieve those who are on their way out or who have already left, structural changes within schools and in the realtionship between school and other public institutions are crucial. Having talked with many young women and analyzed both qualitative and quantitative data on their educational careers, we are compelled to conclude that adolescent females, perhaps more than males, can be assisted by school-based interventions which take seriously the needs and demands of home and community; which promote positive messages about competence and ability, not punishing messages which may be designed to motivate but nevertheless tend to discourage; and which appreciate that all students—and particularly young women—need a safe and intimate space to pursue new ideas, evolving notions of self, and desire to be educated.

*Bridging School-Community Relationships*

For public high schools to interrupt the high rate of female dropouts, the impoverished relationship between schools and low-income communities must be addressed. These communities capture their contradictory affections and loyalties. Many low-income adolescents are fully committed to the neighborhood in which they were raised—to their mothers, fathers, grandmothers, and other relatives who remain— and they are often fearful of the violence associated with drug trafficking. Strong and complex identification with one's culture and community are necessary not only for survival but also for a positive sense of self and for the making of an involved and active community member.[50]

We need to imagine and create schools in which students guide educators through their local streets, churches, and centers, introducing them to the neighborhood woman who "talks to us like we're grown up" and the man who "must be eighty-five years old and seen this community go up and come back down." Students, *particularly those "at risk,"* can be invited to tape oral histories; to investigate the employment patterns in the community; to examine the availability of child care; to conduct surveys on perceptions of race relations, schools, or the police; to visit the courts and follow a criminal trial of bias-related violence; or to interview children about music, dress, or ethnic foods. Students can import the community into school—through exhibits, tapes, documents, visitors, and the arts. They can be the guides to their communities, their histories, and their kin.

Structural arrangements between school and community must also address issues of *employment* for youths. Vocational training for young women should be expressly nontraditional, given the low salaries and job insecurity associated with most pink-collar and domestic work. The New York Technical College program, "Expanding Options for Teen Mothers," offers important nontraditional vocational training for young mothers and pregnant teens.[51] Their interventions stretch the vocational imaginations of girls and women to the nontraditional trades of carpentry and plumbing, open opportunities in male-dominated trades, and give these young women an opportunity to feel entitled to a better life.

Ties with *health care facilities* and social service agencies also need to be established. Low-income women are involved not only with their own health care, but also with that of their kin. Rather than jeopardize a student's education for her family's well-being, schools need to establish links with mental health centers, community health clinics, battered women's shelters, rape crisis centers, and social service agencies to which female students can be referred so that they can assist their families without fully sacrificing their own lives. Better yet, we can engage students in compiling an Adolescent Yellow Pages, with agencies for referrals and the names of individual social workers who will handle the cases stemming from a particular school. If these services can be more broadly made available to kin, the burden on the adolescent female may in part be lifted.

Access to *family planning clinics* is also essential if young women are to flourish and not pay a lifetime price for heterosexual involvement. If a school does not have an on-site or referral health clinic, educators need to advocate one or at least make sure that someone in school becomes sufficiently familiar with community clinics to be able to refer students for contraception or abortion as necessary, and that this someone follows up with these students.[52]

Finally, educators need to be linked with *educational advocacy organizations* nationally and locally. These organizations can provide alternative curricular materials on gender and race;[53] data on sex and race equity issues;[54] strategies for parent empowerment;[55] and professional support for infusing nontraditional and controversial materials into schools and classrooms.[56]

## *Within Schools*

For public high schools to curtail the female dropout rate, schools also need to restructure internally. This means dividing large public high schools into small communities, "houses" or "advisories" in which students meet daily as a community unto themselves, in which they are known to each other, appreciated when present, missed when absent, and tracked down when truant over time.[57] If educators can't arrange schedules to be available during some free time (or even if they can), young women can be involved in peer networks, buddies, "big sisters," and community-based young women's groups, or mother-daughter groups.[58] Peer-tutoring programs have proven to be most effective for tutors, so why not set up a program in which academically marginal high school students tutor young kids, creating both a sense of community and a sense of competence?[59]

In a more proactive, critical stance, there are many projects that educators, community members, and advocates can initiate within schools to *investigate who is discharged,* under what circumstances, with what information, and with how much follow-up. Are students who "choose" to leave high school at age sixteen or seventeen informed that without a high school degree their educational and economic options outside high school are limited, that those options may appear to be more promising than is actually the case, and that those options have grown worse over the past decade? Do they know that the G.E.D. requires passing a tough examination, and that in states like New York the pass rate is less than 50 percent? Are they taught that no branch of the military accepts females who have not graduated from high school and that differential entry standards by sex are well enforced? Have they been informed that proprietary schools have been exposed for their unfulfilled promises of glamour and money? Perhaps students could undertake a class project to study the discharge patterns in a school and follow up some of the dropouts to see what "options" they have pursued, and with what consequence, or to study the impact of retention policies on adolescents.[60]

There are still other intraschool advocacy strategies that educators have found to be useful. Working alone or in concert with other educators, some people have organized to advocate for students who are being pushed out. Others have spoken at Parents' Association meetings to inform parents and guardians of their legal rights with regard to students being discharged or suspended. Some people work one on one with parents to encourage them to come to school and to sit in on classes so that educators come to know and respect the families of low-income adolescents. And still others prefer to work with *long-term truants* who just need personal encouragement to come back, for example, through a Second Chance program.[61] These programs, which were tested effectively across the nation, involve contacting dropouts after a specified period of time (one month or two) and inviting them back into a special program in which classes are small, the curriculum is engaging, and pedagogies are empowering. These students need extra and "accelerated" help, not the routine, dull, and rote pedagogies traditionally associated with "remedial" classes.[62]

## *Within Classrooms*

A variety of *pedagogical strategies* have been developed which appear to enhance the participation of female students in middle and high schools. Teaching cooperatively has recently gained popularity and shown some evidence of effectiveness, particularly with low-income students. Altering the social organization of learning from individualism or competition to cooperation can significantly raise academic achievement, enhance a willingness to pursue academic learning, and foster social learning about community, empathy, and cooperation.[63]

Marlaine Lockheed has developed the notion of 'inoculation groups' in which she recommends that females work in same-sex segregated groups prior to their participation with males in integrated contexts. What Lockheed has discovered is that once young women hear themselves participating on topics, having opinions, and getting a hearing in the all-female group, they then feel better equipped and en-titled to the same hearing in a mixed-sex group.[64]

Educators have found that the introduction of current events which include female activists, protagonists in their own stories, provokes female student involvement. Discussions of the complexities of "being a woman" at work, in families, in classrooms, or on the street can generate much energy from female students. Conversations about the power inequities which surround relations of gender, race and eth-nicity, disability, social class, and sexual orientation are conversations which invite female voices. One notices quickly that when female students are encouraged to analyze the contradictions that organize their lives—the vast space between desire and reality—their voices carry important critical insights into what is, and creative thoughts about what could be.

As we noted in the introduction to this chapter, the traditional at-titudes and sacrifices associated with being female in this society jeop-ardize the educational and ultimately the economic well-being of young women. In the absence of a critical, school-based discussion of gender roles, young women have little choice but to make sense of them alone or default to "tradition." Educators are responsible for creating a context in which *female voices* flourish, get a hearing, pose a critique of the oppressive aspects of the female gender role, and generate novel ways of engaging, resisting, and transforming what it means to be a young woman.

A related issue is *female silence.* The boy who acts out is likely to grab somebody's attention, even if it is only negative attention. Silent females are neglected until they disappear. Educators need to intervene to ensure that young women participate, that their participation is taken seriously and reinforced by peers, and that views through female eyes and experiences are granted legitimacy in the classroom. The female student must be involved in academic activities that enable her to be an expert. If she speaks a language which is not English, let her teach her English-speaking peers. If she lives alone with a grandmother or is the primary caretaker for siblings, involve her in the production of a play or a debate about caretaking in a society without national health insurance, or with inadequate public childcare. If she comes from an economically impoverished and culturally rich neighborhood, let her compile biographies of people, buildings, and blocks to unearth how communities come to be "abandoned."

As we monitor female academic progress, we must note what percentage of female students in our classes and schools are enrolled in science, math, computers, and engineering. If strong gender biases prevail in enrollment patterns, we must be creative about "batch placement" of young women into these classes and vigilant about harassment, stereotyping, and negative, discouraging treatment from male peers and male instructors.[65]

Moving into the social sciences and humanities, once gender is introduced into a class, teachers must be mindful that no single "female" or "feminist" position can prevail. Whether in history, sociology, hygiene, literature, or science, gender perspectives are always mediated by race, ethnicity, and class. The ways in which white, black, and Latina females view romance, marriage, work, lesbian relationships, or having children may vary greatly among themselves and with the views of the teacher. We must allow for the plurality of females' perspectives.

In a similar way, the histories and literatures of all women, women of many colors, and women from different regions of the country must fill the insides of the curriculum.[66] In a remedial reading class, one teacher created original grammar materials which included the following example: Women in Puerto Rico (is, are) oppressed. Math examples should pose Alice as a truck driver trying to estimate the distance across a bridge, and Phillip the homemaker trying to estimate how much flour to include in his cake recipe for eight. Science classes need to note female scientists and the feminist critique of science.[67] Traditional social studies and history must be disrupted by the stories of girls and women, and must engage students in unearthing these herstories through archives, oral histories, newspapers, and even diaries.

We offer these ideas not as models, but as images. Public schools must signify moments of educational empowerment—saying aloud and discovering all that fills the minds, bodies, relationships, dreams, and nightmares of young women. If educators do not permit them the space and the safety to explore what it means to be a woman, with a voice, a body, and a sense of self, and with a race, an ethnicity, and a social class, then who will? What price must they pay for bein' wrapped tight?

## NOTES

1. M. Fine and P. Rosenberg, "Dropping Out of High School: The Ideology of School and Work," *Journal of Education*, 165 (Summer, 1983).

2. M. Fine, "Why Urban Adolescents Drop Into and Out of Public High School," *Teachers College Record*, 87 (Spring, 1986).

3. Michelle Fine's 1984–1985 research, "Voices of Urban Adolescents: Dropping Out as a Moment of Developmental Stress," was funded by the W.T. Grant Foundation and a grant from the University of Pennsylvania Faculty Fellowships; See Fine "Why Urban Adolescents." Nancie Zane's research, "Female Dropouts," was sponsored by the PEER (Projection Educational Equity Resources) WEEA grant, 1987.

4. D. Mann, "Can We Help Dropouts: Thinking about the Undoable," in *School Dropouts, Patterns and Policies*, ed. G. Natriello (New York: Teachers College Press, 1986).

5. Fine, "Dropping Out of High School."

6. A. Kolstad and J. Ownings, *High School Dropouts Who Change Their Minds about School* (Washington, D.C.: Office of Educational Research Improvement, Center for Statistics, 1986).

7. U.S. Department of Labor. *Time of Change: 1983 Handbook of Women Workers* (Washington, D.C., 1983).

8. Ibid.

9. R. Rumberger, *High School Dropouts: A Problem for Research, Policy and Practices* (Stanford, Calif.: Stanford Education Policy Institute, September 1986).

10. See K. Neckerman and W. Wilson, "Schools and Poor Communities," in *School Success for Students At Risk*, ed. The Council of Chief State School Officers (Orlando, Fla.: Harcourt Brace Jovanovich: 1988); T. Williams and W. Kornblum, *Growing Up Poor* (Lexington, Mass.: Lexington Books, 1985); H. Amaro, "Considerations for Prevention of HIV Infection Among Hispanic Women," *Psychology of Women Quarterly*, 12 (1988); LaRaza, "Youth Families Face Economic Disaster," *Education Network News*, 7(Nov/Dec., 1988); D. Scott-

50     *Michelle Fine and Nancie Zane*

Jones and M. Clark, "The School Experiences of Black Girls," *Phi Delta Kappan,* 67 (March, 1986).

11. W. Morgan, "The High School Dropout in an Overeducated Society," Center for Human Resource Research, Ohio State University, February, 1984.

12. R. Ekstrom et al., "Who Drops Out of High School and Why? Findings from a National Study," in *School Dropouts, Patterns and Policies,* ed. G. Natriello (New York: Teachers College Press, 1986).

13. J. Earle, V. Roach, and K. Fraser, *Female Dropouts: A New Persepctive* (Alexandria, Va.: National Association of State Boards of Education, 1987).

14. Ekstrom, et al. "Who Drops Out."

15. Mann, "Can We Help Dropouts?"

16. Fine, forthcoming.

17. Ibid.

18. C. Dweck, "The Role of Expectations and Attributions in the Alleviation of Learned Helplessness," *Journal of Personality and Social Psychology,* 31 (1975), 674–685.

19. T. Clark, "Preventing School Dropout," Citizens Budget Commission Quarterly, 7 (1987), 1–7.

20. C. Gilligan. *In a Different Voice: Psychological Theory and Women's Development.* (Cambridge, Massachusetts: Harvard Unviersity Press, 1982.)

21. Hispanic Policy Development Center, *Make Something Happen: Hispanics and Urban School Reform.* (Washington, D.C.: 1984).

22. Ibid.

23. Ekstrom et al., "Who Drops Out."

24. Kolstad and Ownings, *High School Dropouts.*

25. Ibid., Tables 1 through 6.

26. D. Passmore, "Employment of Young GED Recipients," American Council on Education, Research Brief No. 14, September 1987.

27. New York State Department of Education, Memo from Dennis Hughes, State Administrator on High School Equivalency Programs; Albany, NY, December 4, 1984.

28. R. Rothman, "Black Students Boosting Enrollments in Proprietary Schools," *Education Week,* 18 (June 10, 1987).

29. Ekstrom et al., "Who Drops Out."

30 M. Fine and P. Rosenberg, "Dropping Out of High School: The Ideology of School and Work," *Journal of Education,* 165 (1983), 257–272.

31. P. Collins, "Black Feminist Thought," paper presented at the Penn Mid-Atlantic Seminar (Philadelphia: University of Pennsylvania, 1988); C. Gilkes, "Building in Many Places: Multiple Commitments and Ideologies in Black Women's Community Work," in *Women and the Politics of Empowerment,"* ed. by A. Bookman and S. Morgen (Philadelpha: Temple University Press, 1988); C. Gilligan, *"In a Different Voice";* J. Ladner, *Tomorrow's Tomorrow: The Black Woman.* (New York: Doubleday and Company, 1971); A. McRobbie and Trisha McCabe, *Feminism for Girls, An Adventive Story* (London: Routledge and Kegan Paul, 1981).

32. Z. Elsenstein, *The Radical Future of Liberal Feminism* (New York: Longman, 1981).

33. Ibid.

34. See Z. Eisenstein, "The Radical Future;" and M. Fine and S. Gordon, "Feminist Transformations of/Despite Psychology," in *Gender and Thought* (New York: Springer-Verlag, 1989).

35. R. Connell et al., *Making the Difference* (Sidney, Australia: George Allen and Unwin, 1982); National Committee for Citizens in Education, personal communication on their Empowered Parents program; Fine, "Dropping Out of High School."

36. S. Harding. *The Science Question in Feminism.* (Ithaca: Cornell University Press, 1986).

37. Bell Hooks, *Ain't I a Woman* (Boston: South End Press, 1981).

38 P. Wexler, "Structure, Text and Subject: A Critical Sociology of School Knowledge," in *Cultural and Economic Reproduction in Education* (Boston: Routledge Chapman and Hall, 1982).

39. A. Gramsci, *Selections from Prison Notebooks* (New York: International Publishers, 1971).

40. Harding, *The Science Question.*

41. F. Block et al., *The Mean Season: The Attack on the Welfare State* (New York: Pantheon, 1987).

42. S. Barro, *The Incidence of Dropping Out: A Descriptive Analysis* (Washington, D.C.: Economic Research, Inc., October, 1984).

43. M. Fine, "Sex, Schooling and Adolescent Females: The Missing Discourse of Desire," *Harvard Educational Review,* 58 (February, 1988).

44. C. Smith-Rosenberg, "Sex as Symbol in Victorian Purity: An Ethnohistorical Analysis of Jacksonian America," *American Journal of Sociology,* 84 (1978), 229.

45. B. Omolade, "Hearts of Darkness," in *Powers of Desire,* ed A. Snitow, C. Stanseel, and S. Thompson (New York: Monthly Review Press, 1983), 6.

46. Fine, "Sex, Schooling and Adolescent Females."

47. Ann Snitow, C. Stansell, and S. Thompson, eds., *Powers of Desire: The Politics of Sexuality* (New York: Monthly Review Press, 1983).

48. L. Zabin et al., "Evaluation of a Pregnancy Prevention Program for Urban Teenagers," *Family Planning Perspectives,* 18 (May/June, 1986), 119–126.

49. H. Jordan, *High School Military Recruiting: Recent Developments* (Philadelphia: Militarism Resource Project, 1985).

50. T. Whitehead and K. Gentmann, "The Cultural Broker Concept in Bicultural Education," *Journal of Negro Education,* 52 (1983), 2.

51. New York Technical College, *Expanding Options for Teen Mothers,* Final Report, May 1985.

52. For very exciting results on reduction of teen pregnancy, dropout, and low-birth-weight babies, see Zabin, et al., "Evaluation of a Pregnancy Problem;" J. Dryfoos, "School-Based Health Clinics: A New Approach to Preventing Adolescent Pregnancy?" *Family Planning Perspectives,* 17, No. 2 (March/April 1985), 70–75; Fine, "Sex, Schooling and Adolescent Females."

53. See Educational Equity Concepts, *Materials on Gender, Race and Disability,* 440 Park Avenue South, New York, New York, 1988; J. Hale-Benson, *Black Children: Their Roots, Culture and Learning Styles* (Baltimore, Md.: Johns Hopkins University Press, 1982); A. Hilliard, "Creating a Multi-Ethnic and Racial Curriculum," paper delivered at the Educational Writers Association Meeting, Racine, Wisconsin, 1987.

54. M. Fine and M. Foster, Introduction to PEER's *Handbook on Female Dropouts.* Project on Equal Educational Rights. Washington, D.C. 1988.

55. National Committee for Citizens in Education, personal communication.

56. National Coalition of Advocates for Students, *A Special Analysis of 1982 Elementary and Secondary School Civil Rights Survey Data.* (Boston, 1987); Fine and Foster, *Handbook.*

57. E. Foley and P. Crull, *"Educating the at-Risk Adolescent: More Lessons from Alternative High Schools,* (New York: *Public Education Association,* 1984).

58. T. Vriend, "Utilizing Peer Leaders in Counseling and Study Groups to Modify Academic Achievement," dissertation, New York University, 1982.

59. A. Gartner, M. Kohler, and F. Reissman, *Children Teach Children: Learning by Teaching* (New York: Harper and Row, 1971).

60. New York City Board of Education. "Evaluation Update on the Effectiveness of the Promotion Policy Program," November 12, 1986; Massachusetts Advocacy Center, Memo to Dr. Laval Wilson, May 11, 1987; Massachusetts Advocacy Center, Memo to Boston School Committee, June 5, 1987.

61. La Raza, *Education Network News,* 5 (September/October, 1986).

62. H. Levin, "Accelerating Elementary Education for Disadvantaged Students," in *School Success for Students at Risk,* ed. The Council of Chief State School Officers (Orlando, Fla: Harcourt Brace Jovanovich, 1988).

63. M. Foster, "'Its Cookin' Now': A Performance Analysis of the Speech Events of a Black Teacher in an Urban Community College," paper presented at the Symposium on Afro-American Perspectives on Issues of Learning, Ethnicity and Identity, American Anthropological Association, Chicago, Illinois, 1987; P. Triesman, "A Study of Mathematic Performance of Black Students at the University of California at Berkeley," Ph.D. dissertation, University of California at Berkeley, Department of Mathematics, 1985.

64. M. Lockheed, "Classroom Organization and Climate," in S. Klein (ed.) *Achieving Sex Equity through Education.* (Baltimore, Johns Hopkins University Press, 1986).

65. FARE, "Their Proper Place: A Report on Sex Discrimination in New York City Vocational High Schools," December 1982 (New York: Center for Public Advocacy Research, 1982).

66. Hilliard, "Creating a Multi-Ethnic."

67. E. F. Keller, "Feminism and Science," *Signs: Journal of Women in Culture and Society,* 7 (1982).

ALAN J. DEYOUNG WITH KAREN HUFFMAN AND
MARY ELLEN TURNER

Chapter 3

# Dropout Issues and Problems in Rural America, with a Case Study of One Central Appalachian School District

Most of the rhetoric of contemporary school reform in the United States pinpoints the high school dropout phenomenon as a problem in search of one or more solutions. Given the current crisis of youth unemployment across the nation, paticularly in urban America, the fact that many poor and minority children leave school before they can acquire either the skills or credentials necessary to become producers, consumers, and citizens of this nation is a major problem. Equally vexing, yet perhaps less visible, are dropout issues and problems within many rural regions of the United States. In many American schools in the countryside, both minority and "majority" students have a tendency to leave school before completing the twelfth grade. Importantly, the relationship in rural America between formal education and economic status is also central to the analysis of the problems, issues, and dilemmas signified by frequently higher than average dropout rates.

To be sure, many concerns and problems in rural education are similar to their counterparts in urban and suburban locations. Others, however, are not. Yet it has only been within the past decade in the United States that rural education issues have even been mentioned within the larger arena of educational scholarship, let alone discussed. Ostensibly, the omission of rural education issues and problems, like the high school dropout problem, was based upon the notion that rural communities and rural schools were anachronistic in America, where the future and progress seemed synonymous with urbanization and industrialization. With few exceptions, school reform crusaders from Elwood Cubberly to John Dewey to James Conant to William Bennett have proclaimed that educational problems are outgrowths of urban, national, and now international problems. Americans from the late nineteenth to the late twentieth century have been on the move, and their movement away from rural and agricultural America toward urban, industrial, and cosmopolitan America has precluded any systematic concern with those left behind.

As a number of authors by the 1970s discovered, however, rural America and rural schools were still with us in the late twentieth century.[1] In fact, although the United States is primarily an urban and metropolitan nation, almost two-thirds of all American school districts, half of all public schools, and fully one-third of currently practicing schoolteachers are located in the rural regions of this country. And there seem just as many, if not more, problems and issues in rural schools as there are in urban ones.[2]

The purpose of this essay is to briefly sketch the existing dimensions of rural dropout problems and issues. Central to much of this discussion will be an analysis of how economic and demographic changes in much of rural America are related to individual decisions for leaving the school. Unfortunately, since even less research on the particular dynamics of rural school dropouts is available in the rural education literature than in many urban centers, much of this analysis will focus upon the dilemmas and paradoxes of the rural school per se. Following this general overview, a specific case study of the school dropout problem and the context in which it occurs in one central Appalachian school district will be presented.

## ISSUES IN AMERICAN RURAL EDUCATION

To perhaps overstate the case, the public education phenomenon in modern industrialized nations has been guided by urban and industrial needs and concerns. Therefore, some have argued, rural schooling issues and problems are virtually guaranteed, being a by-product of the evolution of state-mandated and state-controlled educational institutions.[3] In the United States, as elsewhere, public schooling reforms, including the provision of an occupationally relevant secondary school experience, have been brought about by changing economic and demographic conditions. Where urban and industrial conceptions of adequate schooling have been applied to rural regions, one might expect to find important schooling issues and problems. Not surprisingly, the rural school dropout dilemma is one of them.

Specific rural school issues, once considered, are not too difficult to imagine. Frequently, the economic problems of rural schools run parallel to those of our declining central cities. For example, the dwindling economic base to support schools in inner cities is also of concern in depressed rural regions of the country. The decline of agricultural price support systems for many farmers and declining real estate values in the countryside during the 1980s have led to an important erosion of local and state tax bases for public instruction.

On the other hand, some problems in rural areas seem specifically a function of demographic factors very different from those in central cities. Geographical isolation of children in some regions causes many school budgets to be disproportionately allocated for transportation needs, compared with such allocations in urban America. For related reasons, attracting and retaining good teachers in rural areas of the country is frequently difficult, especially given the wide range of competencies needed among instructors having to teach multiple subjects in relatively small schools and school districts. In addition, given that industrialized nations increasingly force or attract rural citizens toward metropolitan areas for job opportunities, losses in the numbers of children to educate typically cause yearly local battles over staffing and capital outlay priorities in the countryside. Furthermore, when outmigration does occur in many rural areas, it seems primarily the aged, the infirm, and the handicapped who are left behind.

Furthermore, some suggest, many federal and state initiatives to compensate for economically and culturally disadvantaged children are biased in favor of the urban poor, as opposed to those in rural areas. Research monies designated by Congress for the analysis and understanding of educational underachievement in America primarily focus upon the bias and discrimination faced by urban minorities in their educational and community settings. Yet the plight of many rural poor children—white, black, Hispanic, and native American, goes unmentioned and unanalyzed in the education journals or at professional meetings around the nation. Similarly, those compensatory programs which have been implemented in the United States over the past few years, although arguably inadequate in urban America, are even more difficult to put into place among widely dispersed schools in the countryside. Coordinating and sharing counselors and reading specialists across hundreds of square miles appears much more problematic than being able to concentrate most district resources in two or three buildings of a central city.

Although the preceding cursory review may appear pessimistic, it would be a grave mistake to argue that every rural school district in the United States has all of the types of problems just mentioned. Even definitions of rurality in America seem problematic. The National Rural Development Institute, for example, defines a rural school district as one containing fewer than 150 inhabitants per square mile, or one in which 60 percent of the population live in communities with less than 5,000 inhabitants. Although most Americans might consider communities falling within such categories quite small, in point of fact, most rural school districts in the United States are far smaller than this.

Not surprisingly, there is as much if not more diversity among rural school districts in the United States than there may be among many urban ones. Moreover, some rural and small school districts have been much more successful at dealing with the educational aspects of their smallness or remoteness than others. Some rural states, particularly in the West, have had, and continue to have, working rural educational models, curricular devlivery systems, and grass roots organizational structures for addressing rural schooling problems.[4] Some states, like Alaska, decided early on that urban and suburban educational polices would never work in their states, and have spent decades decentralizing school decision-making policies and experimenting with telecommunications systems for curriculum implementation.[5]

Other regions, however, have been much less fortunate. In an era of reform in which community support and parental involvement in schooling have become increasingly featured as the best route to educational excellence, we can find literally hundreds of rural and poor county schools around the nation without such input. Public schools whose primary constituents are the children of poor black tenant farmers or Hispanic migrants provide a good case in point. In many such Deep South districts, the schools have literally been abandoned by white fundamentalist groups or by more affluent middle-class families. Thus, compounding the rural economic decline of such regions has been the erosion of local community support for education. As "public" schools decline while private white academies and fundamentalist schools grow in number and size, discussions of public education and the public purpose seem hollow at best, and a mockery of the concept at worst.[6]

Not surprisingly, parental involvement with the school becomes difficult when minority parents, often handicapped by earlier educational experiences, attempt to bridge the gap between themselves and overworked, underpaid, and primarily white teachers. Other community-based strategies for keeping students in school, which have proven popular in metropolitan areas, appear difficult to implement in remote rural regions. Building effective business-school partnerships, for example, becomes virtually impossible when there are not enough businesses to go around. And who knows at this point what sort of psychological harm is done to minority and poor children who have to take long school bus rides past the many predominantly white schools whose primary existence stems from racial fear and distrust? In such circumstances, perhaps a far better question to ask about high school completion rates in much of the Deep South is why any minority and poor children ever *do* finish high school, rather than why they don't.

As the preceding discussion might suggest, many (but not all) rural school districts in the United States do have higher dropout rates than the national average, and usually higher ones than many metropolitan districts. In state-by-state comparisons, primarily rural southern states have always been among the highest. For example, the national dropout rate in 1985–86 (according to the U.S. Department of Education) was 29.4 percent. During that same year, the state of Louisiana reported a dropout rate of 45.3 percent, Mississippi reported a figure of 38.2 percent, and South Carolina, 37.6 percent.[7] Not surprisingly, some individual districts in these states report dropout rates of over 50 percent.

Part of the explanation for comparatively high dropout rates within many rural areas no doubt stems from economic possibilities of just a generation ago. Industrial expansion across the United States has been very uneven, and small-scale farming activities in many rural areas seem to have provided some opportunity for (self) employment without the need for specific educational credentials. It might even be argued that extension agents funded through the U.S. Department of Agriculture made school leaving less occupationally damaging earlier in this century, when they came out to "educate" working farmers and their families about practical agricultural techniques and strategies.

Even with the rural decline of the past several decades, sentiments toward school-based education in some rural areas continue to be mixed. Formal schooling in many rural areas is frequently perceived as the way one prepares to leave the community, since most salaried employment opportunities have only been available some distance from home. Predictably, some rural parents with local roots and extended family networks view school success for their children with uneasiness. The school's success at creating independence and achievement norms may cost the family in terms of losing a child who ideally would marry into another local family and undertake economic activities within the home community.[8]

On the other hand, within rural America the variability among school districts on indicators of educational performance can be quite high. In some rural school districts, critics claim, educational "underperformance" is related to the fact that little outside pressure from middle-class parents, civic groups, or business concerns is placed upon school officials and teachers.[9] Rather, in many rural counties around the nation the school may be the largest employer in the county, and delivering jobs to relatives and friends may be of higher priority to school board members and administrators than keeping up with the latest pedagogical techniques or enhancing existing curricular resources.

## RURAL SCHOOLING ISSUES IN CENTRAL APPALACHIA

Although economic decline, rural out-migration, and frequently less than helpful state and federal schooling policies and intervention strategies may separately plague many rural school districts, within some regions of the country such trends are particularly pronounced. Such is clearly the case in America's central Appalachian region, where each of the authors of this discussion resides. Here, depressed state economies, local school politics, continuing out-migration, and external land ownership patterns virtually guarantee an educational underperformance rivaling only the educational status of Third World countries.

The central Appalachian region includes eastern Kentucky, eastern Tennessee, western Virginia, and all of West Virginia. Although small-scale agriculture has a history in this area, such an economic base has been in continuous decline during the twentieth century. In its recent history, central Appalachia has relied upon (or been exploited for) its mineral and timber resources. This region also differs substantially from contiguous areas of the country in terms of its geographic isolation, sparse population density, and distance from the industrial and commercial hubs of the Northeast and Midwest.

So too, much of this region has a different nineteenth century history than its neighbors to the North, East, or South. Always too remote to develop an industrial base and not flat enough for plantation agriculture, the region, occupied primarily by Scots-Irish immigrants of the late eighteenth and early nineteenth centuries, was never considered affluent even before the Industrial Revolution. The Civil War and its aftermath also took its toll upon many Appalachian families and communities, for it was typically among residents of states like Kentucky, Tennessee, and West Virginia that brothers literally did fight brothers. Many of the family feuds in the mountains, which persisted well into the twentieth century, can be traced directly to hostilities between clans who fought on different sides of the War Between the States.

Most, if not all, of rural Appalachia is poor, and has been so ever since accurate economic figures have been kept. The irony is that such poverty takes place within a region extremely rich in mineral and fossil fuel resources. In addition, discrepancies between the few wealthy and the great majority of impoverished residents of many central Appalachia counties are both profound and very visible. Particularly in coal-dependent regions, coal operators and executives representing distant owners live side by side with ancestors of the miners who once toiled with pick and shovel to eke out a meager living in the Appalachian coal fields. With advances in mining technology, and within an industry once again on the decline (given the "stabilization" of foreign oil prices during the eighties), work for many Appalachians is even harder to come by now than it was just a generation ago. And of course, good jobs were almost impossible to come by even then. As elsewhere in rural America, most Appalachians have been forced to migrate to the North and Midwest in search of employment. And those who haven't migrated typically find themselves either in low-paying and/or dangerous occupations, or waiting for ever promised economic development projects to come their way.

Given that central Appalachia has little agriculture and little industry, that most of the income generated in the region comes from extractive industries with great boom and bust cycles, and that the steel and auto industries which used to attract and employ Appalachians themselves are in decline, it should perhaps come as no great surprise that educational performance in eastern Kentucky, eastern Tennessee, western Virginia, and West Virginia is typically less than ideal. Even within each of these states, significant differences between county schools in the mountains and those in more agriculturally prosperous areas are quite visible. Appalachian districts in each of these states, on average, have fewer taxable resources, lower student achievement test scores, more students receiving free and reduced-price lunches, fewer dollars per student spent on instruction, and so forth than those in non-Appalachian districts.[10]

## A RENEWED FOCUS ON THE DROPOUT PROBLEM IN CENTRAL APPALACHIA

Improving education in central Appalachia, as everywhere else in America, has become an important preoccupation for local communities, states, and regional economic development agencies. For example, the former governors of all four of the states just mentioned, particularly Lamar Alexander of Tennessee and Martha Lane Collins of Kentucky, built much of their political successes upon educational reform planks in their respective states. The role of education in economic development, particularly high school completion rates, has been a focal point of much of this concern.

In some Appalachian regions, like Kentucky's Fifth Congressional District, school improvement projects targeted at the high school dropout problem have reached a fever pitch rhetorically, even if few actual programs have been put into place to improve schooling outcomes.[11] In this congressional district, both the economic and educational indicators are among the worst in the nation. And predictably, school reform is argued to be an important key to revitalizing a region long in decay.

Most recently, federal dollars and programs to enhance educational status in the region have also been targeted at the high school. The Appalachian Regional Commission was instituted several decades ago ostensibly to help stimulate economic growth in Appalachia. Some of their programs have been targeted at developing human resources, and most recently, high school completion rates have been pinpointed as an arena of concern.[12]

## RURAL COMMUNITIES IN DECLINE:
## THE CASE OF BRAXTON COUNTY, WEST VIRGINIA

As this literature review has suggested, dropout issues and problems in rural America and more specifically in Appalachia are complicated and important. And although much of the conventional wisdom around the country seems to be that dropout problems can be significantly remedied via curricular reform,[13] we have attempted to suggest the social and economic base of many of the relatively inferior school performance indicators in many rural places. Rather than continue with broad overviews and sweeping generalizations, however, we would like to shift the terms of the discussion to educational dropout issues as they exist in one central Appalachian school district, recognized throughout the region at the official level as an excellent one.[14]

Braxton County, like most of West Virgina, is primarily poor and quite mountainous, and its inhabitants are almost all white. Aesthetically speaking, the county is gorgeous. Intersected by several rivers, still heavily forested and recently the beneficiary of two man-made lakes, Braxton County could easily be presented as a recreational haven for anyone in the Northeast or Midwest with a car, a fishing rod, and/or a boat. In fact, a major new interstate runs right through the county, and according to one local businessman, over 75 percent of the U.S. population lives within a long day's drive to its natural wonders.

The local school district is one of fifty-five West Virginia districts, and has developed a reputation for educational excellence throughout the state. Three of its eight school principals have attended, and been heavily influenced by conference leaders at the nationally renowned West Virginia Principal's Academy. State-mandated achievement test results for Braxton County have been on the rise for several years, and reading scores for third graders have been amongst the highest in the state throughout this period. In 1988, one of Braxton County's middle schools won a state award for being an exemplary school. And most recently, this rural school district and its efficient operation and high test scores were profiled by the *Charleston Gazette* as the prototype for West Virginia schools. According to story headlines in that publication, the Braxton County case proved that schools can be excellent, even when the school and its clientele are rural and poor.

And there can be no doubt that Braxton County is rural and poor, even by West Virginia standards. In 1980 the official unemployment rate for Braxton County was 13.6 percent, almost twice that for the rest of the state. Although the 1986 rate was somewhat better, such figures may be very misleading in a region where occasional and part-time employment is the norm rather than the exception. Per capita income for county residents suggests how sporadic employment is, the figure for 1983 being $6,879. Although the county ranked thirty-ninth (out of fifty-five) in population in 1983, it ranked forty-seventh in per capita income for the same year. Discounting retail sales personnel, the Braxton County Board of Education employed more individuals in 1980 than all other major employers combined. And teachers in West Virginia are among the poorest paid in the nation.[15]

Poverty data themselves, however, do not tell the entire story about Braxton County or why the high school dropout rate seems high at 25 percent.[16] Rather, the history of the county and its several communities probably holds the key to understanding dropout issues and problems there. We don't want to dwell on "ancient" history in the next few pages or focus on particulars not relevant to educational status in Braxton County. The several communities which do (and did) exist there say plenty of Indian battles, Confederate raids, and commercial activities throughout the nineteenth century. Interestingly, early historical accounts of education in Braxton County suggest that educational undertakings were seen, for the most part, as very important functions and duties of collective life, contrasting greatly with the Appalachian stereotypes from which the region still suffers.

More appropriate for understanding modern-day school dropout issues and problems, however, is the more recent past. In essence, Braxton County, West Virginia, has been economically in decline throughout the twentieth century. As in many other rural areas, once Braxton County communities were thriving, growing, and economically productive. Transected by several navigable rivers, surrounded by timber, clay, and various mineral deposits, having a main railroad line running through the middle of the county, and with a still viable timber industry, the main Braxton County towns of Sutton, Gassaway, and Burnsville seemed still optimistic about their collective futures as late as the 1940s. This optimism is well reflected in West Virginia Writers' Project accounts of each community just prior to World War II. Describing the civic, business and educational climate of Sutton, for example, project writers had the following to say in 1941:

Sutton is situated on the beautiful Elk river, 100 miles east of Charleston and 70 miles from Clarksburg. A rich farming region surrounds the city and contributes to its economic welfare. The river, which divides the town, and the hills on all sides provides a scenic background for the thoroughly up-to-date homes and business houses of the Braxton County seat... City services include sewerage, paved streets, motorized fire department, police and other features of present-day towns. ... Foward-looking, yet anxious to preserve its atmosphere of rural peace while taking advantage of every facility of the age, Sutton has combined the old and new in a delightful blend of easy living and progressive building. The schools of 1941 are an example of this attitude. Special emphasis is placed on social adjustments and vocational guidance. Clubs and intramural activities instruct the pupils in social living. With 300 students, the Sutton High School in its 36th session is representative of the best in modern education... In 1941, Sutton can proudly boast that it has taken full advantage of twentieth-century developments, without losing its character as a pioneer community motivated by pride in its past and present and faith in its future.[17]

The Braxton County of today, however, bears little resemblence to the county as described in 1941. To be sure, it is still a beautiful place, and some look forward to major revitalization through tourism. But economic decline and out-migration of many citizens has been epidemic since the early twentieth century. The picture painted of Braxton County by the West Virginia Department of Employment Security in 1985 suggests little to sustain the "faith in the future" described just forty-four years earlier:

Braxton County lies in the center of the state and, like its neighboring counties, suffers economically from this geographic handicap. Until the building of Interstate 79, the county was isolated to a considerable degree from more metropolitan and affluent areas of the state. Even with completion of the interstate highway in the 1970s, the expected growth and development has been limited... The construction of Sutton Dam and Burnsville Dam have added to the desirability of the area, but have done relatively little in improving the economic status of the county's citizens. In fact, the completion of construction projects in the county has been detrimental, as premium jobs quickly disappear when work is concluded. The population of Braxton Country declined steadily between 1940 and 1970. The county claimed 21,658 residents in 1940 but only 12,666 in 1970, a population loss of 41.5 percent in 30 years. This tremendous loss occurred as individuals were literally forced by economic considerations to abandon hillside farms and seek employment in the factories of Ohio, Michigan and other industrial states.[18]

The language and the statistics used to discuss the very same place forty years apart suggest how profound the economic decline has been in Braxton County. In the 1940s, the county is described as modern, within a "rich agricultural region," and boasting of numerous business houses. In 1980, this rich agricultural region seems ostensibly no longer very rich, as "hillside farms" have been increasingly abandoned by local citizens. Instead, the county is described as geographically isolated, depopulated, and economically handicapped.

## BRAXTON COUNTY SCHOOLS

As mentioned previously, public education in Braxton County seems typically to have been a source of community pride during the late nineteenth and early twentieth centuries. In each of the three community histories on Braxton County towns compiled by the West Virginia Writers' Project, the importance of public schools and in particular their (separate) high schools feature prominently. In fact, community histories of both Gassaway and Burnsville have pictures of their then new and modern high schools on the covers. Yet, faced with economic decline and out-migration since 1940, the schools in each of those communities has had a less than kind fate. By reviewing school enrollment trends and projections commissioned by the Braxton County Board of Education for the years between 1957 and 1964, we get a glimpse of some relatively recent educational difficulties that are suggestive of many current ones:

Within the Sutton Attendence Area, elementary school enrollment dropped from 1122 in 1957–58 to 870 in 1963–64 . . . In this same period, enrollment at the Sutton Elementary dropped from 485 in the 1957–58 school year to 340 in the 1963–64 school year. During this period, the schools of Windy Run, Stoney Creek, Maymond, Bug Ridge, Wolf Creek, and Marpleton were closed and their pupils transferred to the Sutton Elementary school . . . In the last few years, at least 44 elementary schools have been abandoned. This is desirable, because many of the buildings serving as Braxton County schools do not allow the presentation of a well-rounded educational program.

Often, the buildings are structurally obsolete and unsound, without central heat, indoor toilets, and, in some cases, without electricity . . . Even more important than the physical are considerations of program. Without consolidation of one-, two-, three- teacher schools there can be none of the enrichment of program that comes from having specialist teachers. The disadvantages become more critical in the high schools. Sutton's High School Center does not now have the space or the equipment to present the children of Sutton with an education comparable even to the education offered in counties of similar economic status . . . The 1963 Annual Report of the West Virginia Educational Association shows that Braxton County put proportionately less money into its schools than did any comparable county. This is partly because the assessed valuation in Braxton County declined from $29,204,580 in 1958 to $25,658,040 in 1963.[19]

The history of educational decline thus parallels that of economic decline in Braxton County. Once there were over a hundred small schools; now there are eight. Once three communities built three modern new high schools. Now these admittedly decaying structures serve either as a K–8 school (in Burnsville) or grade 5–8 middle schools (in Gassaway and Sutton). Many of the small towns and villages that once existed in Braxton County have literally disappeared from the map, along with their local schools.

The current superintendent of less than fifteen years, Dr. Kenna Seal, came into office just after the great wave of school consolidations previously mentioned. As elsewhere in rural America, school consolidation is a touchy subject in Braxton County. Yet, although consolidation for pedagogical reasons has been frequently urged for rural schools, consolidation pressures in Braxton County seem equally a function of out-migration and lack of local funds to maintain the most isolated of those which still remain. Dr. Seal has closed only one school during his tenure, but he has reorganized the elementary schools and middle schools into grades K–4 and 5–8, respectively. These reorganizations were not primarily accomplished for pedagogical reasons, but rather to enhance enrollment figures in the remaining schools to economically defensible levels. Citizens of several outlying communities had resisted further efforts at closing down their small elementary schools, and thus grade restructuring became the only way the superintendent could keep them open.

Another reason for restructuring the public schools in Braxton County was the resistance of local taxpayers to increased revenues for public schooling. Faced with high unemployment and low per capita incomes, county taxpayers have rejected increases in excess school levies three times in local elections during the past twelve years. Much of this money would have gone to updating old school buildings which many residents agree are in need of repair. Given the lack of finances for building improvement, county maintenance workers have doubled as construction workers since 1980, adding new rooms to existing structures and installing new playgrounds at several elementary schools. Most recently, the citizens of Braxton County in March of 1988 voted 3,319 to 274 against a statewide uniform levy tax which would have moderately increased local school revenues.

Interestingly, the local superintendent is better known and appreciated locally for his financial adeptness at maximizing state funding formulas and for saving money at the central office than he is for the quality of his district's academic programs. It is primarily outside the district where he, his staff, and his students have won recognition for program excellence. Paradoxically, even though Dr. Seal went on record as supporting the statewide excess levy, his own school board opposed the measure. Furthermore, statewide publicity regarding Braxton County's educational success with minimal resources was used locally as an argument against the measure. Even though the district is poor and even though many buildings need work, local taxpayers seem convinced that educational success can be achieved without spending more money.

## BRAXTON COUNTY HIGH SCHOOL AND ITS DROPOUT PROGRAMS

Braxton County no longer has three separate high schools for each of its larger communities. It now has a consolidated high school with approximately eight hundred students. Almost 95 percent of these students are enrolled in vocational education programs of one sort or another, and one wing of the high school building is dedicated to such programs. The high school is centrally located along the new interstate, making travel to and from the building easier for most county residents. As previously mentioned, raising achievement test scores at all grade levels has been a particular concern of late, including those at the high school. And these test scores have improved greatly since the early 1980s.

On the other hand, the dropout rate has always been relatively high in the county, and has hovered between 25 and 30 percent during this decade. Currently, this problem is attracting the attention of the superintendent and much of the high school staff. In order to improve the high school completion rate, Braxton County has put into place several dropout prevention programs during the past year, including the "Context III" program, partially funded by the Appalachian Regional Commission and, on a more limited scale, a student team learning program developed at Johns Hopkins University.[20]

The focus of the Context III program is upon what the authors term "blockages" to student school completion. The rationale behind its intervention strategy is that early school leavers have experienced frustration and lack of concern by adults throughout their educational careers. Therefore, the way to attack the school dropout problem is to open up the channels of communication between students, their teachers, their parents, and the surrounding community. Low self-esteem, poverty, poor previous school performance, and so forth are the types of student problems about which teachers and the community should become aware so that disruptive and withdrawal behaviors exhibited by children can be discussed and dealt with before they become significant events around which blockage occurs.

Importantly, the Context III program emphasizes that dropping out may be but the last of a series of behaviors based upon student inability to communicate frustrations and anxiety to school personnel. Therefore, the program is designed to be put into place at all school building levels, not just at the high school. Moreover, not only the school, but also parents and the community at large are targets of Context III. In Braxton County, all teachers have recently participated in workshops overviewing the program, parents have been informed about its intent, and various civic and community groups have been urged to talk with and support the schools' efforts to keep children in school.

Differing somewhat in focus and content is the KEYS (Keeping Educable Youth in School) cooperative learning program used currently in Braxton County High School. Basically, this program follows a group mastery learning format for specifically identified "at-risk" ninth graders. For this program, dropout prevention specialists chose from among forty academically deficient eighth-grade students. Twelve were selected and put into a special U.S. history class using group mastery techniques. The philosophy behind this initiative is that individuals achieve better when working in small groups, and that mutually pursued group academic projects allow for tutoring and shared problem solving within the group.

In Braxton County High, basic historical concepts and events constitute a specially formulated curriculum, which group members are allowed to pursue collectively. Subsequently, individual assessments of their mastery are made, followed either by further group practice or advancement to new material. Unlike the Context III program, the KEYS program is still very experimental, and full-scale use of the model has not been adopted yet.

## THE BRAXTON COUNTY DROPOUT PROBLEM AS A LEGACY OF THE RURAL ECONOMIC DECLINE

Our suspicion is that much of the extraordinary efforts of Braxton County educators will have a payoff in terms of reducing high school dropouts in that district. Both of these dropout prevention programs have the strong support of the district superintendent, who believes that keeping students in school is vital both to their futures and to that of the county. Importantly, both he and numerous central office staff believe that with federal reductions in health and welfare programs through other social agencies, the public school is one of the few places left which can attempt to deal comprehensively with the educational, health-related, and social needs of children and adolescents in economically depressed areas like Braxton County.

In addition, although there is some hope in Braxton County that future economic development might occur in the region, there seems relatively little local rhetoric regarding the school's role in attracting outside investment through greater rigor in academic programs. Braxton County schools already measure higher on statewide tests than many surrounding districts, and many graduates of the high school (and the three which preceded it) have left the county and been successful. More typically, the county continues to press for economic development in order to retain able graduates. Few citizens blame public education for the economic decline of the region.

On the other hand, although the dropout problem may be positively affected by the merging educational philosophy and programs in

Braxton County, there still remain a number of economic and community-based problems which even energetic educators may not overcome. Specifically, there are a variety of economic and social legacies surrounding and pervading schools and communities in Braxton County which mitigate against some, if not all, of the educational efforts put forward by public school officials. So, too, at the state level there are several academic- and efficiency-motivated initiatives which potentially threaten the new dropout emphases in Braxton County.

For example, even a brief visit to rural West Virginia today should provide a keen appreciation of the many positive historical legacies currently taken for granted by more cosmopolitan citizens of this nation. The pioneer spirit, small-scale agricultural proficiency, strong community identification, and the importance of extended families are clearly less influential today than they probably were fifty or sixty years ago, yet their influence still seems important. On the other hand, such cultural and economic inheritances may have less utility today in modern and "post industrial" America. The driving force behind contemporary American education builds upon many assumptions and ideals quite dissimiliar to those which can still be found in much of rural America, including Braxton County, West Virginia.

From the more distant past, the pioneers who settled in Braxton County were rugged individuals who wrested this territory from the Indians and initiated small-scale agriculture. In the late nineteenth and early twentieth centuries, agriculture, lumbering, and small business ventures provided an economic base for many in Braxton County, and much community pride was reflected in the local schools in and around Sutton, Gassaway, and Burnsville.

Yet, important income-producing agriculture and manufacturing concerns are a thing of the past in Braxton County, and most of the community schools are no more. The successfully educated children of Braxton County, by state and national standards, are the ones most likely to leave either the region or the state. The irony of this turnaround seems not to have escaped some local parents. School officials in the county will be the first to admit that lots of families back in the hollows have little appreciation for the offerings of the public schools. In addition, there are a few remaining citizens of power and wealth in Braxton County whose current status derives from its previous economic strengths. And some have been less than enthusiastic about supporting either economic or educational innovations identified with progress and the future.

On the other hand, many parents, although not philosophically opposed to public education and high school completion for their kids, display mixed reactions when asked to help support public institutions whose ultimate purpose in the late twentieth century is to enable their children to leave the county in search of jobs not available at home. Again, as many school officials in Braxton County are ready to concede, getting parents of high school students to support their endeavors has historically been an almost impossible task. And for those students and parents who have little educational ambition beyond high school, economic arguments regarding why students should finish an extra year or two tend to ring hollow. Even the counselors and dropout prevention specialists at Braxton County High concede that there appear to be just as many unemployed high school graduates in the county as there are unemployed dropouts.

The most recent legacy of school and community relationships in Braxton County also seems to mitigate against central office hopes for involving parents and the community in school improvement efforts. When local communities talk about "our school" in Braxton County, almost never are they referring to the consolidated high school. In the local papers and on the local radio, it seems that the three *former* high schools are the subject of pride and interest, not that newer building next to the interstate. The athletic teams of Braxton County most often talked about and featured in local restaurants and newspapers are also those of the eighth grade, not those of the high school. And in fact the current largest (per capita) high school alumni association in the entire state of West Virginia is the Burnsville Alumni Association. Of course, Burnsville has not even been a high school for more than twenty years. In many ways, then, "Braxton County Schools" as an entity remains somewhat a misnomer in this county. Most county citizens still identify with their smaller communities, and many still seem to view with some mistrust educational officials and programs not from their town.

In addition to the several cultural and economic forces mitigating against dropout remediation programs in Braxton County, three current developments or movements at the state level appear ominous. One is a growing sentiment that some sort of academically rigorous high school exit exam ought to be put into effect throughout the state. Coupled with complaints that the standardized achievement test results in West Virginia are all inflated because of dated national norms, such greatly renewed emphases on academic performance as a prerequisite to high school graduation might negatively affect Braxton County efforts to keep all students in school. While local dropout prevention staff are focusing on improving the classroom and building social climate throughout all county schools, the language of "educational excellence" (in hopes of attracting outside industry to the state) seems to be the language of the state legislature. It seems quite conceivable that significant numbers of high school students already performing poorly might decide to forego the embarrassment of failing a statewide exit exam and leave school early, regardless of the concern shown by local educators.

In addition, although West Virginia classroom teachers are overworked and underpaid, they have increasingly been the target of criticism and ridicule in Charleston, the state capital. Not only have future hopes for increasing educational funding for teacher salaries and programs been diminished of late, but the state's ongoing budget crunch has led to delays in current state payroll obligations. Some local school districts in West Virginia have begun litigation against the state government for failing to provide state funding on time. To say that teacher morale in West Virginia in 1988 was low would be a dramatic understatement. And this lack of appreciation is keenly felt even in Braxton County, where schools are getting good reports.

Finally, there is a statewide initiative to cut back on vocational education funding in West Virginia, which might have serious consequences for high school completion rates in Braxton County. In attempts to save money, "inefficient" vocational programs have been targeted for removal or reduction throughout the state. Inefficient programs, it is argued, are ones which do not place local graduates in the private sector upon completion of vocational training. Unfortunately, since there are few manufacturing, construction, or technical businesses in the county, many graduates of high school trade programs pursue employment opportunities outside the state. In practical terms, then, these vocational programs may be providing exactly the type of experiences which would make students employable. But since many employment opportunities lie outside the state, "official" statistics make vocational training programs look ineffective, and they have become the target of those advocating greater cost effectiveness in public education.

## CONCLUSION

Dropout problems and issues in rural America are frequently just as perplexing and intractable as they are in urban America. Particularly in places like Braxton County, West Virgina, to have good school programs does not ensure that all children will complete them. In many cases, current cultural, social, and economic forces seem potentially to interfere with even the best intentions of educators to keep children in school. Furthermore, commonsense notions about the purposes of formal education in urban America frequently run counter to older notions regarding the mission of public education in rural America. Many small rural communities, for example, still cling to the idea that their social institutions, like the school, ought to serve local and community needs. And the realization that much of the school curriculum at higher levels of education is designed to allow local children to leave the community in search of employment not available at home seems to cause some ambivalence, if not outright hostility, in many rural communities. Even many of the teachers we know in rural American schools vocalize the conflict between careerism and community.

On the other hand, we are sure that many dropout issues and problems faced in rural America have their counterparts in various urban environments. In point of fact, many inner-city youths with very high dropout rates have historically been, and may continue to be, out-migrants from Appalachia and other rural regions of the country.[21] In this essay, we have suggested that economic decline, lack of opportunity, loss of community, and competing expectations among educators and policy makers regarding the purpose of public instruction are all involved with the dropout problem in rural America. We anticipate that a good case can be made for a similar interpretation of dropout issues and problems in many other settings in this country. Yet we hope that this discussion has furthered our understanding of such concerns as they exist in places not frequently talked about in the national context.

## NOTES

1. See Jonathan Sher's important edited collection entitled *Education in Rural America: A Reassessment of the Conventional Wisdom* (Boulder, Colo.: Westview Press, 1977).

2. See Alan J. DeYoung's more recent overview of rural education statistics and issues earlier addressed in the Sher collection in "The Status of American Rural Education Research: An Integrated Review and Commentary," *Review of Educational Research,* 57(2), 1987, pp. 132–148.

3. Jonathan Sher, *Rural Education in Urbanized Nations: Issues and Innovations* (Boulder, Colo.: Westview Press, 1981).

4. See, for example, Paul Nachtigal's (1982) edited collection entitled *Rural Education: In Search of a Better Way* (Boulder, Colo.: Westview Press).

5. See K. Hecht's chapter, "The Educational Challenge in Rural Alaska: Era of Local Control" in Sher, *Education in Rural America.*

6. For a good example of such problems, see the story on Marengo County schools in Alabama which appeared in *Education Week,* 7(21), February 1988, pp. 7 and 22.

7. Southern Regional Education Board, *A Progress Report and Recommendations on Educational Improvement in the S.R.E.B. States.* (Atlanta, Georgia: Southern Regional Education Board, 1987).

8. Robert Dreeben argues that the primary mission of contemporary American education is the transmission of "modern" norms useful for individual performance in business and industry. Such norms may be relatively difficult to transmit in rural areas, where more traditional, community-based norms still have utility within the social and occupational worlds of adults. See *On What is Learned in School* (Reading, Mass.: Addison Wesley, 1968).

9. See, for example, H. D. Plunkett and M. J. Bowman, *Elites and Change in the Kentucky Mountains* (Lexington, Ky.: Universtiy Press of Kentucky, 1973).

10. See Alan J. DeYoung, "The Status of Formal Education in Central Appalachia," *Appalachian Journal,* 10(4), 1983, pp. 321–334. Also see Alan J. DeYoung, "Economic Development and Educational Status in Appalachian Kentucky," *Comparative Education Review,* 29(1), 1985, pp. 47–67.

11. See, for example, the publication *Would You Like to Swing On a Star?: Opportunities to Improve Education in Kentucky's Fifth Congressional District* (Berea, Ky.: Mountain Association for Community Economic Development, 1986).

12. See J. Cox, J. Holley, R. Kite, and W. Durham, *Study of High School Dropouts in Appalachia* (Washington, D.C.: Appalachian Regional Commission, 1985).

13. See, for example, F. Newmann and J. Thompson, *Effects of Cooperative Learning on Achievement in Secondary School: A Summary of Research* (Madison, Wisc.: National Center on Effective Secondary Schools and Wisconsin Center

for Educational Research, 1987). See also W. Brookover et al., *Creating Effective Schools* (Holmes Beach, Fla.: Learning Publications, 1982).

14. The research upon which this case study is based was facilitated by a grant from the Office of Educational Research and Improvement. The larger study involves an evaluation of the Appalachia Educational Laboratory's Rural/Small School demonstration project. The views expressed here are those of the authors, and do not necessarily represent those of either agency or those of the Braxton County Board of Education.

15. These data were culled from a variety of West Virginia state documents, as well as from *West Virginia County Profiles* (see Note 18).

16. The calculation of dropout data seems truly one of the most puzzling undertakings of the current school reform era. Different states use different measures and different beginning points, and few follow up assessments to find out whether students have actually dropped out, transferred, or remain a semester away from graduation. The 25 percent dropout rate for Braxton County probably exceeds the state average by several percentage points. Of the 1983–84 freshmen class at Braxton County High School, only 55 percent actually completed school as of January, 1988.

17. This account is taken from a document published by the West Virginia Writers' Project, entitled *Sutton on the Elk* (Charleston, W. Va.: Works Projects Administration, August, 1941), pp. 32–35. There is in fact good reason to believe that Braxton County had already been economically in decline since at least the early thirties. See Otis Rice's *West Virginia: A History* (Lexington, Ky.: University Press of Kentucky, 1985) for details on statewide economic decline and educational status in the twentieth century.

18. West Virginia Department of Employment Security (Labor and Economic Research Section), *West Virginia County Profiles* (Charleston, W. Va., 1985), pp. 5–6. Appalachian migration patterns have been well documented during this period by a number of scholars at the University of Kentucky. See, for example, the study by Clyde McCoy and James Brown entitled "Appalachian Migration to Midwestern Cities" in W. Philliber and C. McCoy (eds), *The Invisible Minority: Urban Appalachians* (Lexington: University Press of Kentucky, 1981).

19. Weston Community Planning Commission, *Sutton West Virginia: A Comprehensive Development Plan* (chapter seven pp. 4–6) (West Chester, Pa., 1967).

20. See Robert Slavins's cooperative learning approach outlined in *Using Student Team Learning,* 3rd ed. (Baltimore, Md.: Center for Research on Elementary and Middle Schools, Johns Hopkins University, 1986; *Catch a Falling*

*S.T.A.R.: How to Prevent Dropouts,* by R. Hayman Kite (Winter Park, Florida: Continuing Education Institute, 1987).

21. Current out-migration patterns from Appalachia and the plight of many urban Appalachian children are discussed in P. Obermiller and W. Philliber (eds.), *Too Few Tomorrows: Urban Appalachians in the 1980's* (Boone, N.C.: Appalachian Consortium Press, 1987).

R. PATRICK SOLOMON

Chapter 4

# Dropping Out of Academics: Black Youth and the Sports Subculture In a Cross-National Perspective

## INTRODUCTION

In recent years educators, policy makers, and researchers concerned about school dropouts have focused on students who leave high school prior to completing their academic program. Very little attention has been paid to another form of dropping out: remaining in school but disengaging from the pursuit of academic credentials. For both categories of dropouts the end results are the same: they fail to acquire the competencies and credentials necessary for social and economic advancement in adult life. Who are these "in-school" dropouts and what prevents them from pursuing academic credentials?

Trends in dropout rates among various social groups reveal that black students, who traditionally have left school at a higher rate than whites, are reversing this pattern. This trend is noticeable across national settings. Research data accumulated from national samples of high school students in the United States and analyzed by such researchers as Ekstrom and Rumberger indicate that with factors such as socioeconomic status and student grades held constant, black students are less likely than their white and other minority-group peers to drop out of high school.[1] In Canada, data from a large urban school district reflect a similar pattern: black students are less likely than their native Canadian and white counterparts to terminate in the early years of their high school education. The same study also showed that although black students remain in school longer, they accumulate fewer diploma credits than other groups over the same time period.[2] Although British school dropout data are not readily comparable to those of the U.S. and Canada, because of differences in defining and computing dropout rates, available data indicate that black students are remaining in school longer and are having better attendance records than their white peers.[3]

Given this increasing propensity of black students to remain in school longer than some other social groups, why has this trend not been reflected in their academic work? Researchers studying the schooling process of black working-class students have concluded that these students commit themselves to a nonacademic, sports subculture that limits their academic participation. As early as 1961, Coleman's study pointed to the deleterious effects of athletic and peer subculture on the academic process and the consequences of commitment to such alternative reward structures.[4]

This chapter examines the process of black working-class students dropping out of the academic culture of the school and adopting the alternative sport culture. To capture the cross-national dimensions of this problem, I will review the works of researchers in Canada, Britain, and the United States. The Canadian data will be drawn from my ethnographic study, which was conducted over a two-year period at Humberville, a Metropolitan Toronto vocational high school. This school is located within a racially diversified working-class community.

At Humberville High, I studied a cohesive group of black working-class boys of West Indian origin whose intense involvement in school sports earned them the label *Jocks.*[5] Using participant observation techniques, I recorded the interactions and experiences of these boys in their everyday school life. From the British perspective, the works of Carrington, Cashmore, and other researchers provide a comprehensive picture of black students' preoccupation with school sports and the emergent issues. For data on black youth disengagement from the conventional areas of education in the U.S. schools, I drew on the research of Fordham and Ogbu, Petroni, and others.

In comparing the findings of these ethnographies of black schooling in these national settings, I will focus my analysis on two main issues: the crucial influence of school processes and the cultural significance of sports in the school life of black students. The remainder of this chapter will seek to answer such questions as the following: What is the nature of black students' commitment to school sports? Who, or what, contributes to their adoption of this nonacademic alternative culture? What are some of the long-term consequences of "dropping out" of academic life? I will conclude with suggestions for "getting black students out of the gym and back into the classroom."

## SCHOOL SPORTS: BLACK YOUTHS' PREOCCUPATION

Athletic participation, not academic pursuits, has been the central life interest of black youth in some mixed-race high schools. In the case of the Canadian students in my own ethnographic work, the Jocks at Humberville were completely immersed in the athletic subculture. Their involvement was intensely routinized:

> Preclass workout each morning was followed at lunchtime by intermural athletic competitions in which the Jocks either played or officiated. Immediately following classes the Jocks took part in either try-outs for school teams, team practices or competitions. For tournaments and other interschool league programs, the Jocks and other school team members were excused from academic instruction to represent their school.[6]

This preoccupation continued throughout the school year, beginning with "vocational school" soccer in the fall and rotating to basketball, volleyball, badminton, track and field athletics, and "collegiate" soccer toward the end of the school year. In the limited time left for academic pursuits, the Jocks still remained mentally tuned to sports. They capitalized on the less structured shop classes to plan team selection and game strategies for upcoming sports competitions. In the classes of teachers who were also team coaches, the Jocks skillfully sidetracked planned academic work into discussions of topical issues in sports.

This sports involvement continued beyond the boundaries of the school and into the community gymnasium, where black boys labored for hours, perfecting skills in, say, basketball or volleyball. The centrality of sports in black students' school life was especially borne out by one school's refusal to accept promotion to a higher-track academic program if curricular sports was not timetabled: "I was going to attend

Eastway [High School] and I forgot to put gym down [on my option sheet]. When I went back to change my timetable I couldn't get sports anymore; so I didn't accept the promotion to Eastway. If I don't have gym I'm spaced out; I'm bored to death."[7] The total immersion of the Humberville Jocks in the sports subculture signifies a declining significance of the mainsteam curriculum in their school life. They have simply dropped out of the academic mainstream, and thereby run the risk of abandoning school completely when the athletic flame burns out.

Researchers in Britain and the United States have captured similar images of black youths' adoption of a nonacademic culture. The influx of West Indian immigrants to Britain during the 1950s and 1960s created a more multiracial school population. A noticeable feature of this mixed-race phenomenon which emerged was that students of Afro-Caribbean origins were more likely than other ethnoracial students to become intensely involved in school sports. Cashmore's research alludes to the fact that "a great many black youths find their central life-interest not in a possible career or in further education, but in sport."[8] He continues this discourse in *Black Sportsmen:* "So immersed are many black kids in their sport or sports, they sometimes neglect their academic work . . . [One youth] was training seriously at least four times a week and attributed her total lack of educational qualifications to her athletic indulgences."[9] Cashmore's study shows how black students' "gradual intensification of involvement with sport" quite often caused academic failure and school dropout.

Black youths' adoption of a sports subculture also seems to bring about debilitating social consequences within the social system of the school. Leaman and Carrington have highlighted some of these: "The comparative popularity of sport with black youth effectively excludes them from other areas of social life, since it fulfills a public stereotype of physical skill being the only sort of achievement of which blacks may be capable."[10]

Black students' involvement in nonathletic extracurricular activities in U.S. schools also appears to be severely restricted. Petroni found that black athletes "do not generally participate in activities such as speech, madrigals and drama."[11] More surprisingly, his research showed that dropping out of such academic-oriented activities as the college preparatory curriculum, the senior play, and student government was encouraged and applauded by fellow black students. Participation in such "white activities" earned black students the pejorative label *Uncle Toms,* and seriously threatened black group solidarity. Petroni saw such withdrawal from mainstream activities as contributing to and perpetuating the cultural stereotype of blacks as athletically superior but academically inferior.[12]

The trend toward contrived academic marginality among black students in U.S. schools is also documented in the ethnographic research of Fordham and Ogbu. Here, black students were faced with the dilemma of wanting to achieve academically, but of giving in to peer pressure that denigrates academic pursuits as "acting white." The researchers describe a black student with a bright potential in the "advanced placement course" whose academic underachievement represented his effort to validate his black identity. "His low [academic] performance is due to his greater emphasis on athletic achievement and his emerging manhood, and his less emphasis on the core curriculum. He does not study. He spends very little time completing his homework assignments . . . he does not feel he can change the direction of his school career because he does not want to be known as a 'brainiac.'"[13] To cope with this "burden of 'acting white,'" many black students with academic potential adopt strategies such as camouflaging their academic ability and interest or overindulging in athletic activities. By doing so, these students become academically marginal and, in effect, withdraw from the mainstream curriculum. Spady concludes that, for any category of students, complete athletic involvement without other extracurricular participation tends to depress academic aspiration and attainment.[14]

Equally seriously, the adoption of a nonacademic culture by black students has had a negative impact on intergroup relations within the social system of the school. A comparative analysis of black-white relationships in Canadian, U.S., and British mixed-race schools reveals a well-established pattern of racial in-groups in sports. At Humberville, where team sports is dominated by black students, there are subtle but distinct strategies employed by this group to protect this territory. Quite often black cliques emerge from the team selection process, with white students being excluded from stronger teams or used as "fillers" for weaker teams. Black-white separation occurs when white students express the feeling that "we are not as good as the black guys" and then gradually withdraw.

In British comprehensive schools, where black students have "colonized" extracurricular sports and regard this area of school life as their territory, Carrington observed: "White lads were frequently overlooked unless they were friendly with coloured lads in the team."[15] Racial separation in sports, moreover, is not motivated entirely by black students. Carrington's British study shows that the withdrawal of white students may be attributed to white racism. One of his white respondents conceded: "There is a lot of prejudice at this school . . . some kids won't play for the school because they just don't like West Indians."[16] Racism was also identified by Oliver's study of the U.S. situation as a factor contributing to the overrepresentation of blacks in a community baseball program and the withdrawal of whites from the program. White parents perceived this sport as a black activity and discouraged their sons' participation. As Oliver pointed out, white children are redirected into tennis, golf, and racquetball, which require monetary resources, thus excluding many blacks who may not be able to afford these sports.[17]

Furthermore, spectators of extracurricular sporting events dominated by black athletes are also predominatly black. Their white peers identify more with nonathletic extracurricular activities, even as spectators. So, contrary to the belief that sports strengthens intergroup relationships, research shows that the sporting prowess of black students may have little or no effect in bringing about intergroup friendships or may even cause dissension between races. Actual friendship patterns are of a racial in-group nature.[18] So, although sports may have the potential for racial in-group and athlete spectator binding, it is, in fact, more of an arena for negative intergroup social relations.

To summarize, dropping out of the academic culture of the school and adopting the alternative sports culture may lead to serious in-school dysfunctional consequences for black youth. First, it tends to interfere with their academic progress: students miss classes, shortcut homework, and do poorly on exams. Second, black students who are preoccupied with sports are excluded from other areas of school life, especially those that are academically oriented, such as speech, drama, or student government. Finally, black sports culture negatively influences intergroup relations; black control of sports, coupled with white withdrawal, contributes to divisiveness within the social system of the school.

## SPONSORSHIP AND SOCIALIZATION OF
## BLACK STUDENTS INTO SPORTS

Who or what causes the "sidetracking" of black students away from the academic mainstream and into the sports culture? We have already examined how black students in U.S. schools pressure fellow blacks to relinquish academic aspirations and commit themselves to the sports culture they perceive as validating black identity. Here we examine two other factors: teachers as socializing agents, and the media's presentation of black professional athletes as models. Commenting on the socializing impact of schools with teachers as agents, Carrington writes: "Schools are sponsoring black academic failure by channeling black pupils away from the academic mainstream and into sport."[19] Researchers are convinced that teachers' perception of black students as having superior physical skills but an inferior intellectual endowment contributes to the erection of barriers to opportunity within schools for this racial group.[20] With such denigrative images of black youth, incidents of "channeling" were captured vividly in the claims of teachers themselves in Carrington's study: "Sports gives them [West Indian pupils] a chance of success. Whereas they're not successful in the classroom they can show their ability on the sports field."[21] A black student in Cashmore's study summarized the effects of teacher's perceptions on student outcome in this fashion:

> Teachers definitely think of you as a good athlete if you are black. They seem to have this idea about natural talent and any kid who shows the slightest promise is put into sport and made to concentrate on that. It's as if they're expecting you to fail academically; and if the teacher expects you to fail, then you begin to believe it yourself and you do.[22]

Academic failure was clearly an outcome of teachers channeling black students out of the mainstream curriculum and into sports, as one of Cashmore's respondents related: "[The] games teachers would say 'There's a [track] meeting at such and such a place on Wednesday afternoon; would you ask your teacher if you could miss your lessons?' and I'd get the afternoon off. It was quite nice."[23] Cashmore labels teachers' impact as the "push" factor supplying the impetus necessary to instigate and sustain black students' interest in sports as an alternative to academics. But to what end? Some educational critics have suggested that sports are used as a social control mechanism, curbing, containing, and neutralizing black resistance to schooling.[24] Others have speculated that black students are channeled into sports to provide them with some measure of success, since "sports are the things they are good at." Still others see this sidetracking as a "cooling out" process for black youth and a diversion away from their pursuit of academic credentials.[25] Whatever the imputed motive of teachers for prioritizing the schooling of black children, the end result is the same: without the expectation of or encouragement to pursue an academic curriculum, black students will continue to fulfill the stereotype of outstanding athletes but be underachievers scholastically.

McPherson has suggested that beyond the socializing environment of the school and the socializing agents such as teachers and coaches, successful black athletes presented in the mass media also inspire black youth.[26] Print and electronic media have become influential in projecting and publicizing black professional athletes as role models. These images are thought to have a significant impact on the psyche of black children, who internalize them as proof of success for "their kind." The effect of such modeling on young blacks aspiring to be career athletes was captured cogently by one of Cashmore's black respondents: "If you can relate to somebody, it's a big spur to you 'cause if someone else has done it you can follow him ... And like James Brown said on TV the other day, 'Black kids need black people to associate themselves with.'"[27] The teachers themselves, though, accuse the media of creating in black youth the aspirations of becoming career sportsmen: "Part of the reason for getting this business of professional sports is because of a predominant number of blacks in the media playing professional football, baseball ... The examples are there for these kids when they watch professional sports on TV. Players in high exposure positions are usually black."[28] To what extent, then, have black students organized their aspirations around the professional athletes they see in the media? Black students at Humberville Vocational move beyond aspirations and actively strategize to make their dreams a reality. The way to acquire athletic scholarships to U.S. colleges, they argue, is to be scouted by agents who travel around the city's collegiates seeking out talented athletes. Since agents do not scout vocational (low-track) schools, the boys embark on an "underground railroad" to higher-track schools. A teacher and coach at Humberville confirmed the athletes' aspirations and efforts to achieve them:

> The [black] boys do aspire to be professional athletes. But the fact that they are in a vocational school that does not prepare students for college is an indication of their unrealistic expectations ... The trek of boys to schools such as East Park [higher track] is in chase of an elusive dream. Many of them cannot make it there and have returned [to Humberville] to hang around.[29]

At the same time that the black sportsmen portrayed in the media provide conspicuous models for black students to emulate, they also negatively influence these students' scholarly commitment. Thus, when black aspiring athletes fall short of the goals they set for themselves, they have little or no academic qualifications to fall back on. Cashmore concludes: "Guided by images of success, role models and teachers they [black students] set their sights immovably on sports careers. Sports become their central preoccupying interest in life, displacing more down to earth possibilities of education."[30] Conspicuously absent from the list of significant others who encourage and nurture black youths' preoccupation with school sports are their parents. Commentators have hinted at parents' resentment of the media presentation of black athletic success and the school's support for black students' concentration in sports and not in academic achievement.[31]

## LONG-TERM CONSEQUENCES

Cashmore's sad commentary sums up the predicament of black men rooted in school sports: "There are thousands upon thousands of unsuccessful black, would-be sportsmen, with careers in shreds, having placed too much hope on the precarious sporting world."[32] The process of dropping out of the academic mainstream in favor of school sports inevitably leads to leaving school without academic credentials or job skills. Cashmore's work, *Black Sportsmen,* captures the rapidity with which self-esteem, sense of accomplishment, and the prestige of black high school athletes disappear outside the supportive and protective school environment. This change of status from "star athlete" to unskilled, generalized laborer was described by a teacher and coach in my ethnographic study: "This student lived, ate, slept basketball; he always had a basketball in his hand. He ended up making the all-star team. But as he got older his focus changed quickly from sport to earning money. He ended up dropping out of school to earn money."[33] Picou and other researchers conclude that for working-class blacks, athletics are of significance neither to achieving their mobility goals nor to the occupational status of the school leaver.[34] Facing the harsh, uncompromising job market with inadequate credentials and job skills, young black dropouts, with their sports dreams aborted, have to settle for a lifetime of unskilled wage labor or even unemployment.

To summarize, researchers critical of the schooling of black working-class students in Canadian, British, and U.S. mixed-race schools have focused on another form of dropping out. These students have disengaged from the academic curriculum and have committed themselves to an alternative reward structure: the sports culture. As Rumberger points out, this in-school academic disengagement quite often culminates in the final act of leaving.[35] Without intervention these students are destined for an adult world of unskilled labor or unemployment. But intervention strategies designed to revise teachers' perceptions of black students and black students' construction of their own identities need to be creatively developed and implemented.


## OUT OF THE GYM, BACK INTO THE CLASSROOM

To begin the process of getting black students back to the classroom, a number of intervention strategies have to be employed with teachers, black students, and their parents all working cooperatively. To start, the opportunity structure within the socializing environment of the school needs re-evaluation and change. Teachers as socializing agents need to alter their stereotypical images of black children as physically superior, but intellectually inferior, to other racial and ethnic groups. The "white mind–black body" ideology that has influenced the opportunity structure within mixed-race schools has to give way to the concept of truly equal educational opportunities for all students. To initiate this process, Cashmore urges that teachers "raise their expectations of Blacks in intellectual spheres and lower them in relation to 'natural sports ability.'"[26]

A useful starting point is for schools to make a conceptual distinction between blacks' physical education classes and their extracurricular sports programs, since there is the tendency for the latter to engulf the former. Lawson points out that when there is no separation, emphasis is placed on athletic performance for the highly skilled students instead of on physical education instruction for all.[37] Making a clear, conceptual separation of physical education from sports, and implementing this within schools, will help blur the "ethnic territorial boundaries" and foster better intergroup social relations. Lawson concludes that black students could benefit educationally, since the distinction between physical education and sports makes it more difficult for sports to be employed by schools as compensation for academic involvement or social control.[38]

Another strategy for reintroducing sports-minded black students to the academic mainstream is to establish guidelines that limit their involvement in school sports. Such a limitation is crucial for those minority students who are marginal in their academic performance and need to spend more time and effort on classroom work.

By the same token, teachers should become aware of the effects of the high profile given to sports within the school community. For example, some schools lavish their athletes with awards in recognition of their dedication and contribution to their sports program. Presented at elaborate sports banquets held in the athletes' honor are such awards as Male Athlete of the Year, Female Athlete of the Year, Special Award Plaque, Honor Athletic Letter, and Second Athletic Letter. Black students monopolize this area of success in school, but they present no competition to their white peers for academic awards.[39] Leaman and Carrington find it ironic that the one area of school life that blacks dominate is, in itself, marginal: "Marginality is also a matter of one's life being in some ways at the disposal of others and not really under one's own control ... Their [young blacks'] very marginality [is] a result of their identification with physical activities."[40] Instead of reproducing racial minority students as adult marginal workers at the bottom of the socioeconomic structure, schools should, without reservations, guarantee black students full exposure to the mainstream curriculum. Academics should be stressed as the only means for working-class blacks to achieve upward socioeconomic mobility.

Black students who adopt the alternative sports culture as an entree to professional sports should be sensitized to the long odds against achieving any success. This reality could be communicated much more cogently by having both successful sportsmen and unsuccessful "would-be" sportsmen share their life experiences with overzealous student athletes. Such an intervention strategy should have a lasting effect. As Lawson reminds us, "The successes of a few have served to conceal the limited opportunities for the majority."[41] Employment as recreational sports leaders—a logical alternative for the enthusiasts—will also be closed to blacks who may have acquired skills in "playing the game" but lack the academic and professional credentials to assume leadership positions. Career counseling services should be available to alert students to the employment opportunities in the field of recreational sports and to the credentials required for entry into this field. Emphasizing this harsh reality may serve to jolt black students out of the false consciousness, created by socializing agents, that a career in sports is theirs for the asking.

Finally, the black community (including parents) has to assume leadership in erasing from the consciousness of black youth the impact of the "white mind–black body" socialization. Because black students perceive sports as their own "ethnic territory" and the pursuit of academic credentials as "acting white," the black community has two urgent tasks. The first, as Fordham and Ogbu direct, is to "help students learn to divorce academic pursuit from the idea of acting white."[42] To achieve this end, the black community should publicly recognize those who achieve academic success. The second task is for the black community to communicate a strong message to the school system to relinquish the ideology that guides the differential development of black students for the world of sports and whites for academic pursuits. Equality of educational opportunity must be foremost in the minds of both the school officials and the black community. Until both sides cooperate in redirecting black youth out of the gym and back into the classroom, they must take joint responsibility for the reproduction of inferior black alternative culture within schools.

To conclude, effective intervention starts with school personnel raising their expectations of black students. They must then reduce the high profile afforded sports within the school community while at the same time making the academic curriculum more accessible and attractive to these "would-be sportsmen." The black students themselves need to downgrade the importance of sports as a cement for their ethnic group and as a route to socioeconomic advancement. If the school presents the academic curriculum as a rational alternative to sports and the black community highlights black role models in other fields of endeavor, the life chances of working-class blacks will be greatly enhanced.

## NOTES

1. For the U.S. data, see Ruth B. Ekstrom et al., "Who Drops out of High School and Why? Findings from a National Study," in *School Dropouts: Patterns and Policies,* ed. Gary Natriello (New York: Teachers College Press, 1987); Russel W. Rumberger, "Dropping out of High School: The Influence of Race, Sex and Family Background," *American Eduational Research Journal,* 20, No. 2 (1983), 199–213.

2. For Canada, see data from the city of Toronto, in E. N. Wright, *The Retention and Credit Accumulation of Students in Secondary Schools,* (Toronto: Board of Education, Research Department, 1985), pp. 25–28.

3. For the purposes of this study, dropping out in the British schools means leaving school at the earliest legal age and, also, persistent absenteeism. The following references carry quantitative and qualitiative data on attendance and ethnic origin: Grace Gray, Allan Smith, and Michael Rutter, "School Attendance and the First Year of Employment," in *Out of School: Modern Perspectives in Truancy and School Refusal,* ed. L. Hersov and I. Berg (Toronto: John Wiley and Sons, 1980), 353–354; John Furlong, "Black Resistance in the Liberal Comprehensive," in *Readings on Interaction in the Classroom,* ed. Sara Delamont (London: Methuen, 1984), 227–228.

4. James Coleman, *The Adolescent Society* (New York: The Free Press, 1961). See also Richard Rehberg and Walter Schafer, "Participation in Interscholastic Athletics, and College Expectations," *American Journal of Sociology,* 73 (May, 1968), 732–740.

5. All names of schools in this Canadian study are pseudonyms. The rationale for selecting black working-class boys for this study is based on the importance of gender and class dynamics in the schooling process. First, sports are culturally and ideologically significant to black males' identity formation, so boys are more intensely involved than girls in school sports. As a result, this involvement in school sports is more likely to affect the structure of opportunity for boys. Second, it is generally believed that black middle-class boys are more committed than their working-class counterparts to academic pursuits. Their involvement in school sports tends to complement rather than detract from their academic achievements.

6. See R. Patrick Solomon, "The Creation of Separatism: The Lived Culture of West Indian Boys in a Toronto High School," State University of New York, Ph.D. dissertation, (1987), chapter 5.

7. Solomon, "The Creation of Separatism," 120.

8. Ernest Cashmore, "Black Youth, Sport and Education," *New Community,* 10, No. 2 (1982), 216.

9. Ernest Cashmore, *Black Sportsmen* (London: Routledge and Kegan Paul, 1982), 100.

10. Oliver Leaman and Bruce Carrington, "Athleticism and the Reproduction of Gender and Ethnic Marginality," *Leisure Studies,* 4 (1985), 214.

11. F.A. Petroni, "'Uncle Toms': White Stereotypes in the Black Movement," *Human Organization,* 29, No. 4 (1970), 260.

12. Ibid., 260–266.

13. Signithia Fordham and John Ogbu, "Black Students' School Success: Coping with the 'Burden of Acting White,'" *The Urban Review,* 18, No. 3 (1986), 188–189.

14. See William G. Spady, "Lament for the Letterman: Effects of Peer Status and Extra-curricular Activities on Goals and Achievement," *American Journal of Sociology,* 75 (January, 1970), 608–702; see also Lloyd Lueptow and Brian Kayser, "Athletic Involvment, Academic Achievement and Aspiration," *Sociological Focus,* 7 (1973–74), 24–36.

15. Bruce Carrington, "Sport as a Side-track. An Analysis of West Indian Involvement in Extra-curricular Sport," in *Race, Class and Education,* ed. Len Barton and Steven Walker (London: Croom Helm, 1983), 14.

16. Ibid., 59.

17. Melvin L. Oliver, "The Transmission of Sport Mobility Orientation in the Family," *International Review of Sport Sociology,* 2, No. 15 (1980), 51–73.

18. The perception of West Indian boys that sports is *their* ethnic territory and their strategies to protect this territory prove counterproductive in building better intergroup relations. See A.J. Sargeant's study, "Participation of West Indian Boys in English Schools' Sports Teams," *Educational Research,* 14, No. 3 (1972), 225–230.

19. Carrington, "Sports as a Side-track," 45.

20. For a more in-depth look at teachers' perceptions and behavior, see Cashmore, "Black Youth, Sport and Education"; Cashmore, *Black Sportsmen;* Carrington, "Sport as a Side-track"; Leaman and Carrington, "Athleticism"; and Solomon, "The Creation of Separatism."

21. Carrington, "Sport as a Side-track," 52.

22. Cashmore, *Black Sportsmen,* 106.

23. Ibid., 101.

24. Hal Lawson, "Physical Education and Sport in the Black Community: The Hidden Perspective," *Journal of Negro Education,* 48, No. 2 (1979), 187–195. See also Cashmore, *Black Sportsmen;* Carrington, "Sport as a Side-track"; and Cashmore, "Black Youth, Sport and Education."

25. Maureen Stone, *The Education of the Black Child in Britain: The Myth of Multiracial Education* (London: Fontana, 1981).

26. B. McPherson, "The Black Athlete: An Overview and Analysis," in D. Landers, ed. *Social Problems in Athletes* (Urbana, Illinois: University of Illinois Press, 1976).

27. Cashmore, "Black Youth, Sport and Education," 215.

28. Solomon, "The Creation of Separatism," 129.

29. Ibid., 122, 126.

30. Cashmore, "Black Youth, Sport and Education," 216.

31. Department of Education and Science, *Interim Report of the Committee of Inquiry into the Education of Children from Ethnic Minority Groups, Cmnd 8273* (Rampton Report) (London: Her Majesty's Stationery Office, 1981). See also H. Lashley, "The New Black Magic," *British Journal of Physical Education,* 2, No. 1 (1981), 5–6; and Cashmore, *Black Sportsmen.*

32. Cashmore, "Black Youth, Sport and Education," 217.

33. From field notes for study, Solomon, "The Creation of Separatism."

34. See J. Steven Picou, "Race, Athletic Achievement and Educational Aspiration," *The Sociological Quarterly,* 19(1978), 429–438.

35. Russell Rumberger, "High School Dropouts: A Review of Issues and Evidence," *Review of Educational Research,* 57, No. 2 (1987) 111.

36. Cashmore, "Black Youth, Sport and Education," 219.

37. See Lawson, "Physical Education and Sport in the Black Community," 191.

38. Ibid.

39. Solomon, "The Creation of Separatism," 120.

40. Leaman and Carrington, "Athleticism," 214–215.

41. Lawson, "Physical Education and Sport in the Black Community," 190–191.

42. Fordham and Ogbu, "Black Students' School Success," 203.

# Part II

## *Inside Schools*

ELEANOR FARRAR AND ROBERT L. HAMPEL

Chapter 5

# Social Services in High Schools*

Quitting school often caps a series of unfortunate experiences. We know that weak classroom performance is only part of that series. Nonacademic problems usually precede the decision to leave. We also know that most high schools, especially the largest urban schools, try to salvage students through an array of programs and specialists. Recently we've even heard the American high school called a "social service center for adolescents at loose ends."[1] What goes on inside that center, however, is rarely examined closely. We don't know very much about the organization and operation of the activities designed for the at-risk populations. Because dropout prevention can be classified as one of the social services, it behooves us to look at the recent history and present condition of the help offered by counselors, social workers, nurses, and other specialists.

The nonacademic complications of adolescence are remarkably diverse. In one suburban Boston high school, a school nurse knew of twenty cases of anorexia or bulimia, a one-year total far above previous figures. Incidents of sexual abuse and incest come to the attention of school people. Suicides, attempted suicides, and contemplated suicides are recurring crises. So are the woes of "emancipated youth," teenagers living alone and supporting themselves.

*Research for this paper was sponsored by the Carnegie Corporation. An earlier version appeared in *Phi Delta Kappan,* December 1987.

Those startling misfortunes are dramatic material for television documentaries; but equally compelling is the prevalence and severity of more familiar patterns of behavior. The entanglements of divorce often affect half the school's students. Drug abuse may be down in some places, but teenage drinking rarely is. Sex presents many challenges in this age of legalized abortion, reliable contraception, and peer pressure to be active. Less visible symptoms attend the problem of stress, but school people see many students who feel unconstructively pressured. Depression is another troublesome state of mind, reportedly on the increase.

How do our high schools identify and respond to such complications in youngsters' lives? This chapter offers an interpretation of the organization and delivery of social services. Contrasting the formal organization and the informal delivery of social services is the key to understanding what happens (and doesn't happen) in high schools. On paper, the division of labor is tidy: many different people are responsible for specific tasks. In practice, the segmentation often becomes fragmentation. Staff can do as they see fit, coordination in house is minimal, follow-up is haphazard, and relations with outsiders are uneven. That informality, we argue, can only be fully understood in light of the *ambiguous* and *volatile* nature of the work social service staff do.

## PROCEDURES

This sketch of social services had its origins in Theodore Sizer's national study, A Study of High Schools. Both Sizer and one of the authors of this chapter worked for several years as principal investigators and field researchers. That project involved classroom observations and interviews with students, teachers, administrators, and parents in fifteen public and private high schools, and examined various aspects of high school life, especially instruction. The study did not focus on social services, but our colleagues gathered much information about how schools respond to student problems, information which was barely described in the study's publications.

During our visits to these schools and in reading the reports of others' visits, we were struck by the tremendous staff concern and school resources devoted to students whose emotional problems interfered with their ability to take advantage of the schools' academic programs. We also noticed the ambivalence and uncertainty that characterized the schools' responses to these problems. Although many students received services, it appeared that many with the same problem were served in different ways. Many fell through the cracks. The Carnegie Corporation encouraged our interest in exploring these matters further, and with its help we reconsidered social services in eight of the fifteen schools we had studied earlier.[2]

The eight schools which we revisited in the spring of 1984 varied in size from 1,200 students to over 3,000. Most of the schools had substantial nonwhite enrollments and drew from the least advantaged sections of town; two schools were in upper-middle-class communities. Private schools, rural schools, and schools with few or no social services are not in our sample; our remarks apply to suburban and urban schools with a diverse student population.[3]

We asked staff open-ended questions. How does the school know which students need help? What assistance is available? What is the role of community agencies? Those and other questions sought information on common patterns and overarching themes, not minute details or specific problems. What follows is an aerial snapshot, not a detailed road map, of territory too often ignored. Case studies would be welcome; here we offer general thoughts on what impressed us as the crucial aspects of social service provision in high schools.

## THE FORMAL STRUCTURE

The social services are not a place where each person has common responsibilities. A counselor and a social worker are less interchangeable than teachers of Shakespeare and Business English. Although specialization in academic departments is common, differentiation is much more extensive among the nonacademic staff.

Before the 1970s, generic responsibilities were more prevalent than they are today. Guidance staff handled college recommendations, scheduling, personal counseling, career planning, and (sometimes) discipline. Specialists were either outsiders or central office staff. Many counselors lacked professional preparation; indeed, counseling was often seen as training for future principals.

Staff differentiation came about for several reasons. All social services expanded rapidly in the same years, but the cause of growth in one area was not the same cause as in other services. Heightened concern for school safety gave rise to security departments, thereby reducing the disciplinary duties of counselors. Federal funding in the early 1970s for career counseling, a popular reform then, encouraged specialization in that subfield. Another important development was the growing strength of special education, an enclave fortified by state and federal laws. Although many adult members of that enclave teach, they often advise students on nonacademic issues.

In addition to the growth of those three subspecialties—school security, career planning, and special education—the segmentation of social service specialties cannot be explained without reference to the changing problems adolescents brought to school. Substance abuse, sexual activity, and teen parenting became classified as medical and pyschological issues, suitable for nurses and social workers. Many veteran counselors resisted a therapeutic approach to behavior that previously had been punished as willful delinquency. The influence of nurses and social workers expanded when traditionalists were unable or unwilling to treat problems which, in their school days, were either nonexistent, quietly hushed up, handled by parents, or punished by the deans.

Differentiation persisted in the 1980s. The organizational chart of social service departments is usually a complicated chart. The arrangements at one urban Massachusetts high school illustrate the balkanization found in other schools. There are eighteen counselors, and few of them share the same duties. Each of the four houses has a counselor for scheduling and college recommendations. They leave discussion of personal issues to the two group counselors who are not in any house. Other counseling staff without house affiliation include career and bilingual specialists. Several special programs—one for occupational education, another with participatory governance, a third featuring no-nonsense rules and regulations—have their own counselors. Several "school adjustment counselors" work with students referred by the weekly meeting of a child study team. For delinquents and youth on probation, a court liaison is available in the schools. Moreover, nurses offer information on sex, psychologists do diagnostic tests for special education students, and a child parenting program helps young mothers raise their babies. This assortment of specialists works in a school that had no guidance department (aside from truant officers for nonattendance) until the mid-1960s.

In some schools the division of tasks is compounded by the assignment of several schools to the same social service staff. In one California district, a career counselor is available two days each week, which is less time than the nurse has (four days) or the district counselor (two and a half days, for attendance, parent conferences, and troubleshooting), but more than the social concerns (sex, drugs, alcohol) counselor's short daily visits or the appearances of the psychologist, who is responsible for two other schools. Specialization, in other words, applies to time and place as well as task. Further scattering stems from the existence of different lines of authority. Some staff report to superiors in the building, whereas others work for administrators in the central offices.

The organization of social services varies from school to school. There is no one best system uniformly copied. The only common pattern is the recent triumph of specialization over the older generic delivery of (fewer) services by (fewer) counselors. Growth and differentiation, each promoting the other, are what the different districts share.

To be sure, many schools have tinkered with their staffing arrangements. The division of labor is rarely set in stone. For instance, reassigning counselors to work side by side with class coordinators isolated counselors from each other. Clerical chores sometimes (not usually) recede, thanks to more secretaries or aides. The most frequent organizational change is the coming and going of little pushcarts in the shopping mall high school—peer counseling, substance abuse workshops, human relations lessons, and alternative programs for truants. Those programs usually have a precarious future because their funding is often from state or federal money in risk of disappearing whenever budget cutting happens.

None of those refinements significantly affect the organization of social service delivery. Even the teamwork gained by having counselors and coordinators in adjacent offices is lost by isolating counselors from other counselors. Clerical help for paperwork does not change the number of professional staff. The ephemeral programs are manned by teachers, students, or outsiders as often as by counselors, thus increasing the number of different people with different jobs. The organizational changes reinforce rather than reduce the balkanization of the social services.

## THE INFORMAL FUNCTIONING

When somebody says, "I'll handle it," it doesn't mean the same thing from one person to another. Treating the assortment of student problems varies greatly according to personal style and preferences. There is considerable informality in matching students with services. Individuals enjoy substantial autonomy and discretion in their daily work. Rigid policies and clear-cut regulations are the exception, not the rule.

How social service staff deal with each other depends on the people involved. In one Colorado high school, only one of the four counselors consults with either the nurse or the social worker. The head of a parenting program in California refuses to refer her students to the counselors (who concentrate on college recommendations and counseling). Regular contact, in any school, is more likely if mandated by laws or regulations—periodic core evaluation team meetings, for example—and when the staff get along nicely with each other. Intradepartmental cooperation is not uncommon, to be sure, but when it occurs, agreeable personalities influence the coordination more than printed job descriptions.

What is particularly negotiable is the power a social service provider can exercise over colleagues. That murkiness was evident in one high school where a student was suspended for fighting. The boy was employed in a school work program at one of the school's best job placements, a site the school hated to jeopardize. Suspended from school, was he also out of a job as important to his economic well-being as to the school's program? The social worker wanted to tell the employer what happened in school and let the employer decide what to do. The teacher in charge of the work program refused to contact the employer. Each insisted it was the other's responsibility. After several weeks, the social worker did so. Never was it predetermined that a teacher or a social worker can tell the other to do something. Furthermore, the rules from Washington, D.C. stipulated that a student must be enrolled in school to be eligible for the work program, without saying if suspension was the same as nonenrollment. Throughout this episode there was no certainty as to who could or should make what decision.

Informality also characterizes much of the contact between students and social service staff. Appointments are rarely necessary. The typical counseling department is more like a walk-in clinic than a doctor's office. "Everything in my day just sort of mooshes together," one woman aptly remarked. Students do not have to rely on one and only one adult for help. Some ignore their counselor, preferring instead a different adult they seek out. Some know from their friends that one or another counselor is unusually accommodating, so they ask for reassignment or (more commonly) just visit that person for conversation, advice, and assistance.

The social service staff's effectiveness with teachers often presupposes cordial relations. "A lot of my work depends on good will," one counselor said. One way she retains friendship is by refusing to pull students from academic classes for group counseling (her chairman agreed—"kids get too uptight if they miss a Latin quiz"). Special education staff often choose to act like counselors, negotiating directly with classroom teachers on behalf of their students. "We tell them what our kids can do, convincing them that they're not going to take on a raving maniac." Another influence on teacher-counselor relations is availability. Classroom teachers prefer immediate solutions to the problems they bring to the counselors, and time spent outside the office complicates fast troubleshooting. "They want a piece of advice, or they want the kid to disappear." Frequently counselors try to establish informal alliances with teachers able to get otherwise silent students to open up.

How many teachers can do personal counseling varies from school to school, but nowhere can the counselor assume that everyone is able or willing to be an ally. Frequently we heard comments like this psychologist's remark: "Teachers tend to view mental health very concretely. If a kid is doing all right in school, they think that's all that matters. They never understand that behavior that may be quiet and controlled can lead to trouble down the line." In schools with teacher-led classes on human relations, many counselors questioned teacher qualifications to discuss personal issues, aware that some led excellent conversations while others were terrible. Some teachers close to students stood too close, promising troubled kids confidentiality and later refusing to share the privileged information with social service staff. The unevenness in the staff's therapeutic aptitude means that counselors forge stronger links with some teachers than with others. Of course the reverse is also true. Teachers evaluate, rightly so, some counselors as better than others, and they hesitate to work with someone they either do not respect or dislike.

There is also much flexibility in how far an individual social service provider chooses to expand his or her workload. For many staff an important area of discretion is whether or not to involve parents. In regard to pregnancies, some staff prefer not to break the news to the parents (unless the law mandates disclosure). Allotment of time between various tasks is another important area where no rules or regulations dictate how much has to be done in a given block of hours.

That might happen in classrooms—three periods of Emily Dickinson, a movie, then a quiz—but social service staff are less constrained by the clock. A boy depressed by his parents' divorce may spend ten minutes, one hour, or more speaking with a social worker; it all depends on the adults' judgment of the situation.

Sometimes job responsibilities can be reconfigured to suit individual temperaments. "Here we are more counselors than we are police officers," said one school security director. His staff do not wear uniforms, and the only weapons they have are those taken from kids. He put a coke machine in his office, and keeps a side door open for those who do not want friends to see them going in. Every person in the department either coaches or sponsors a club. As one student exclaimed, "They try to be like kids instead of like security." The director takes special education students on wildlife hikes, and also spends many late afternoon hours in pinball arcades, "just shooting the breeze."

Administrators have considerable discretion in deciding how to supervise social service staff. Quite a few choose to do very little, we found. One Colorado vice-principal, when asked what services schools should provide, confessed, "You know, I really don't feel qualified to answer that question. For three years I have had administrative responsibility for social services and the assumption is that I know something about these areas. But I don't." A vice-principal in California said that he did not know the attendance and parent relations counselor in the school, nor did he know the alcohol, sex, and drugs counselor. He knew they existed, but he had never referred students to them. Furthermore, he had never sent students to the school guidance department for counseling. He was also aware of a district directory of outside agencies to which kids can be referred, but he never recommends those agencies.

We rarely saw administrators try to coordinate the different social service staff activities. In six of the eight high schools, the position of department head was either nonexistent or weak. In none of those schools did a vice-principal, assistant headmaster, or principal monitor day-to-day events; the only meaningful oversight (which was usually quite modest) came from central office staff in positions like director of health services. The absence of strong leadership perpetuates the informal practices. Without much supervision, staff can use their autonomy to do their work as they see fit. Fragmentation is not reduced by energetic coordination from vigorous department heads or other administrators.

A final sign of informal operations is the lack of systematic record keeping. Nearly everyone complained of endless paperwork, but in the schools we visited not enough data existed to analyze the frequency of different student problems, the number or kind of referrals outside the school, or the results of the cases. Although some staff, admittedly, kept meticulous files, thoroughness was an exception, not the rule. Usually staff were free to use whatever notational systems they preferred. One school nurse had a private code for recording student pregnancies. Even the conscientious tabulators used catch-all classifications too broad to analyze meaningfully; for example, one school nurse's monthly report counted as "counseling" any and every conversation on non-medical issues.

Informality not only characterizes the ways that social service staff deliver services within high schools, but it also fits their dealing with community service providers in agencies, health clinics, and private practice. High schools, particularly urban high schools, have many resources available for referrals. But whether students are referred, and then followed to see that they get outside help, is left to the discretion of social service personnel. "You'd think there would be some policy about what to do with some of these problems," one principal mused, "but as it is, each of the high schools deal with things differently— except in those cases where there are laws, such as child abuse or illegal weapons."

There is no confusion with respect to child abuse, possession of illegal weapons, and suicide threats. Each of those dangers is covered by either laws or district policies that spell out staff responsibility to act. Physical impairments and medical problems also rank high on the list of likely referrals. Professional help for pregnant teens is often available; girls are more likely to get it when the school has a parenting program. (But often girls have to transfer to a different school to enroll in those programs, and since many do not want to switch, they receive little help with prenatal care. A school nurse said that she and the school's social worker tried to "meet with these girls from time to time," and when they suspected the absence of medical care, "worked on" the girls to get it.)

Drug and alcohol abuse are more complicated problems for social service personnel. Here are serious health risks, but they frequently signal deeper mental distress. It is in this domain of psychological and emotional disorder that the staff's comfort level begins to drop and their discretion in referral decisions increases. The reasons for not referring are quite varied. Sometimes they are habit and past practice. Sometimes the lack of information about agencies is important. Anxiety about job security is not uncommon: a principal said, "[counselors] are afraid their kids will be pulled into that agency and the staff will lose their raison d'être and be replaced by clerical technicians." Most common is skepticism of parents' support.

Whatever the different reasons social service staff give for not referring students, the sheer numbers who want or need help result in many referrals. But there is rarely much follow-up by the school. Many agencies either won't share information about students involved in counseling or, as one counselor put it, they act "uppity" and treat school staff "like a bunch of professional incompetents." Agency snippiness of that sort has led school staff to hold various criteria for outside referrals. They care about the amount of feedback they get. They prefer to refer to practitioners whom they know. The agencies' theoretical orientation— directive versus nondirective counseling, for instance— is of consequence. Staff also consider the location of the agency ("kids won't travel into strange sections of town") and the rate of agency staff turnover ("So many kids already have to cope with loss in their lives, and we shouldn't make that worse"). One counselor nicely summarized the referral guidelines: "We go to people we have faith in. The key is trust, past experience, a good relationship, and their personalities." But those criteria mean different things to different people. No codified rules define standards like "past experience." Each social service staff member supplies the definitions, an individualism in keeping with the informality of referrals both within and outside the school.

## AMBIGUITY AND VOLATILITY

Why does this combination of formality and informality exist in the effort to meet social service needs? In part, it accommodates the different responsibilities placed on schools to provide services. Where the expectation is clear, as with abuse and suicide threats, policies and procedures have been delineated, and the organization's roles and rules are straightforward. But often responsibilities are unclear. In that vacuum, social service staff can work with students, each other, and outsiders in ways they deem proper and find comfortable. That informality accommodates the ambiguity surrounding the diagnosis of the need and determination of who is best qualified to meet it.

In America, the educational system asks its staff to answer questions that often confound outside professionals. Who should be served? What is the best treatment? Clear guidelines are absent except in the most serious cases. In schools where depression is supposedly pervasive, how does staff know who to counsel and refer in light of the fact that so many kids will happily grow out of their problems as they get older? The director of an alternative program for troubled students frequently meets former students on the street and is astonished at their reports of stable jobs and home lives, which he never would have predicted. Some think that the best course of action is no action. But others, like this guidance chairperson, said, "Should the school deal with student problems? Of course. The kid brings that with him to school and we should deal with it." But who among the school staff is fully qualified to decide on a course of action?

Sometimes the decisions are simple, as with suspected medical problems, because the diagnosis and the response are technically easy to see. The appropriate specialists can be identified; they are professionally trained and certified, so questions about the proper treatment are seldom an issue. The possible channels of referral are also clear—for instance, the straight path from the school nurse's vision screening to the optometrist. The less ambiguous the condition that requires treatment, the more likely it is that formal procedures exist to guide the school's response. Moreover, social service staff are not fearful of possibly adverse student or parent reactions in these cases. There is public consensus on the need for treatment in medical cases, and agreement that schools should provide some screening and treatment.

But a school nurse, on her own, hesitates to say, "She is depressed and needs a psychiatrist." What qualifies her to say so? Can she defend that judgment to upset or angry parents? Moreover, the line between medical and psychological problems is hard to see. Does a pregnant student need counseling? Is a thin girl potentially anorexic? Are substance abusers chemically addicted or mainly psychologically impaired? Many school staff waver, unsure whether or not to refer. But what if a student is potentially suicidal? The mere mention of the word by a student or his or her friends activates a district policy; it must be reported.

The combination of formality and informality in the social services encourages staff to respond in ways that are consistent with their treatment philosophies and personal comfort levels. It lets them refer everyone or no one, to counsel some students themselves if they wish, to involve parents or leave them alone. It enables them to match students to particular agencies or therapists, or to hand out a list of resources without any descriptions alongside the dozens of names and phone numbers.

But even with the decision rules, problems abound, often as the result of differing value systems and conflicting policies that dictate conflicting responses. Whether schools should ignore at-risk students or respond therapeutically is far from settled. Many schools sit astride the same fence on which American correctional facilities squirm, unsure whether punishment or treatment is the best approach.

Many staff can make (or reject) reasonable claims to responsibility if they wish. Individual counseling can be done by the nurse, the social worker, the adjustment counselor, or others. In fact, we're not sure how schools define counseling—whether it's anything that a psychologist would recognize, whether it's giving advice, whether it's just listening and saying nothing, or whether it's a pat on the shoulder and a pep talk. We sometimes got the impression that counseling is defined by the topic under discussion, not by the process, the methods, or the amount of time spent. In this highly informal arrangement, we suspect there are some kinds of problems that people are unwilling to talk about whenever they lack the necessary time, interest, competence, and self-confidence.

The pervasive informality also helps achieve a major social service staff priority: conflict avoidance. Schools can minimize dispute by permitting individual staff to decide who will receive social services, what kind, and from whom. There are several reasons why confrontations are feared. Part of the anxiety stems from the delicacy of relations with parents and taxpayers, but insiders also seem to need careful handling.

The external diplomacy is necessary because social services are more volatile, or potentially volatile, than a split infinitive or a geometry theorem. Many problems can only be attacked with the family's cooperation, but an alliance between home and school on behalf of the student cannot be assumed. Frequently it is hard to make even an initial telephone contact with a parent. Coming to school for a conference might cost a day's pay. Some cases, especially child abuse and incest, can catch counselors between a student's allegations and angry parental denial. Some parents scorn therapeutic solutions and rely instead on physical punishments. A few parents well versed in the law try to demand that the school pay for services, particularly if school staff recommend them. Other parents become acquainted with the law when they lose welfare checks because their children are truant, a point brought to the welfare department's attention by the school social workers. Furthermore, the enactment of disclosure laws in the 1970s gave parents easier access to school records. An assistant principal said, "I am very careful about what I say about the psychological condition of the kid. I can find myself in a lot of hot water." One counselor recalled the days when "seeing psychiatrist—mother alcoholic" would be a routine entry; today such bluntness could be troublesome if the parents read the record.

Informality also minimizes public awareness of, and alarm at, the size and severity of the problems. The public is already sure that violence and drugs bedevil most high schools; they assume that a movie like *Teachers* accurately depicts the true state of affairs. Even publicizing a spectacular success with a new social service program might broadcast too loudly the existence or pervasiveness of the original deficiency that was remedied. Victories cannot be celebrated in the style of a great basketball season or higher reading scores.

Moreover, personality clashes and power struggles can be finessed by not insisting on hard and fast procedures. Social service staff have to see more of each other than two classroom teachers from the same department. Yet they vary enormously in age, experiences, and philosophy. One California staff included a born-again Christian, a horse racing enthusiast, and an art collector. Putting them together would invite trouble. By letting staff concentrate on what they feel they do best, order is maintained with live-and-let-live agreements not to force each other to do business one set way.

## SUMMARY

Whatever one's opinion of the place of social services in high schools, adolescents deal with issues as major as pregnancy, alcoholism, parental divorce, weight disorders, and suicide. The array of school specialists available for help is striking. Many people can assist a student. The social service domain is not only larger than in the past, but also more segmented. At one time, a counselor was assigned a wider range of tasks than is now the case. Social services, at first glance, seem tightly scripted, with responsibilities parceled out in narrowly defined roles.

But in practice social service delivery is exceedingly informal. Staff enjoy substantial discretion in shaping their work. Within the school, their performance reflects idiosyncrasies like relations with other staff. Referrals to outside agencies also hinge on individual judgments, except in serious cases, like child abuse, that set in motion well-defined responses. The autonomy is rarely hedged in by careful administrative supervision.

The formal organization and the informal delivery of services is not just a case in point of the familiar maxim that our schools are "loosely coupled" institutions rather than rigid bureaucracies. Many adolescent problems are either ambiguous in diagnosis and treatment or potentially controversial. Sometimes they are both ambiguous and controversial, which makes it doubly difficult to find better ways to organize the delivery system so that students who need help can get it.

One approach might be to expand and redesign the role of community agencies by locating them in or near high schools to collaborate with staff and to work with students. Agencies would replace schools as the main service providers to students whose problems are both ambiguous and clearly serious; they might also help to deflect controversy from schools. An arrangement of this sort would narrow the scope of responsibilities schools now carry and would help them focus attention and resources on the academic lives of their students.

## NOTES

1. David K. Cohen and Barbara Neufeld, "The Failure of High Schools and the Progress of Education," *Daedalus,* Summer 1981, 83.

2. With the schools' permission, we reanalyzed the earlier study's field notes for information on social services. We also visited the eight schools. We interviewed administrators; counseling staff; social workers, nurses, and psychologists; social service staff who work out of the central offices but spend some time in each school; and staff in charge of special programs for pregnant girls, substance abusers, potential dropouts, and other adolescents at risk. We also reread earlier notes from interviews with students as well as classroom teachers.

3. In this article we discuss the schools as if they were utterly similar in their attitudes toward, and approaches to, social services. However, we found considerable variation between schools, especially in whether they counseled students in house or referred them to outside agencies. The number of staff

available to provide services also varied from place to place, as did the extent to which staff wanted to be involved. We found much variation in the number of school programs for such things as pregnancy, drug and alcohol abuse, divorce counseling, and dropout prevention. In some schools, the number of those programs was astonishingly large, particularly when supported by outside money. We also found differences in social services between rich and poor schools. Wealthier parents were more likely to ask schools for help and use their referrals than poor families.

Our comments focus on central tendencies and shared patterns; we do not analyze why one school differs from another, although that variation is indeed part of the theme of informal practice presented in the essay.

Chapter 6

# Urban Teachers and Dropout-Prone Students: The Uneasy Partners

One of the most difficult aspects of learning to teach in the inner city is learning to deny, in a sense, the plain evidence of one's own eyes. By the time they are of junior high age, if not sooner, many inner-city youngsters behave in ways that seem to unambiguously proclaim their lack of interest in schooling. Teachers are literally bombarded with these signals. Those teachers who hope to work successfully with such youngsters have to convince themselves that the signals do not mean what they so clearly appear to mean but are only symptoms of other problems. Similarly, I think that those of us who study or work with inner-city teachers have to remember that what we see of their day-to-day behavior may only be a reflection of more fundamental problems. The quality of teaching in urban school systems is frequently so poor that it is easy to portray teachers as the enemies of their students and we can prove the charges with words from the teachers' own mouths. In doing so, however, we run the risk of confusing symptoms with causes.

In both popular conceptions of the dropout problem and the research literature on the subject, two themes are common. One is the notion that the dropout problem is essentially a function of the characteristics of the kids who drop out. They have weak self-images, or they cannot defer gratification, or they come from unsupportive families. The other approach sees the problem basically as one of poor teaching. If teachers would only reach out to students, if they would only make a real effort to teach, the problem would at least be greatly ameliorated.

The problem with these positions is not so much that they are wrong as that they are both potentially very misleading. As different as the two approaches appear at first glance, they are similar in that both strip the issue of dropping out from its context. Focusing on the characteristics of those who drop out implies some sort of qualitative difference between them and those who stay in school and also minimizes the need to examine the schooling process. On the other hand, focusing just on the abysmal quality of teaching in the inner city minimizes the very real difficulties involved in trying to teach there, difficulties that do have something to do with the kinds of children who are there and something to do with the climate and structure of such schools. Stretch forth your hand in kindness and you may draw back a nub. The same climate that teaches a seventh-grade boy that there is no reason to do homework may teach his teacher that there is no point in trying to reach out.

This essay will argue that fragmented conceptions of the dropout problem, conceptions which separate the problems of dropouts from those of stay-ins or which separate the problems of teachers from those of their students, may undermine our ability to speak effectively to any part of the problem.

## TEACHERS AS THE ENEMY

For at least the last five years we have seen well-publicized efforts to reform American education. It has frequently been predicted that these efforts will lead to an increase in the dropout rate.[1] I suspect this will be the case not only because of the frustration for students involved in raising standards without otherwise improving the conditions for learning but also because of the assumptions undergirding many of the reforms. Many of the current reform initiatives are grounded in the tendency to separate the problems of teachers from those of students; some of the initiatives coming from state legislatures, in particular, denigrate teachers outright.[2] Calls for accountability are often codes for cracking down on teachers. Even the push for better salaries is based partly on the perception that the teachers we have now are inept and that better people have to be attracted to the field.

We have come full circle in a sense. The cultural deprivationists of the 1960s implied that all we needed to do was change the inner-city child; much of the current wave of reform, fragmenting reality in the opposite way, implies that all we have to do is control the teacher. Thus, we mandate more testing of both teachers and students, tighter certification procedures, a more centrally prescribed curriculum, and a longer school day or year. The list is prescriptive and restrictive rather than enabling. In a preliminary report of his study of factors making for school effectiveness, John Chubb predicts that these reforms are unlikely to do much good and may do additional damage, especially in large urban systems:

> Schools that have problems—disruptive students, poor test scores, parent apathy—tend to generate more demands for remedial action, to which responsible outside authorities respond in the most obvious manner: by imposing new rules governing school practice and carefully monitoring compliance with them. Some of these requirements, such as those that enforce discipline and maintain a requisite level of order, may well prove effective. But the restriction of school autonomy has the potential to backfire.[3]

As schools lose the autonomy which Chubb finds to be one of the keys to organizational effectiveness, student performance may deteriorate, leading to calls for even more restrictions on teachers and principals, leading to even poorer performance, and so on. Similarly, Deborah Meier, principal of a highly regarded school in East Harlem, notes that genuine reform requires fewer constraints on teachers: fewer rules, not more. What would matter most, she says—giving greater control to those closest to the classroom—is unlikely to appeal to legislators and administrators who are looking for obvious answers.[4] What would matter can be centrally encouraged, but cannot be mandated.

The kinds of reforms coming from state legislatures make sense only if one assumes that the problems in the inner city reduce to bad teaching. If bad teaching, on the other hand, is itself partly symptomatic of structural problems, including the fact that inner-city teachers already have too little autonomy, the reforms may add to the problems.

Legislators are hardly alone in seeing teachers as the heart of the problem. Over the last few years, I have become increasingly aware of a contradiction in the efforts of many groups working reform in urban education. I recently saw the problem illustrated at a meeting of a parents' reform group. Part of the program involved giving the Chicago

Board of Education a report card. Parents graded the board for its fiscal integrity, its respect for parents, its effectiveness with children, and so on. The meeting's organizers had intended that someone would grade the board on how well it met the needs of teachers. The woman chosen to speak about that, though, misunderstood her charge. She thought she was supposed to grade teachers, not the conditions they work under. To much applause from the audience, she gave teachers a failing grade.

She stands for many others who have difficulty seeing the structural conditions of teachers' working lives as clearly as they do the problematic sides of teacher behavior. The kinds of experiences which are likely to lead people to feel a sense of personal urgency about the problems are also likely to leave them feeling angry and disgusted with teachers as a group. Teachers are easy to blame, in part because many teachers in inner-city schools do so much that is, in fact, wrong. Teachers, well aware of how they are perceived by reform groups, react as though they are under siege, which is often not far from the truth. Thus, even when reforms are formally initiated, the teachers, who in the end have to implement them, do so defensively and hesitantly, in a fashion likely to vitiate even the best-intentioned and most sensible reforms. No matter how well justified, the anger that energizes activists, parents, and other reformers can, by causing them to see only a fragment of what they need to see, generate its own contradiction.

It is not just angry parents and reformers who focus on partial truths. The intellectual baggage of educational researchers often leads us to disaggregate the world of schooling into its constituent elements to an extent that obscures the importance of the larger context in which those elements play themselves out. We can't see the world for the variables. The dropout problem goes in this box, the working conditions of teachers goes in that one, the problem of kids who stay in school without learning anything goes over here. We discuss all of the problems at great length but we do so separately, and, thus, even when what we say is true, it may not be very helpful. Thus, we have people confidently saying that holding children back a grade only leads to their dropping out later, and saying this without paying attention to what is done with the children held back. Being held back often means just repeating the kinds of teaching that failed the first time, but it does not have to mean that. It could mean more concentrated attention on that child or exposing the child to different teaching strategies, in which case it might have very different implications for the subsequent likelihood of dropping out, but we won't know that if we only look at the relationship between two easily measured variables, ignoring the context in which they operate.

One of the issues we tend to obscure when we fail to concentrate on the overall context of schooling is how similar teachers and students can be. Although they may appear at first to be natural enemies, the more closely one looks at students most at risk of dropping out in urban high schools and the teachers who work with them (at-risk teachers), the clearer it becomes that the behavior of one side frequently informs and mirrors the behavior of the other. If many inner-city students are apparently undisciplined and lackadaisical about their class work, some of their teachers are just as lackadaisical about preparing for class. The behavior of students who skip as many classes as they think they can get away with has its analogue in the behavior of those teachers who come to work as late as they can, leave as early as they can, take off as many days as they can, and steal as much time as possible from the working day. The disrespect of students for the authority of teachers has its analogue in the disrespect many urban teachers exhibit toward their administrators. As students live down to the low expectations of teachers, teachers frequently live down to the low expectations of their supervisors. I have never seen any direct data on the sense of on-the-job fate control among inner-city teachers, but I do not doubt that it would parallel what we know about the sense of academic fate control among at-risk students. Indeed, the working ideology that characterizes teacher culture in many inner-city schools, the beliefs centering on how impossible it is to work with *these* students and *these* parents, amounts to an admission that teachers are not in control of what is going on, an admission of alienation.

Caught up in the same alienating structures, teachers and students respond in similar fashion—with cynicism and with withdrawal of effort. Like lovers, they help to create one another and, like lovers, they are ordinarily unaware of the dialectical quality of the relationship. Neither side can see clearly the extent to which it helps to mold the problematic behavior of the other side. Each side sees the negative behavior of the other side more clearly than it sees the social context in which that behavior evolves, even though both are partly responding to the same situation. Thus they go on in their uneasy partnership, jointly helping to create schools that satisfy no one.

Some years ago, I studied student behavior at a Chicago high school which had a reputation for being among the city's very worst. Although the overall levels of student misbehavior were quite high, it varied substantially from teacher to teacher. Students who behaved like rogues in some classrooms behaved perfectly well in others. Students systematically skipped certain teachers more than others, cut up in certain classrooms more than in others, and ignored the assignments of some teachers more than those of other teachers. Students explained these variations partly in terms of how serious they took a particular teacher to be: that is, the more demanding the teacher was and the more committed to teaching, the less likely students were to take liberties.

Teacher misbehavior followed a similar pattern. Ordinarily, teachers seldom troubled themselves about such minor responsibilities as hall duty or enforcing school regulations or responding to administrative requests for information. A great many did little to suggest that they were even concerned with trying to look like they were seriously involved in teaching. Nonetheless, when the climate of the school changed because of changes in administrative behavior, teacher behavior changed as well. When they thought that the administration was clearly focused on educational priorities and that positive efforts would be rewarded, the staff performed at a much more satisfactory level.

Too frequently the climate in these schools encourages and even rewards negative behavior from all parties. In the worst of our urban schools, teachers, students who drop out, and students who stay in are similarly demeaned and devalued by the physical conditions of their schools, by the impersonal nature of the environment, by supervision founded in distrust, by a lack of basic supplies, by capricious rules selectively enforced, by their inability to trust the people with whom they work, and by their inability to participate in the decision-making process.[5] If, in fact, we focus only on how teachers ordinarily behave without taking into account the degree to which we may be focusing on teacher reactions to an alienating environment, it is easy for parents, reformers, and researchers to conclude that teachers are indeed the problem, are in fact the enemy. When we do so, we are fragmenting the shared realities of teachers and students.

## DROPOUTS AND STAY-INS

We may also underestimate the realities shared by those who drop out and those who manage to hang on long enough to graduate. The sheer numbers of students dropping out—40 to 50 percent in our larger urban centers—are so dramatic as to encourage us to think of the dropout problem as something dramatically different from the rest of what goes on inner-city schools. We have a sizeable research literature

concentrating on the characteristics of dropouts—on the size and structure of their families, ethnicity, work patterns in and out of school, and
psychological characteristics.[6] Two of the presumptions of this literature are that dropouts will have considerably less favorable life chances
than those of graduates and that dropouts are different—generally less
effective—sorts of people. Both points may involve a degree of
exaggeration.

A recent Chicago study raises some questions about how much better it is to stay in school. Rather than asking how many students
dropped out and why, it asked what it cost the city to produce one well-
prepared high school graduate, taking "well-prepared" to mean reading
at least on grade level at the time of graduation.[7] From the nearly 40,000
freshmen entering the city's high schools in 1980, the yield in 1984 was
about 6,000 well-prepared graduates, about 18,000 dropouts, and 12,000
students who graduated reading below grade level.

Over the course of the four years of high school, the city had expended about $58,000 for each well-prepared graduate, nearly twice the
national average. Schools with low dropout rates, of course, have lower
costs per well-prepared graduate. In these schools, some of them
academically selective, the cost was below $25,000. In twenty of the non-
selective schools, may of them in the inner city, the figure rose to more
than $200,000. At the top of the list was a school that started with almost
three hundred freshmen and managed to produce five seniors reading
at grade level, at a staggering average cost of over $700,000.

These figures suggest again the enormity of the human and
material waste in our poorest schools, but they also remind us that
many of those who hang on to graduate are not developing the kinds of
skills they need. At sixteen of the inner-city schools, at least half of the
graduating seniors read below the eighth-grade level. On the face of it, it
is difficult to believe that their life chances are going to be significantly
better than those of their fellow students who left school early.

Michelle Fine and Pearl Rosenberg argue that much of the discussion concerning the dropout issue obscures more than it illuminates.[8]
The stress on the psychological problems of dropouts, their family
problems, and their educational weaknesses diverts attention from the
possibility that dropouts are offering a critique of schooling and its
relationship to society. By leaving school some students are expressing
a very reasonable skepticism about traditional beliefs with regard to occupational mobility and are also expressing their unwillingness to
tolerate injustices and discrimination in the classroom as well as their

refusal to legitimate forms of authority that are ultimately geared to keeping them in their place.

Fine and Rosenberg contend that, contrary to common belief, dropouts do not, in fact, have weaker self-images than stay-ins, a point confirmed by Wehlage and Rutter, who found that dropouts had higher self-esteem than non-college-bound youth who remained in school and that the difference actually grows after they have been out of school a couple of years.[9] Fine and Rosenberg also found that the dropouts they studied were more likely than other students to protest perceived injustices from teachers, which is also inconsistent with the image of the dropout being the self-hating loser. Although there certainly are costs associated with dropping out, they argue that we may be overestimating them. The unemployment rate among dropouts is high, but for urban black youth, one of the most dropout-prone groups, it is high, period. In 1981, 71 percent of black dropouts were unemployed, but so were 53 percent of black youth with diplomas. Some dropouts may very clearly understand that staying in school offers them only marginally better opportunities. Thus, Fine and Rosenberg both reject the notion that the personalities of dropouts are in some sense weaker than those of stay-ins and suggest that, although there are clearly benefits to staying in school, we may easily exaggerate them.

The most obvious point to be made about the literature on the characteristics of dropouts is that it tells us little or nothing about the institutions they are leaving. Wehlage and Rutter note that

> Implicit in much research on school dropouts is the assumption that a better understanding of the characteristics of dropouts will permit educators to develop policies and provide practices that will reduce the number of adolescents who fail to graduate. The intent is noble, but the results have been negligible because the focus on social, family and personal characteristics does not carry any obvious implications for shaping school policy and practice.[10]

Wehlage and Rutter also note that the focus on the characteristics of dropouts may be counterproductive in that it gives educators an excuse for failure. Put differently, concentrating on the characteristics of dropouts reinforces the tendency of educators to locate the problem someplace other than in an environment that both teachers and students find debilitating. A survey in Illinois (cited in Kaplan and Luck) asked high school administrators to rate the effectiveness of various kinds of dropout prevention programs.[11] At the top of their list, they put work study programs, improved guidance programs, improved transportation, and more vocational classes—a list that does not imply the need for any substantial change in the school itself. To assume that dropouts are dramatically different from those students who remain in schools which serve them poorly, like assuming that teachers are the enemy, discourages us from concentrating on the nature of school life.

## THE ASSUMPTIONS OF DROPOUT PROGRAMS

Much of the research on successful dropout prevention and re-entry programs reflects the tendency to conceive of the problem in ways that minimize the importance of what happens in school. We are certainly not lacking for a variety of programs to study. Dale Mann notes that an amazing array of approaches are being tried. His list, far from exhaustive, includes programs aimed at enhancing self-image, alternative high schools, Big Brother programs, computer-based instructional programs, storefront academies, drug abuse counseling, smaller class sizes, having students agree to performance contracts, and providing them with an ombudsman. Programs may be vocational or academic; they may be preventive or remedial; they may focus on the school staff, the student, the student's family, or the organization of the learning environment. Mann cites one case where just a dozen school districts reported a staggering 360 different approaches to the problem.[12] In part, one suspects, the endless varieties of strategies is a reflection of the conceptual fragmentation of issue, the tendency to separate one part of the problem from the larger whole and to design practices to address that fragment.

Looking at more or less the same literature, different writers have taken very different practical implications from it, depending in part on how holistic their underlying assumptions are. Some are very explicitly aware that teachers, dropouts, and stay-ins are in pretty much the same boat; other writers are much less aware. Hamilton represents one variant of the position that stresses discontinuity between the experiences of dropouts and those of other students.[13] His survey of the literature concludes that successful dropout prevention programs separate potential dropouts from other students, have a strong vocational emphasis, stress learning outside the classroom, and are intensive in that they offer individualized instruction and strong counseling components.

Comparing the U.S. educational system to that of West Germany, in terms of how well they serve the least academically inclined students, Hamilton finds that the West German system does a much better job of pointing students to meaningful careers. Students are placed into academic tracks sooner than they are here, and track placement has traditionally been very rigid; even the lowest tracks lead to good employment, largely because high school students in those tracks are involved in vocational schooling combined with apprenticeship programs leading to stable careers. Half of the country's sixteen-to-eighteen-year-olds are involved in this system.

In contrast, vocational education in this country seldom leads anywhere. Only a minority of those graduating from such programs actually go to work in the area for which they were trained; employers are more concerned with basic academic and interpersonal skills than with specific job training. For all of its weaknesses, Hamilton takes the nearly universal presence of vocational training in successful dropout prevention programs—and the fact that students say they prefer them to more academic programs—as evidence that vocational education prevents the dropout rate from being even higher. Since the United States lacks the tradition of employer-school cooperation which exists in West Germany, he suggests that more emphasis be placed on using vocational programs as a vehicle for teaching academic skills as well as for experiential learning.

There is little in Hamilton's analysis that would suggest a critique of the overall school environment (curriculum aside) and nothing that suggests that dropouts and teachers may be suffering from some of the same problems. Although many successful programs for dropouts do separate them from other students, it is not clear to what extent it is a programmatic necessity and to what extent it is merely a reflection of the fact that the assumption—that dropouts are qualitatively different from other students—is so widespread that it gets built into most programs. The emphasis on curricular change is particularly problematic. Apart from the fact that Mann finds that vocational programs actually have higher dropout rates, I suspect that changing the curriculum without changes in the overall school climate is unlikely to be productive. Given the current climate in too many schools, whatever the curriculum is, teachers are going to teach it poorly and students are going to approach it with indifference.

Wehlage and Rutter, on the other hand, are a good deal more explicit about the role of the school, taking the finding that dropouts widely perceive teachers as being uninterested and the discipline system as being ineffective and unfair as an indication of an institutional lack of legitimacy. They are also aware that teachers and students are in the same boat: "The comprehensive high school of today may create adult/student relationships that result in skepticism and cynicism in both parties."[14]

Seeing the parallels between the needs of teachers and those of students leads to a somewhat different reading of the literature on successful programs. Wehlage, Rutter, and Turnbaugh maintain that the literature on what works implies that a model program should be structured as an independent alternative school with fewer than one hundred students within a regular school.[15] The small size facilitates the development of positive teacher-student relationships, as well as the individualization of instruction and cooperative faculty planning. A model program should also be built around teachers who are willing to extend their roles, which means a willingness to address problems in the home or the community or in students' peer groups if necessary. Participation should be voluntary, and those who wish to be admitted should undergo some sort of admissions process in which one criterion taken into account in deciding whom to admit is the willingness of the student to be honest about the nature of his or her past school difficulties. There should be clear rules about attendance, behavior, and class work. Those who can't follow the rule should be taken out of the program, which helps in building a positive peer culture. The curriculum should offer prompt feedback and be responsive to student interests. It should include some experiental learning, perhaps dealing with social skills, career education, and community service. The University of Wisconsin is currently in the process of implementing models like this.

One might criticize several points in the model on value-related grounds, but I have no doubt that carefully run programs of this sort would be of value to many dropout-prone youth. For students already in high school, these programs may be among the better short-term options. Nonetheless, despite the explicit recognition of the school's role in pushing students out and despite the recognition of the need to link programs for dropouts to the working conditions of teachers, the emphasis is still on separating dropouts from others.

Levin describes a more holistic model currently being implemented by a group at Stanford University.[16] He argues that the experience of the last twenty years shows that many dropout programs have an element of

stigma associated with them partly because they are seen as academically undemanding. Individualization of instruction easily becomes in
practice a way of allowing students to plod along at a pace slower than
their capabilities would allow. Levin advocates taking the opposite tack:
offering high-intensity, accelerated programs that get to students before
their deficiencies become very serious, setting an explicit deadline for
bringing disadvantaged students to the point where they can profit from
mainstream education. These transitional elementary schools are
aimed at preventing dropouts by eliminating academic deficiencies
before they lead to dropping out. If such schools are to work, he main-
tains, teachers cannot be expected to implement programs that are imposed on them. Instead, teachers, as well as parents, need to have extensive involvement in the design and implementation of programs.

The emphasis here on the school as a "total institution," in Levin's
phrase, strikes me as a more powerful model than the more discrete,
pull-out models, both in the centrality given teachers and parents in
decision making and in what I take to be an implicit recognition that
dropouts are far from the only ones poorly served by schools as schools
are now structured. Almost by definition, alternative programs reinforce the comforting notion that the problem is something that only affects a distinct minority, a minority that can and should be isolated from
normal people. There is something frightening about saying, in effect,
that bringing the most at-risk students up to a level of functioning that
typifies their fellow inner-city high school students is some kind of
victory.

Arnove and Stout note several other potential problems with alternative programs.[17] In their comprehensive examination of alternative
programs for what they call "dis" students—disenchanted, disaffected,
disaffiliated, disturbed, and disruptive—they leave little doubt that well-
managed programs improve self-concept, attitudes about school, sense
of efficacy, attendance rates, and rates of disruption. Nevertheless, such
programs can have their negative sides. Administrators sometimes treat
them as dumping grounds for troublesome students and, I would add,
for troublesome teachers as well. Even the best programs can be
stigmatizing, as Levin notes, and can increase racial segregation. Some
of the vocationally oriented programs prepare students for menial or
nonexistent jobs, and some programs try to control student behavior
through such morally repugnant means as operant conditioning.

Levin is very explicit about expanding the authority of teachers, a
point made by many others in recent years.[18] Although such changes are
long overdue, it is important to be careful in thinking about what they

mean, if only because for many of us they resonate with deeply held biases about the value of participatory governance, values which may lead us to underestimate the difficulties involved. For one thing, teacher participation is as easily trivialized as parent participation. We can be certain that in many cases giving teachers a voice will come in practice to mean letting them decide whether bulletin boards will be hung vertically or horizontally. Even in the article by Levin, there is a potential tension between the stress on teacher involvement in decision making and the fact that the Stanford group already seems committed to certain program features (a language-based curriculum, peer tutoring, cooperative learning) which reflect some of the very areas about which teachers would most like to have some say.

Even when they are given a real voice, it may take some teachers a while to learn to use it in a positive manner. Accustomed to the protect-your-own-behind, get-as-much-for-yourself-as-you-can atmosphere that characterizes our worst schools, some teachers are likely to misuse expanded authority. The irony is that the lack of meaningful supervision in many inner-city schools means that teachers already have too much freedom, enough freedom to stop participating, if they choose, in anything that resembles teaching. Given what they are accustomed to doing, it would be naive not to think that expanded autonomy will not seem to some teachers like expanded license, which I take to underscore the arguments found in Comer for shared governance models in which the authority of teachers is counterbalanced by the authority of other parties.[19] Similarly, while arguing for more autonomy at the school level, Chubb notes that in the most out-of-control schools, a period of restrictiveness may be beneficial.[20]

Wehlage and his associates are aware that successful programs for dropouts are often successful because of the depth of the relationships that develop between teachers and students.[21] These programs are often underfunded, ill-housed, and staffed by teachers with nontraditional credentials. In my experience, the pedagogy of these programs is frequently strictly unimaginative and routine, not at all dissimilar to the styles of teaching which have failed these students in the past, but that seems to matter relatively little when teachers and students are mutually invested in one another.

Saying that fewer students would drop out if teachers were more supportive may not say much that is actually useful. It again ignores the context. No doubt we should all be nicer to the people we see everyday. If teachers frequently fail to extend themselves to the students most in need, that is not because we have a generation of particularly mean-spirited teachers. If student-teacher relationships are formed under structural conditions that are as alienating for teachers as for students, as confusing, as damaging to self-esteem, there is no reason to expect that many teachers will extend themselves. Even when very positive relationships are established, that factor, in isolation from other factors, may not matter much. Arnove and Strout report finding that even when students have developed warm relationships with their teachers and feel good about their own academic progress, their sense of efficacy—which may be more important for their futures than whether or not they stay in school—is not necessarily enhanced.[22] The most important determinant of efficacy, as well as of disruptive behavior, was whether the school program was perceived as really making it possible for youngsters to attain higher-status roles in the future. Niceness has its place, but so does articulation with future economic realities.

In her examination of the literature on successful programs, Raywid holds that the important program features are a personalized environment and a sense of community, providing students some choice about the nature of their academic program, providing them with opportunities to learn how to function as a member of a social group, and providing them with opportunities for encountering some real success in their work.[23] The tragedy is that we are likely to overlook the fact that such a list could serve as a wish list for inner-city teachers and for inner-city students in general, not just for those who drop out.

Commenting on the past twenty years of school reform in New York City, Deborah Meier claims that public discussion has been dominated by ersatz issues. People have talked about things like low reading scores and violent children while ignoring the real issue, the fundamental lack of respect for all the people involved in the life of schools. Depending on the assumptions we surround it with, the dropout issue may be another ersatz problem. If we conceive of it in ways that lead to policies which will further alienate teachers, in ways that exaggerate the differences between dropouts and stay-ins, in ways that lead to the designing of programs for a few students to create the kind of school climate that all students are entitled to, then our very concern for dropouts may not result in better schooling for children. Good intentions notwithstanding, it can become a way to *not* think about fundamental school reform in the inner city. We may be fooling ourselves to think there are shortcuts.

## NOTES

1. Stephen Hamilton, "Raising Standards and Reducing Dropout Rates," *Teachers College Record*, 87 (1986), 410–429; Gary Natriello, Edward McDill, and Aaron Pallas, "School Reform and Potential Dropouts," *Educational Leadership*, 43 (1985), 10–14.

2. Richard Denoyer and Michael White, "Legislating School Reform: Denigrating Educators," *High School Journal*, 70 (1987), 69–71.

3. John Chubb, "Why the Current Wave of School Reform Will Fail," *The Public Interest*, 90 (1988), 28–49.

4. Deborah Meier, "Good Schools Are Still Possible, But . . . ," *Dissent*, 34 (1987), 543–549.

5. Raymond Calabrese, "Teaching as a Dehumanizing Experience," *High School Journal*, 69 (1986), 255–259; Charles Payne, *Getting What We Ask For: The Ambiguity of Success and Failure in Urban Education* (Westport, Ct.: Greenwood Press, 1984); Rick Ginsberg et al., "Working Conditions in Urban Schools," *The Urban Review*, 19 (1987), 3–23.

6. For summaries of this literature, see Dale Mann, "Can We Help Dropouts: Thinking About the Undoable," *Teachers College Record*, 87 (1986), 307–323; Robert Pittman, "Importance of Personal, Social Factors as Potential Means for Reducing High School Dropout Rates," *High School Journal*, 70 (1986), 7–13; Jay Kaplan and Edward Luck, "The Dropout Phenomenon as a Social Problem," *Educational Forum*, 42 (1977), 41–56; Henry Svec, "Youth Advocacy and High School Dropout," *High School Journal*, 70 (1987), 185–192.

7. Designs for Change, *The Bottom Line: Chicago's Failing Schools And How to Save Them*, 220 S. State Street: Chicago (1985).

8. Michelle Fine and Pearl Rosenberg, "Dropping Out of High School: The Ideology of School and Work," *Journal of Education*, 165, (1983), 257–272.

9. Gary Wehlage And Robert Rutter, "Dropping Out: How Much Do Schools Contribute to the Problem?" *Teachers College Record*, 87 (1986), 374–392.

10. Ibid., 376.

11. Kaplan and Luck, "The Dropout Phenomenon."

12. Mann, "Can We Help Dropouts."

13. Hamilton, "Raising Standards."

14. Wehlage and Rutter, "Dropping Out," 391.

15. Gary Wehlage, Robert Rutter, and Anne Turnbaugh, "A Program Model for At-Risk High School Students," *Educational Leadership*, 44 (1987), 70–73.

16. Harry Levin, "Accelerated Schools for Disadvantaged Students," *Educational Leadership*, 44 (1987), 19–21.

17. Robert Arnove and Toby Strout, "Alternative Schools for Disruptive Youth," *Educational Forum*, 44 (1980), 452–471.

18. Ginsberg et al., "Working Conditions"; Chubb, "Why the Current Wave"; William Bailey and Daniel Neal, "Teachers and School Improvement," *Educational Forum*, 45 (1980), 68–86; James Comer, *School Power* (New York: Free Press, 1980).

19. Comer, *School Power*.

20. Chubb, "Why the Current Wave."

21. See also John Simon, *To Become Somebody: Growing Up Against the Grain* (New York: Houghton Mifflin, 1982).

22. Arnove and Strout, "Alternative Schools," 462.

23. Mary Ann Raywid, "Finding Educations's 'Lost' Children: The Status, Cost and Prevention of Dropout Prone Youth," *School Leader*, 27 (1987), 27–31.

AMELIA E. KREITZER, GEORGE F. MADAUS, WALT HANEY

Chapter 7

# Competency Testing and Dropouts

After more than a decade of being eclipsed by concerns about educational quality, the topic of dropouts is once again interesting researchers and policy makers. One question addressed in the recent dropout literature is how the reform to raise standards has affected students who are at risk of leaving school early.[1] This question is not new. Since the mid-1970s, when the call to raise standards spurred minimum competency testing (MCT) legislation, student advocacy organizations and others have speculated that reforms such as MCT programs would increase dropout rates. In particular, concerns have been raised that MCT used for graduation or grade-to-grade promotion increases the likelihood that high-risk students will not complete their education.[2]

This chapter explores available evidence of links between minimum competency testing and dropping out. This line of inquiry is not easily pursued because there is very little literature on the relationship of MCT and school leaving. We begin our discussion by comparing the nature of the testing programs in states with extremely high dropout rates and those with extremely low rates. We discuss apparent effects of failing MCT on self-esteem. The impact of competency tests on retention rates and curricular content are also explored.

Before the relationship between MCT and dropping out is examined, a clarification of terms is in order. Although in some contexts it might be useful to distinguish between pushouts, dropouts, and other

'ers, in this chapter a dropout is any school leaver who fails
: from high school. Some of these school leavers may even-
n to school or pursue a G.E.D.; however, we do not consider
this development here. By minimum competency testing, we refer to
tests administered at the elementary or secondary level, mandated by
state or local government agencies, and used to make decisions about
students or institutions. A student's performance relative to a standard
of performance set on these tests determines, at least in part, that
student's immediate educational future. Examples of minimum competency tests are examinations which determine whether a student will
graduate from high school, be promoted to the next grade, or qualify for
remediation. Currently, local or state education agencies use MCT for
graduation decisions in twenty-four states and for promotion decisions
in at least twelve states.[3] Twenty-four states also use MCT in decisions
about remediation.[4] One state, Georgia, has just broken new MCT
ground by requiring a test as one of the criteria in admitting a child to
the first grade.[5]

## WHERE IS THE RESEARCH?

An immediate stumbling block in exploring the effect of MCT on
dropping out is the paucity of the available evidence. A routine search
of the ERIC data base revealed that the data base from January 1979
until September 1987 contained 2,400 entries including the word
*dropout* and over a thousand documents containing the term *minimum
competency testing.* Yet, when querying ERIC for entries that contained
both the term *minimum competency testing* and the term "dropout, only
five entries over the almost nine-year period met the double criteria.[6]
Why has so little been published or presented on the effect of minimum
competency testing on dropouts?

Several explanations can be posited for the lack of literature and
empirical data concerning the relationship between dropping out and
minimum competency testing. First, even though opponents of the
MCT movement have persistently raised questions about the MCT-
dropout connection, general concern about dropouts among policy
makers and researchers has only recently been revived. Before the
1980s, one needs to go back to the sixties, in other words, before the
MCT era, to find substantial literature on early school leavers. Un-
resolved issues from this earlier dropout research, such as how to define
a dropout or calculate a dropout rate, have returned to challenge a new

generation of dropout researchers. Perhaps the greater urgency of these more fundamental questions about dropouts precludes addressing substantive questions, such as whether MCT influences early school leaving.

Another possible reason that the link between early school leavers and minimum competency tests has not been investigated may be a gap in the dropout literature itself. Wehlage and Rutter note that the traditional focus in dropout research has been on the social, family, and personal characteristics of dropouts.[7] Only more recently, they assert, has the influence of school policy and practice on school leaving been explored.

A third reason for the lack of literature on dropouts and MCT is that concern about dropouts and the push for minimum competency testing find their origins in what some observers would consider opposite camps. Minimum competency testing arose as a response to the perceived crisis in American education in the mid-1970s. Declining SAT scores, grade inflation, increasingly costly school systems, the widespread practice of social promotion, and growing numbers of functional illiterates led policy makers, the media, and the public to clamor for reforms and accountability.[8] In many states, the ensuing legislation designed to raise sagging standards included minimum competency testing. Minimum competency testing, then, is historically and philosophically associated with the movement targeting educational excellence.

The dropout topic, on the other hand, belongs on a different agenda, rooted in a different era. In 1961, Secretary of Health, Education, and Welfare Abraham Ribicoff urged that the federal government take responsibility for the alarming dropout rate.[9] Throughout the 1960s, early school leavers continued to be perceived as a pressing educational problem, along with more general issues about equality of educational opportunity. The dropout problem is still viewed against the backdrop of concerns about education for the economically disadvantaged. In other words, it belongs on what Harold Howe, former U.S. commissioner of education, called the "continuing equity agenda."[10]

Evidence that MCT and dropouts are perceived to be on different agendas is the conspicuous absence of concern about dropouts in the major reform reports issued in the early 1980s. Although reports such as *A Nation at Risk* addressed equity issues and were egalitarian in language, their central motif was the goal of educational excellence. The topic of dropouts was largely overlooked. In fact, in a review of these reports, Harold Howe topped his list of major criticisms of reform recommendations with the reports' neglect of the dropout problem.[11] Only now, after embarrassingly high dropout rates have moved policy makers to address the problem, does it seem that the third wave of reform efforts will address the needs of students at risk of dropping out.[12]

The fourth and strongest explanation for the paucity of literature on the MCT-dropout connection lies in a void in the MCT research. Although competency testing receives a great deal of exposure in both the popular and scholarly press, there is very little empirical evidence concerning the impact of MCT programs. In 1986, Ellwein and Glass undertook a review of the literature on standards and competency tests and described what they found as "the record of academic advice and aspirations, but [containing] little about what is truly done in the name of raising standards and with what consequences."[13] Further, this lack of empirical data on the consequences of MCT is not due to an editorial conspiracy to keep such findings out of print; the gap exists because questions about impact do not get asked or investigated. The data from Ellwein and Glass's intensive six-site case study of standard setting in MCT confirm this thesis: "Beyond the fairly tangible or technical outcome of passing rates, agency attention to consequences was generally vague, impressionistic and haphazard ... Planned evaluation efforts were scant or focused on mundane, peripheral questions that could be answered using available technical expertise. The more complex and relevant questions of impact and utility were ignored."[14]

Understanding why questions of impact are ignored requires knowledge of the role of minimum competency testing. Airasian has analyzed the continuing appeal of minimum competency testing despite the very obvious lack of research evidence as to its efficacy; he concludes, as has an existing chorus of educational observers, that the tests function more as symbols than as anything else.[15] Easily legislated and conveniently administered, MCT programs are meant to signify to the public that its legislators have taken a tough stance on educational quality. For many legislators and citizens, the mere fact of legislation seems to be enough.

The public does not demand a rigorous accounting of the effects of MCT. Further, powerful deterrents keep other stakeholders in MCT programs, such as policy makers, state testing agencies, and test contractors, from investigating the impact of MCT. As Madaus has stressed, policy makers have a vested political interest in the success of any program that they support.[16] Thus, if the mere existence of a "get-tough" MCT program can reassure a nervous public that education is again steaming down the right track, policy makers have no incentive to fund MCT evaluation programs that might turn up bad news. Quite simply, the political will is not there. State testing agencies which implement MCT decisions also have little incentive to invest time or resources in investigations that are not on their political agenda or which could prove embarrassing. Similarly, it would be a violation of common business sense if the test contractors who design MCT batteries took it upon themselves to follow up on MCT programs; it is expensive, and if they uncovered any problems, they would become unlikely choices for future contracts.

Once minimum competency testing is viewed as a powerful and politically expedient symbol, whose existence alone satisfies the demand for educational rigor, it is easy to understand why questions about impact do not get raised, let alone investigated. Thus, the impact of MCT on dropping out is one of many topics that remains empirically unexplored. As will become evident below, this interpretation of MCT, as symbolic but not substantive intervention, sheds light on the nature of the effects of MCT on dropout rates.

## MCT AND STATE-LEVEL DROPOUT RATES

One way of gaining a perspective on MCT and dropout rates is to examine state-level data. There are two problems with this approach. First, the well-documented inconsistency in calculating dropout rates muddies any comparative investigation.[17] Even at the national level, the Bureau of Census and the Department of Education differ in their approaches to calculating rates.[18] Further, what can be gleaned from the scattered bits of information available from individual states does not paint a clear picture. In Virginia, for example, the dropout rate increased when MCT was implemented, but then it leveled off.[19] In Mississippi, education officials note that the 1982 educational reform, which included a high school functional literacy test, has resulted in improved test scores but an unchanged dropout rate of about 38 percent.[20] A correlational study of New Jersey's High School Proficiency Test found that district-level 1985 dropout rates and average scores on the proficiency test were negatively correlated—ranging from −.51 to −.59 for different subtests.[21] Bureau of Census data indicates that national dropout rates have decreased in recent years;[22] state-level graduation rates, derived by dividing the number of high school

Chapter 7 table

Table 7.1
State-Level Attrition Rates and MCT Activity
States with highest 1986 attrition rates

| State | 1982 (percent) | 1986 (percent) | MCT purpose | Government level[a] | Year[b] |
|---|---|---|---|---|---|
| Florida | 39.8 | 38.0 | graduation; promotion; remediation | state/local | 83 |
| Georgia | 35.0 | 37.3 | graduation; remediation | state | 83 |
| Louisiana | 47.1 | 37.3 | promotion; remediation | state | |
| Arizona | 35.6 | 37.0 | graduation | state/local | 76 |
| Mississippi | 38.7 | 36.7 | graduation | state | 87 |
| New York | 36.6 | 35.8 | graduation; remediation | state | 79 |
| Texas | 36.4 | 35.7 | graduation; remediation | state | 87 |
| S. Carolina | 36.2 | 35.5 | graduation; promotion; remediation | state | 90 |
| Nevada | 35.2 | 34.8 | graduation | state | 82 |
| California | 39.9 | 33.3 | graduation; promotion; remediation | state/local | 79 |

States with lowest 1986 attrition rates

| State | 1982 (percent) | 1986 (percent) | MCT purpose | Government level[a] |
|---|---|---|---|---|
| Minnesota | 1.8 | 8.6 | no MCT | |
| Connecticut | 9.4 | 10.2 | remediation | state |
| N. Dakota | 6.1 | 10.3 | no MCT | |
| Nebraska | 8.1 | 11.9 | remediation | local |
| Iowa | 5.9 | 12.5 | no MCT | |
| Montana | 1.3 | 12.8 | no MCT | |
| Wisconsin | 6.9 | 13.7 | remediation; by local option, for promotion | local |
| S. Dakota | 7.3 | 18.5 | no MCT | |
| Kansas | 9.3 | 18.5 | remediation | state |
| Wyoming | 7.6 | 18.8 | remediation | local |

NOTE: Attrition rates are obtained by subtracting state-level graduation rates from 100 percent. Graduation rates are obtained by dividing the number of public high school graduates by the number of ninth-grade students four years earlier, then adjusting for migration and unclassified students.

a. Refers to the level of government which sets standards.

b. Refers to graduation year of first graduating class assessed.

Sources: Office of Technology Assessment, U.S. Congress, "State Educational Testing Practices: Background Paper" (Washington, D.C.: By the Author, December 1987), 102–129; Thomas D. Snyder, Center for Education Statistics, *Digest of Education Statistics 1987* (Washington, D.C.: Office of Educational Research and Improvement, Department of Education, 1987), 105; "State Education Statistics," *Education Week*, 2 March 1988, 18–19.

graduates by the number of ninth-grade students enrolled four years earlier, have increased in thirty-eight states from 1982 until 1986.[23]

An overall, albeit quite crude, view of the relationship between MCT and dropout rates is afforded by comparing the MCT activity in the ten states with the highest 1986 dropout rates and the ten states with the lowest dropout rates, here calculated as what is sometimes called "attrition rate."[24] As is evident from Table 7.1 there seems to be a correlation between attrition rates and the existence of MCT programs. Half of the ten states with the lowest dropout rates have no minimum competency testing programs as of 1987. The other five states with low dropout rates have MCT programs that can be characterized as involving relatively low stakes: four use the tests for decisions about remediation; one uses them only for accountability. None require the tests for critical decisions about graduation or grade promotion. Furthermore, in three of these five states, the standards are set by local, not state, education agencies.

States with the highest dropout rates, on the other hand, have MCT programs where standards are set, at least in part, at the state level. Nine of the ten use the tests in decisions about high school graduation; four use them in decisions about promotion. In sum, these ten states with the highest dropout rates employ minimum competency tests with higher stakes and less flexible standards than the states with the lowest dropout rates.

These data are not presented here as evidence of a causal relationship between high-stakes MCT programs and dropout rates. The states with the highest dropout rates differ in obvious ways from the states with the lowest dropout rates. The latter are largely western and midwestern, and they have a relatively low representation of minority and poor students among their school-age populations.[25] However, the pattern in the data should provoke thought about the MCT-dropout connection. Perhaps high dropout rates are symptoms of the educational system's failure that spurred legislators to mandate MCT programs in the first place. Perhaps MCT does contribute in some way to the dropout problem, although the decreasing dropout rates in most states—even those with MCT—argue against this thesis. In any case, crude as the above data may be, they underline the need to address these hypotheses.

## STUDENTS WHO FAIL MCT

Another way of shedding light on the connection between MCT and dropout rates is to piece together what we know about minimum competency tests and what we know about dropouts. Perhaps most obviously, the literature on both topics shows that racial and language minorities and students from families of low socioeconomic status are disproportionately represented among both early school leavers and students who fail competency tests. For example, the 1985 data from the Bureau of Census indicated a 14 percent overall dropout rate among eighteen- and nineteen-year-olds. The dropout rate for blacks, however, was 17 percent; among Hispanics, the rate jumped to 31 percent.[26] Similar patterns are reported in individual states. Indeed, the proportion of students classified as "poor" in a school can help predict the dropout rates for that school.

Students who fail competency tests are also more likely to be poor and from minority groups. During the National Institute of Education MCT hearings in 1981, many witnesses, including Lita Taracido, formerly with the Puerto Rican Legal Defense and Education Fund; Mary Berry, commissioner and vice-chair of the U.S. Commission on Civil Rights; U.S. Representative Shirley Chisholm; and Federico Pena, former Colorado state legislator and current mayor of Denver, offered testimony to this effect.[27] Data from MCT administrations confirm that MCT most adversely affects students already having academic difficulties, poor children, racial and language minority children, and vocational and special education students. For example, on the first administration of the Texas Educational Assessment of Basic Skills, about 48 percent of the bilingual students taking the test failed the language arts portion and 39 percent failed the mathematics test.[28] Similarly, about 25 percent of the black eleventh graders who sat for the first administration of the North Carolina High School Competency Test failed the reading test, whereas only 4 percent of the whites did.[29] The percent minority enrollment in school districts in New Jersey was found to be highly negatively correlated with pass rates on the High School Proficiency Test.[30]

As with the state-level data presented above, these trends cannot support a causal hypothesis between dropping out and failing MCT.

They do, however, increase the urgency of finding out if MCT programs affect dropout rates. After all, language and ethnic minorities make up most of the school-age population in our largest cities, and their enrollments are increasing much more rapidly than those of other groups.[31] These students are already ill-served by the educational system; policy makers should be certain their reforms do not harm these groups most in need of help.

Unfortunately, there is evidence that MCT can harm these at-risk groups in ways that might increase their likelihood of dropping out. One study looked at the effects of failing the North Carolina Minimum Competency Test on the attitudes and personality of low-achieving students. Students whose grades, achievement test scores, and academic track predicted failure on the MCT were given pre- and post-measures of self-esteem, attitude, and personality. Those students who failed the competency test showed increased tendencies toward alienation, anxiety, neuroticism, and apprehension after the test. They also demonstrated lower self-esteem. Interestingly, passing the test did not increase the self-esteem of the students who were predicted to fail but then succeeded.[32] Because low self-esteem and alienation have been related to dropping out, this study suggests that MCT can encourage at-risk students to leave school early.

## MCT AND RETENTION RATES

Another overlap in the literature on MCT and at-risk students is that both dropping out and failing MCT are linked to retention. There is a substantial body of evidence concerning the relationship between nonpromotion and the likelihood of dropping out of school. Research on retention indicates rather clearly that nonpromotion has a negative effect on achievement gains as well as on personal adjustment, self-esteem, and attitudes toward school.[33] It is not surprising then, given the strong relationship between achievement, school attitudes, and self-esteem on the one hand, and school leaving on the other, that being overage greatly increases the likelihood of a student's dropping out. One study from 1971 showed that students who were retained one grade were four times more likely to drop out than students who had never been retained.[34] More recent work from the Chicago Panel on Public Schools found that the risk of dropping out increased directly with a student's age upon entering ninth grade. Ninth graders who were fourteen years old (the modal age for ninth grade) dropped out at the rate of

37 percent; ninth graders who were one year older dropped out at the rate of 60 percent; 69 percent of the students who were two years older than their grade-mates dropped out.[35] Even when ability level is controlled, overage students are more likely to drop out: an analysis of data from Chicago revealed that overage students left school at a rate about 13 percentage points higher than normal-age students of equal ability, as measured by reading test scores.[36] Furthermore, even when overage students have achievement test scores higher than normal-age students, they are still more likely to drop out than their younger grade-mates.[37]

Clearly, the extent to which MCT programs fulfill promises that social promotion will end and that graduation and promotion will be tied strictly to test results determines the extent to which MCT programs will increase dropout rates. In Boston, for example, since the institution of the Student Promotion Policy in 1983, which requires attendance rates of 85 percent, satisfactory grades in classes, meeting standards on curriculum-referenced tests, and in some grades, passing a Degrees of Reading Power "gate" test, retention rates have increased. In 1982–83, 13.5 percent of middle school students were held back; in 1984–85, 16.8 percent stayed an extra year in middle school.[38] It is, of course, not possible to attribute the increased retention to the tests alone; nonetheless, rigid enforcement of promotion policy, be it based on tests, grades, or attendance, will likely increase nonpromotion rates, which in turn should have a negative impact on the holding power of high schools.

Further evidence of the likelihood of MCT to increase the rate of grade repetition is provided by the state of Louisiana, which initiated a MCT program in 1982. The Basic Skills Test (BST) battery (criterion-referenced tests in mathematics and language arts) was administered to students in grades two through five. The BST was to have been the primary, but not the only, consideration in retention decisions. Analysis of data from 1980 to 1985 revealed that in all four grades retention rates increased after implementation of the BST program.[39]

The New York City Public Schools also employed test results in promotion decisions with the much heralded implementation of its Promotional Gates Program in 1981. The California Achievement Test served as the hurdle to passage into fourth and seventh grades. Even though the school system provided a great deal of extra remedial help to the students who were held back, an independent audit of the program revealed that the retained students did not subsequently perform significantly better than students with similar scores who had not been retained. Furthermore, students who had been held back in seventh grade in the Gates program were more likely to leave school early than the comparison group which was not held back. Specifically, 23.2 percent of the retained Gates students dropped out, whereas 16.0 percent of the comparison group did.[40]

Only one of the above examples, the New York Gates program, completes the chain from MCT to dropping out. However, all strongly suggest that rigorous enforcement of standards-based promotion results in retention; and retention highly predicts dropping out. Moreover, the practice of retaining children in grade seems to be on the upswing. Despite the lack of reliable longitudinal data on retention, U.S. Census Bureau estimates show that the percentage of children enrolled in a grade below the normal grade for their age has been increasing since the mid-1970s.[41] The mid-1970s also saw the institution of the first wave of state-mandated competency tests; however, because the decision to retain is frequently based on criteria other than tests, it would not be reasonable to ascribe the national increase in retention rates solely to MCT.

Potentially good news for those who oppose retention is that standards-based promotion is often not strictly enforced; in other words, some students fail to meet MCT standards but are promoted nonetheless. For example, in South Carolina, where test results must count at least 25 percent in decisions about retention, about 60 percent of the students who do not meet state-defined test standards are promoted anyway.[42] In Chicago, where the Chicago Mastery Learning Reading Program (CMLR) was in place from 1981 until 1985, students had to meet an 80 percent criterion on 80 percent of the CMLR tests in order to be promoted. In fact, purportedly because too many students would fail, students who did not meet the standard moved to the next grade along with their age-mates, but continued to follow the CMLR materials that they could not master at the lower grade.[43]

Similarly, in one of the six sites investigated by Ellwein and Glass, district-level criterion-referenced tests were designed to put an end to social promotion. Supposedly scientifically determined cut-scores were to be the main criteria in determining who would be held back. Although the school system researchers knew how many had passed and failed the tests, they had not collected data on the performance-promotion connection. Ellwein and Glass reanalyzed available data and estimated that between 29 and 50 percent of the students who failed to meet the test standard were promoted anyway.[44]

These findings mesh neatly with the discussion above concerning MCT programs as political gestures rather than substantive reforms. As Bruce Eckland remarked in 1980, standards of minimum competency must sometimes be traded off against "whatever is a politically tolerable number of failing students."[45] Holding too many students back represents not only a political embarrassment; it also presents a tremendous financial burden to school districts. Given this context, the conclusion reached by Ellwein and Glass in their study of standard setting is not surprising: they found that normative considerations—that is, a concern with how many examinees would fail—greatly influence MCT standard setting. Furthermore, they noted that "as standards are erected, safety nets are strung up to catch those who fall."[46] The cases above provide examples of one kind of safety net: flexibility in applying the test standard to the decision. In other cases, examinees are allowed to retake competency tests numerous times, until the passing rate is virtually 100 percent.[47] Exemption, too, is employed as a safety net. For example, special education students are frequently exempted from meeting MCT standards. Indeed, this kind of safety net can spare institutions from embarrassment: there have been unsubstantiated allegations that low-achieving nonhandicapped students sometimes get assigned to special education classes so that they do not have to take competency tests, and their low scores do not influence average scores for the classroom, school, or district.[48] Even when students fail graduation tests and are denied diplomas, school officials have privately acknowledged that virtually no one failed who would not have been denied a diploma for another reason as well—for example, lack of Carnegie units.[49]

The effect of MCT on retention rates is less severe than feared when safety nets are strung up. The effect may also be attenuated over time, because, generally, average scores on the minimum competency tests rise over time. For example, Popham, Cruse, Rankin, Sandifer, and Williams reported that since the implementation of MCT programs, average student test scores on competency tests have increased dramatically in Texas, South Carolina, Maryland, and Detroit.[50] The likely cause of this phenomenon, that teachers teach to the competency test, will be discussed below. For now, the relevant point is that fewer students seem to fail competency tests over time. When passing rates are high, however, one must ask what happens to the self-esteem of children who fail tests that are universally acknowledged to be easy.

Another cause for concern is that even when average scores go up, at-risk students may still be harmed. For example, in Boston, average test scores have gone up, but so has the retention rate.[51] In addition, it has been charged that sometimes scores rise because schools remove low-scoring students from the test pool, for example, by not following up on truants and dropouts, whose scores could lower averages.[52]

What does all the above evidence suggest about the impact of MCT on dropout rates? Clearly, the effect depends on the degree to which standards are rigidly enforced. Certainly, where there is some flexibility in the degree of compliance to promotion standards, MCT may not affect retention rates, and hence, dropout rates, as greatly as is sometimes feared. When promotion decisions or institutional benefits are based strictly on test results, however, MCT can, it seems, increase the likelihood of a student dropping out.

## MCT AND THE CURRICULUM

Why do students drop out of school? To answer this question, researchers have looked at what dropouts themselves give as reasons, and at what correlates of dropping out suggest. Dropouts respond in varied ways when asked to identify their reasons for leaving school, but they commonly mention school-related issues.[53] For example, dropouts in the High School and Beyond Study most frequently agreed with "did not like school" and "poor grades" as reasons for leaving school.[54] These self-report data confirm conclusions drawn from other sources; many other school-related indicators, such as grade point average, test scores, absenteeism, and records of disciplinary problems correlate highly with the likelihood of dropping out. Our analysis of the data from the 1985 administration of the Pennsylvania Educational Quality Assessment battery provides additional evidence. Eleventh graders' scores on reading, writing, and mathematics tests were correlated positively ($+.44$ to $+.46$) with the students' expectations of educational attainment. Further, students who expected not to graduate from high school had significantly lower scores than students who anticipated getting a diploma on another school-related indicator: attitudes toward tests. Of course, as Rumberger reminds us, these sources still do not tell us much about the underlying causal factors.[55] One thing, though, is certain: the fit is slippery between what students at risk of dropping out want or need from school and what schools provide for these students.

When examining the bad fit between at-risk students and school programs, researchers often used to blame the victim by searching for problems with the students themselves. Now, however, many are pointing an accusing finger at the schools. A report by the National Coalition of Advocates for Students (NCAS) stated, "The rising number of school dropouts is the single most dramatic indicator of the degree to which *the schools are failing children* [italics added]."[56] The ways in which schools are believed to fail children are many. NCAS includes inflexibility of school structure, narrowness of the curriculum, and lack of support services in its list. Andrew Hahn notes that students at risk of dropping out rebel against "the social control, competition, and order that characterize classrooms."[57] Michelle Fine and Pearl Rosenberg summarize their work with New York City dropouts by noting that "standard curricula tend not to reflect [dropouts'] lived experiences, nor provide much encouragement for their pursuit of education."[58] Gary Wehlage reviewed dropout research and concluded, "The data suggest that schools send out signals to at-risk youth that they are neither able nor worthy enough to continue to graduation."[59] Evidence supporting these assertions that schools are to blame is that variation in dropout rates can be explained in part by school characteristics—even when adjusted for differences in student traits.[60]

Not surprisingly, given the above kinds of criticisms of schools, existing dropout prevention programs generally involve education that somehow differs from the schools that at-risk students already attend. As Hahn summarized, "Conventional education and remediation are not by themselves effective for the at-risk population."[61] The recent flurry of attention to dropouts has prompted numerous recommendations for improving the schools' holding power for the at-risk groups. The recommendations we have seen invariably include a suggestion to tailor the curriculum to the needs of at-risk students, for example, by including job training, building flexibility into the curriculum and the school day, and focusing on challenging yet attainable goals. In addition, recommendations almost always call for small student-teacher ratios, individualized instruction, and teachers and counselors who genuinely care.[62]

Unfortunately, although recommendations abound, hard evidence as to what really works in dropout prevention is scarce. There is some evidence that vocational education programs have lower dropout rates than general (i.e., not college preparatory) high school programs.[63] In a review of dropout prevention programs, Hamilton noted that effective programs include a strong vocational component. He found, in addition, that successful programs "differ markedly from the ordinary high school experience."[64] Other reviews reach similar conclusions.[65] We need to know more specific information about what kinds of programs succeed in keeping marginal students in school so that better programs can be designed. Nonetheless, we know enough to hypothesize about the match between the kinds of programs potential dropouts need and the kinds of curricula that MCT produces.

The effect of minimum competency testing on the curriculum is acknowledged by both proponents and opponents of MCT to be very strong. Indeed, one of the most vocal proponents of MCT asserts that "a high-stakes test of educational achievement ... serves as a powerful curricular magnet" by spurring teachers to "focus a significant portion of their instructional activities on the knowledge and skill assessed by such tests."[66] In other words, MCT encourages teaching to the test.[67] There is little disagreement on this assertion. Proponents and opponents of MCT also agree that scores on competency tests increase over time because the curriculum comes to mirror the test. For example, Popham relates that the percentage of students meeting minimum standards has increased by as much as 25 percentage points in states mandating MCT.[68]

Where MCT supporters and naysayers part company is on the value of the redirected curriculum. Although advocates of so-called measurement-driven instruction claim that MCT can focus and clarify instruction, Jaeger points out that "to sustain such an argument, it would have to be agreed that the content of the tests constituted an appropriate curriculum for the schools."[69] There is little evidence that this is so. In an early review of MCT programs, Gorth and Perkins found that about half of the state MCT programs emphasized only academic skills, to the exclusion of other educational objectives.[70] The tests narrowly limit content, and further, frequently demand nothing more than recognition-level knowledge of basic skills. One MCT critic noted: "If teachers have 'targets' and are using tests whose answers converge on those targets, it is hard to see how divergent thinking and other higher-order skills will be developed."[71] As a teacher from Chicago during the days of the Chicago Mastery Learning Reading program (CMLR) testified to the NCAS Board of Inquiry:

> Because CMLR is mandatory and accountability is emphasized with charts and reports about how many students have passed 80 percent of their tests, and because in many schools basal readers and other real

books are in short supply, or even nonexistent, CMLR becomes the central part of the reading instruction, and children never get a chance to read real books. CMLR crowds out real reading.[72]

Although we agree that MCT does not, in theory, have to affect the curriculum in such a pernicious manner, it seems that it often does. As in any issue of MCT impact, clear evidence is missing. But anecdotal evidence points to a fractured curriculum where MCT drives instruction. An illuminating example of this comes from the MCT program in Virginia. Gerald Bracey, formerly director of research, evaluation, and testing at the state department of education, related in testimony to the National Institute of Education hearings that the mathematics test included parallel lines as part of the published and distributed test specifications; 90 percent of all examinees passed the test question covering parallel lines. One year, however, a question about perpendicular lines showed up on the test instead of the parallel line item. Only 40 percent of the examinees passed this item; what's more, school administrators from around the state complained that perpendicular lines were not justifiable content for the test because they were not part of the test specifications. A similar example is provided by a principal in New York City, who noted that reading instruction has come to resemble reading tests. In class, students practice "reading" by answering multiple-choice questions about dozens of little paragraphs. When synonyms and antonyms were dropped from the reading tests there, teachers dropped instructional materials that stressed them.[73]

The worst case is that MCT atomizes the curriculum into components that closely match the form and content of the competency tests. At best, MCT merely delivers more structured, standardized, and focused doses of traditional schooling. As Spaulding reported in 1938 about the New York State Regents Exam "Examinations, instead of leading the way toward better teaching, have often tended merely to perpetuate the kind of teaching to which a majority of teachers had become accustomed."[74] In either case, the resulting curriculum should hold little allure for students who have already begun the disengagement process from school. In short, MCT does not at all drive the curriculum in the direction presumed best for students at risk. What ought to drive the curriculum for these students is their need for engaging and pertinent instruction—not the content of minimum competency tests.

## MCT IN REMEDIATION DECISIONS

Our discussion has been largely confined to MCT when used for promotion or graduation decisions. But what of MCT when it is used in decisions about remediation? Proponents of MCT argue that MCT can help teachers identify those students most in need of extra help. Leaving aside the argument that teachers can quite reliably depend on daily classroom contact to identify students having trouble, we cannot enthusiastically embrace the optimistic notion that MCT aids remediation efforts. Too often, remediation equals test preparation. For example, in studying the Florida Functional Literacy Test, the State Task Force on Educational Assessment found that "in all cases observed, spot remediation was being practiced."[75] Testimony to the NIE MCT Clarification Hearings confirms that this is not an isolated case. Further, extra funds for promised remediation are not always forthcoming. The Children's Defense Fund undertook a national survey in 1984 and determined that of the thirty-one states mandating retention standards, only twelve allocated enough money for "a significant level of remediation."[76] For example, in Boston, even when a child was identified by a test as needing extra attention, "promised remedial services and smaller classes have not materialized to meet the need."[77]

## THE BOTTOM LINE

The lack of good evidence on the impact of MCT programs hampers the investigation of the effect of competency testing on dropout rates. In our review of available evidence, nothing suggested that MCT decreases the likelihood of dropping out. We did, however, uncover several indications that MCT may give students at risk of dropping out an extra push out the school door. Clearly, the damage done to at-risk students depends on how the MCT program is implemented. In an ideal world, MCT-based curricula taught by caring teachers in small classrooms could engage marginal students in the learning process. In the real world, MCT tends to corrupt the curriculum, converting it into practice for the test. The result must surely be at least as unpalatable to marginal students as status quo schooling, if not more so. We have seen, however, that MCT programs sometimes have no real teeth. When this is the case, one might argue that the potential damage to at-risk groups is minimized. The fact is that we simply do not know.

It is alarming that even though we have no clear indication of the effects of minimum competency testing programs, despite their existence now for well over a decade, some testing proponents are arguing for what has been called "maximum competency tests." Both *A Nation at Risk* and the Carnegie Commission Report[78] called for nationwide systems of standardized tests which would measure, not basic skills, but subject-matter- or program-specific material. Such tests might even further diminish local control over decisions about students. Moreover, pitching the test well above "minimum skills" might result in even greater numbers of at-risk students being labeled as failures and denied opportunities for further education.

The clearest conclusion drawn from our exploration of MCT and dropping out is that the consequences of competency tests must be more thoroughly studied. Competency testing programs must include funding for carefully designed evaluations of the effects on students and curricula—evaluations that go beyond the mere reporting of rising pass rates. Until then, policy makers would do well to keep in mind the needs of those students most in need of help and most likely to be hurt by such testing reforms.

## NOTES

1. See, for example, Edward McDill, Gary Natriello, and Aaron Pallas, "A Population at Risk: Potential Consequences of Tougher School Standards for Student Dropouts," *American Journal of Education,* 94 (February 1986): 135–181; Henry M. Levin, *Educational Reform for Disadvantaged Students: An Emerging Crisis* (West Haven, CT: National Education Association, 1986); and Stephen F. Hamilton, "Raising Standards and Reducing Dropout Rates," in *School Dropouts: Patterns and Policies,* ed. Gary Natriello (New York: Teachers College Press, 1986), 148–167.

2. See, for example, the Minimum Competency Testing Clarification Hearings, sponsored by the National Institute of Education, Washington, D.C., July 8, 9, and 10, 1981 (transcript available through ERIC, Documents ED215000, ED215001, ED215002); National Coalition of Advocates for Students, *Barriers to Excellence: Our Children at Risk* (Boston: By the Author, 1985); and Thomas F. Green, *Predicting the Behavior of the Educational System* (Syracuse: Syracuse University Press, 1980).

3. "State Education Statistics," *Education Week,* 2 (March 1988): 18–19.

4. Thomas D. Snyder, Center for Education Statistics, *Digest of Educational Statistics 1987* (Washington, D.C.: Office of Educational Research and Improvement, Department of Education, 1987), 14.

148

Kreitzer, Madaus, and Haney

5. Deborah L. Gold, "Georgia to Test Kindergartners for Promotion," *Education Week*, 2 March 1988, 1, 15.

6. In ERIC our search request was "dropout* and minimum competency testing." The term *dropout* retrieved all official ERIC descriptors concerning dropouts, including dropouts, dropout attitudes, dropout characteristics, dropout prevention, dropout programs, dropout rates, and dropout research. To increase the chance of finding a match, the field of search was not restricted. The search began with documents published in 1979, when the term *minimum competency testing* was first added to the thesaurus of ERIC descriptors.

7. Gary Wehlage and Robert Rutter, "Dropping Out: How Much Do Schools Contribute to the Problem?" in *School Dropouts: Patterns and Policies*, ed. Natriello, 70–88.

8. Joseph J. Pedulla and Edward F. Reidy Jr., "The Rise of the Minimal Competency Testing Movement," in *Minimal Competency Testing*, eds. Peter Airasian, George Madaus, and Joseph Pedulla (Englewood Cliffs, NJ: Educational Technology Publications, 1979), 23–32.

9. Abraham Ribicoff, "Plain Words from Mr. Ribicoff on Dropouts," cited in Jerald Bachman, Swayzer Green, and Ilona Wirtanen, *Youth in Transition. Volume III: Dropping Out—Problem or Symptom?* (Ann Arbor, MI: Institute for Social Research, 1971), 2.

10 Harold Howe, "Giving Equity a Chance in the Excellence Game," cited in McDill, Natriello, and Pallas, "A Population at Risk," 139.

11. Ibid.

12. Debra Viadero, "Study Finds 'At Risk' Efforts Hindered," *Education Week*, 13 (January 1988): 8.

13. Mary Catherine Ellwein and Gene V. Glass, "Standards of Competence: Propositions on the Nature of Testing Reforms" (under review, 1988)

14. Ibid.

15. Peter Airasian, "Symbolic Validation: The Case of State-Mandated, High-Stakes Testing" (under review, 1988). See also Ellwein and Glass, "Standards of Competence: Propositions" and George F. Madaus, "Public Policy and the Testing Profession; You've Never Had it So Good?" *Educational Measurement: Issues and Practice*, 4 (Winter 1985): 5–11.

16. Madaus, "Public Policy and the Testing Profession."

17. See, for example, Aaron M. Pallas, "School Dropouts in the United States" in *The Condition of Education*, eds. Joyce D. Stern and Mary Frase Williams (Washington, D.C: Center for Education Statistics, U.S. Department of Education, 1986), 158–174; Floyd Morgan Hammack, "Large School Systems' Dropout Reports: An Analysis of Definitions, Procedures, and Findings," in *School Dropouts: Patterns and Policies*, ed. Natriello 20–37; and George Morrow, "Standardizing Practice in the Analysis of School Dropouts," in *School Dropouts: Patterns and Policies*, ed. Natriello, 38–51.

18. Russell W. Rumberger, "High School Dropouts: A Review of Issues and Evidence," *Review of Educational Research* 57 (Summer 1987): 103–107.

19. Gerald Bracey, in testimony to the Minimum Competency Testing Clarification Hearing, July 10th, 1981 (Transcript: ERIC Document ED215002, p. 725).

20. William Montague, "Mississippi Gauges 5 Years of Reform," *Education Week,* 18 (November 1987): 8.

21. Center for the Study of Testing, Evaluation, and Educational Policy, "Observed and Anticipated Effects of the New Jersey High School Proficiency Test on At-Risk Students and the Dropout Rate" (Chestnut Hill, MA: By the Author, August 1986), 19.

22. Rumberger, "High School Dropouts", 107.

23. "State Education Statistics," *Education Week.*

24. Attrition rates are calculated by subtracting the graduation rate from 100 percent. The graduation rates were calculated by the Department of Education by dividing the number of public school graduates by the ninth-grade enrollment four years earlier. The rates were adjusted by DOE for migration and students who are unclassified by grade.

25. "State Education Statistics," *Education Week.*

26. Snyder, *Digest of Educational Statistics 1987,* 86.

27. Minimum Competency Testing Clarification Hearings.

28. Edith Archer and Judith Dresden, "A New Kind of Dropout: The Effect of Minimum Competency Testing on High School Graduation in Texas," paper presented at the annual meeting of the American Educational Research Association, San Francisco, April 1986.

29. Richard Jaeger, "The Final Hurdle: Minimum Competency Achievement Testing," in *The Rise and Fall of National Test Scores,* eds. Gilbert R. Austin and Herbert Garber (New York: Academic Press, 1982), 241.

30. Center for the Study of Testing, "Observed and Anticipated Effects of the New Jersey High School Proficiency Test," 25.

31. Levin, *Educational Reform for Disadvantaged Students.*

32. Charles L. Richman, Kathryn P. Brown, and Maxine Clark, "Personality Changes as a Function of Minimum Competency Test Success or Failure," *Contemporary Educational Psychology,* 12 (1987): 7–16.

33. C. Thomas Holmes and Kenneth M. Matthews, "The Effects of Nonpromotion on Elementary and Junior High School Pupils," *Review of Educational Research,* 54 (1984): 225–236.

34. Bachman, Green, and Wirtanen, *Youth in Transition, Volume III, 34.*

35. G. Alfred Hess and Diana Lauber, *Dropouts from the Chicago Public Schools: An Analysis of the Classes of 1982–1983–1984* (Chicago: Chicago Panel on Public School Finances, 1985), 22.

36. E. Matthew Schulz, Ronald Toles, and William K. Rice, JR., "The Association of Dropout Rates with Student Attributes," in *Dropouts, Pushouts,*

*and Other Casualties*, ed. William Denton (Bloomington, IN: Phi Delta Kappa, 1987), 94.

37. Hess and Lauber, *Dropouts from the Chicago Public Schools*, 12.

38. Massachusetts Advocacy Center, *The Way Out: Student Exclusion Practices in Boston Middle Schools* (Boston: By the Author, November 1986), 36–37.

39. Janella Rachal, "Student Placement Study: 1985–86 State-Funded Conpensatory/Remedial Program Evaluation, Placement Report #1765" (Baton Rouge: Louisiana State Department of Education, 1986).

40. New York City Board of Education, Office of Educational Attainment, "Evaluation Update on the Effects of the Promotional Policy Program" (New York: By the Author, 1986), 2.

41. Mary Lee Smith and Lorrie A. Shepard, "What Doesn't Work: Explaining Policies of Retention in the Early Grades, *Phi Delta Kappan*, 69 (October 1987): 130.

42. "South Carolina Students Promoted Despite Poor Test Performance," *Education Week*, 28 (October 1987): 2.

43. Kenneth S. Goodman, "Chicago Mastery Learning Reading: 'A Program with Three Left Feet,'" *Education Week*, 9 (October 1985): 20.

44. Mary Catherine Ellwein and Gene V. Glass, "Ending Social Promotion in Waterford: Appearances and Reality," in *Flunking Grades: Research on Policy and Practice*, eds. Lorrie A. Shepard and Mary Lee Smith (in press).

45. Bruce K. Eckland, "Sociodemographic Implications of Minimum Competency Testing," in *Minimum Competency Achievement Testing*, eds. Richard M. Jaeger and Carol Kehr Tittle, (Berkeley, CA: McCutchan Publishing Corporation, 1980), 134.

46. Ellwein and Glass, "Standards of Competence: Propositions."

47. Mary Catherine Ellwein and Gene V. Glass, *Standards of Competence: A Multi-Site Case Study of School Reform*, Technical Report to OERI (Los Angeles: University of California, Los Angeles, Center for Research on Evaluation, Standards, and Student Testing, 1987), 116.

48. Illinois Fair Schools Coalition, "Holding Students Back: An Expensive School Reform that Doesn't Work" (Chicago: By the Author, 1985), 9.

49. Ellwein and Glass, *Standards of Competence: A Multi-Site Case Study*, 118.

50. W. James Popham, Keith L. Cruse, Stuart C. Ranking, Paul D. Sandifer, and Paul L. Williams, "Measurement Driven Instruction: It's on the Road," *Phi Delta Kappan*, 63 (October 1985): 628–635.

51. Massachusetts Advocacy Center, *Status Report: The Way Out* (Boston: By the Author, January 1988), 1.

52. Joan McCarty First and Jose Cardenas, "A Minority View on Testing," *Educational Measurement: Issues and Practice*, 5 (Spring 1986): 7.

53. Rumberger, "High School Dropouts" 101–122.

54. Ruth B. Eckstrom, Margaret E. Goertz, Judith M. Pollack, and Donald

A. Rock, "Who Drops Out of High School and Why? Findings from a National Study," in *School Dropouts: Patterns and Policies*, ed. Natriello, 52–69.

55. Rumberger, "High School Dropouts," 111.

56. National Coalition of Advocates for Students, *Barriers to Excellence: Our Children at Risk*, p. xi.

57. Andrew Hahn, "Reaching Out to America's Dropouts," *Phi Delta Kappan*, 69 (December 1987): 258.

58. Michelle Fine and Pearl Rosenberg, "Dropping out of High School: The Ideology of School and Work," *Journal of Education*, 165 (Summer 1983): 269–270.

59. Gary G. Wehlage, "At-Risk Students and the Need for High School Reform," *Education*, 107 (Fall 1986): 21.

60. Ronald Toles, E. Matthew Schulz, and William K. Rice, Jr. "A Study of Variation in Dropout Rates Attributable to Effects of High Schools" in *Dropouts, Pushouts, and Other Casualties*, ed. William Denton (Bloomington, IN: Phi Delta Kappa, 1987), 105–114.

61. Hahn, "Reaching Out to America's Dropouts," 263.

62. See, for example, Anthony Cipollone, "Research, Program, and Policy Trends in Dropout Prevention" (Cambridge, MA: Education Matters, Inc., July 1986); Hahn, "Reaching Out to America's Dropouts"; Dale Mann, "Can We Help Dropouts? Thinking about the Undoable," in *School Dropouts: Patterns and Policies*, ed. Natriello, 3–19; and Rumberger, "High School Dropouts."

63. Elinor M. Woods and Walter Haney, *Does Vocational Education Make a Difference? A Review of Previous Research and Reanalyses of National Longitudinal Data Sets* (Cambridge, MA: The Huron Institute, 1981), 8-5-4 and 8-5-5.

64. Hamilton, "Raising Standards and Reducing Dropout Rates," 154.

65. See for example, Rumberger, "High School Dropouts" 116–117; and Gary G. Wehlage, *Effective Programs for the Marginal High School Student* (Bloomington, IN: Phi Delta Kappa, 1983).

66. W. James Popham, "The Merits of Measurement-Driven Instruction," *Phi Delta Kappan*, 68 (May 1987): 680.

67. For an extended discussion of how high-stakes testing affects curriculum, see George F. Madaus, "Testing and the Curriculum: From Compliant Servant to Dictatorial Master," in *Critical Issues in Curriculum: The 1988 NSSE Yearbook*, ed. L. Tanner (Chicago: University of Chicago Press, 1988).

68. Popham, "The Merits of Measurement-Driven Instruction," 682.

69. Jaeger, "The Final Hurdle," 236.

70. W. P. Gorth and M. R. Perkins, "A Study of Minimum Competency Programs," cited in Jaeger, "The Final Hurdle," 236–237

71. Gerald Bracey, "The Muddles of Measurement Driven Instruction," *Phi Delta Kappan*, 68 (May 1987): 689.

72. National Coalition of Advocates for Students, *Barriers to Excellence*, 49.

73. Minimum Competency Testing Clarification Hearings.

74. F.T. Spaulding, *High School Life: The Regent's Inquiry into the Character and Cost of Public Education in the State of New York* (New York: McGraw-Hill, 1938), 198.

75. Task Force on Educational Assessment Programs, "Competency Testing in Florida: Report to the Florida Cabinet, Part I," Tallahassee, Florida, 1979, 10.

76. Illinois Fair Schools Coalition, "Holding Students Back," 7.

77. Massachusetts Advocacy Center, *The Way Out*, 36.

78. E.L. Boyer, *High School: A Report of the Carnegie Foundation for the Advancement of Teaching* (New York: Harper and Row, 1983).

FRED M. NEWMANN

Chapter 8

# Reducing Student Alienation in High Schools: Implications of Theory*

Social science inquiry into alienation blossomed from 1950 to the early 1970s. Though not recognized as a central concept in the study of schooling, the essential aspects of alienation—estrangement, detachment, fragmentation, isolation—contribute powerfully to the interpretation of such common problems as dropouts, vandalism, and low commitment to schoolwork. Many efforts at school improvement, such as reducing school size, increasing student input in school governance,

This article is based on my final report, "Orgainizational Factors and Student Alienation in High Schools: Implications for Theory for School Improvement," prepared under a grant from the National Institute of Education, No. NIE-G-79-0150, September 1980.

I am indebted to many who contributed to this study: Michael Apple, Jay Berger, Frank Crowther, Donald Erickson, Burton Fisher, James Garbarino, Maurice Gibbons, Gerald Grant, Bruce Haslam, Jim Jirsa, Tom Kelly, Jim Kielsmeyer, Nancy Lesko, Jim Lindemann, James Lipham, Cora Marrett, Linda McNeil, Mary Heywood Metz, Joy Newmann, Donald Oliver, Michael Olneck, Jerry Patterson, Gary Phillips, John Quillan, Baxter Richardson, Richard Schoenherr, Cal Stone, Marilyn Watkins, Gary Wehlage, Tom Wilson, Helen Wood, and Ed Wynne.
The footnote style has been changed from the original in order to be consistent with the other chapters in the book.

individualizing instruction, and humanizing school climate, can be viewed as efforts to reduce student alienation: that is, to increase students' involvement, engagement, and integration in school. Used too loosely, however, the term alienation conveys such a broad sense of malaise as to be useless for guiding school improvement. This essay clarifies the concept of alienation, suggests guidelines for its reduction based on sociological and administrative theory, and assesses the extent to which current efforts at reform in secondary education conform to these guidelines. Although this analysis could be applied to all levels of schooling, the study focuses on comprehensive public high schools because, in comparison to elementary schools and higher education institutions, they seem to reflect high levels of student alienation.

Initially discussed as a metaphysical or theological phenomenon, alienation represented the discrepancy between one unified principle of Being or God, and the lower-order, material, and differentiated aspects of nature. In its evolution through Christian thought to Hegel, Feuerbach, Marx, Durkheim, and contemporary sociology, we find the persistent themes of separation, estrangement, fragmentation, and lack of engagement.[1]

Discussion of these themes raises the issue of whether to regard alienation as an objective structural feature of human situations or as a subjective individual psychological state. The structural perspective, derived largely from Marx and Durkheim, considers alienation an aspect of social structure, roles, and functions. Work, for example, is alienating to the extent that workers are prevented from controlling their working conditions, from owning the processes and products of their labor, and from engaging in complex and integrated tasks. Human relationships are alienating when people are treated as objects or standardized abstract units, as, for example, in the use of grade-point averages; when people are manipulated to serve the objectives of others; and when high mobility and specialization in the society prevent people from developing affectional and moral bonds to a community. Because such conditions reflect fragmentation of experience, they are, by definition, alienating. People will not always have negative feelings about alienating conditions; they may report satisfaction, especially if such extrinsic rewards as high salaries are available. Thus, the objective structural perspective assumes that alienation is an important social reality existing somewhat independently from people's perceptions of it.

On the other hand, those who consider alienation a personal psychological phenomenon contend that people's perceptions of their world constitute a critical part of social reality. Seeman identified the following dimensions: powerlessness, the sense of low control, low mastery over events; meaninglessness, the sense of incomprehensibility of personal and social affairs; normlessness, the sense that social ideals to which most people profess are continually violated in practice; cultural estrangement, the individual's refection of values commonly held in society; self-estrangement, the individual's engagement in activities that are not instrinsically rewarding; and social isolation, the sense of exclusion from or rejection by social groups.[2] Alienation may be reported as diffuse feelings of estrangement in which these analytically distinct affective states are blurred or highly correlated.[3] The distinctions remain important, however, because they imply different remedies and alert us to the likelihood that improvement in one area will not necessarily entail progress in another: helping persons to sense power and mastery, or to find rewarding work, is different from helping them to become socially integrated or to resolve conflicts between individual values and the culture at large.

To construe alienation only in psychological terms is not enough; human beliefs and feelings are subject to manipulation, false consciousness, and accommodation. Students, for example, may express contentment and a sense of mastery with easy homework assignments, only to discover at a later time that they have no actual mastery of the subject. To gain a complete picture we need to step beyond feelings, to view human situations from more general perspectives that portray systems of political-economic control, the organization of work, and patterns of affiliation.

I am not proposing that an objective structural perspective is superior to a subjective personal view of alienation. Rather, I find value in their combination. Reduction of alienation requires altering structural aspects of labor and human relations in ways that affect subjective states. This position seems necessary to avoid deception. One might intervene only to create more positive perceptions, perhaps by convincing students that they can count on teachers for help, without actually changing conditions in the school to facilitate this. Or one might change conditions so that teachers are in fact available, but students may fail to seek help, because they perceive the teachers as inaccessible. In either case the separation between student and teacher remains.

Assessing and reducing alienation therefore requires attending to conditions that transcend reported perceptions of participants, even though those perceptions are critical in determining the degree of alienation.

## ALIENATION IN THE SCHOOLS

There have been no systematic national studies of student alienation, but reports on vandalism, absenteeism, and declining achievement portray large numbers of students as estranged from high school.[4] Examples of dedication, school spirit, and satisfaction seem overshadowed by persistent reports of student apathy and hostility toward school.

The goal is not to design schools where students feel only euphoric comfort and passive contentment. Extensive scholarship shows that alienation is an inevitable and not totally undesirable aspect of the human condition. Survival depends in part upon harmony-integration with nature, but also upon humans differentiating themselves from the physical environment. Individuality presupposes separation and distinctions among people, and experience has shown persistent efforts by individuals and groups to differentiate themselves from one another. The development of art, science, and social innovation requires argument and specialization, as well as integration and synthesis. Paradoxically, the quest for harmony-integration (the reduction of alienation) through learning requires a differentiation of self from experience, an analytic detachment, but this must be pursued with effort and struggle, engagement. Reducing alienation, then, is not tantamount to eliminating stress or effort; rather, it is arranging conditions so that people expend energy in ways that enhance engagement with work, people, and physical surroundings.

Increasing student involvement in school life, however, is not in itself a sufficient educational goal. Students may be energetically engaged in schoolwork, but their activities may have only limited educational value. Students may become committed participants in group life, but direct their energies in morally indefensible ways, such as gang wars or Nazi youth groups. Nevertheless, it makes sense to reduce alienation in schools, for three reasons. First, student involvement-engagement is necessary for learning. Teachers consistently complain of the difficulty of teaching passive, withdrawn students. Tremendous resources are wasted when students remain "tuned out" in school, even while fulfilling minimal requirements. Second, it is socially and psychologically valuable for people to work with and relate to one another as integrated, active participants rather than in a withdrawn, passive manner. Third, additional educational and ethical criteria—based, for example, on the principles of individuality and communality—can be developed as guidelines to deter us from supporting activities that elicit nonalienating participation but that violate human dignity.

Alienation may be seen as a result of pervasive social forces beyond school, such as specialization, mobility, bureaucratization, rationalization, capitalism, or other features of modernization that fragment human experience. This perspective, though valuable in suggesting limits to school improvement, does not justify abandoning the effort to create less alienating schools. So long as there is some possibility of improving school life, the well-documented human need to diminish alienating experiences as much as possible establishes a moral obligation to work in that direction. Nisbet summarized the contributions of Marx, Weber, and Durkheim relevant to this argument.[5] The fact that schools vary considerably in the extent of student and staff commitment and engagement[6] indicates that the ills of modernization do not fall uniformly on all schools. The evidence that some schools are operated in ways that minimize the alienating features of modern life offers reason enough to continue the quest.

Having defined alienation in the negative sense of fragmentation, estrangement, separation, how would we recognize a school characterized by its implied opposites, such as integration, engagement, connectedness? First, one would expect that students would participate actively in the work of the classroom, showing serious effort and considering that work meaningful. Students would also have civil relationships with one another and with school staff, extending common courtesy to one another—friendly greetings, casual conversation, and acts of caring in times of personal hardship. Finally, the school's facilities would be treated with care, and vandalism would be rare. These criteria for student involvement in their work, in the people around them, and in the physical surroundings of the school may help to identify schools with low levels of alienation, but additional principles are necessary to provide guidance on how to design schools to inspire involvement.

As Ollman has shown so well, plans for attacking alienation are derived ultimately from assumptions about human nature. I assume that three fundamental human needs must be met to minimize alienation: the need for integration, or consistency and continuity in one's experience; the need for individuality; and the need for communality. The need for integration is affirmed in philosophical work and in social psychological research illustrated especially by Erikson.[7]

Individuality refers to expression of ideas, interests, values, temperament and personality that distinguish one person from another. It represents individual striving for personal competence as well as personal choice in a variety of matters, from work and politics to intimate relationships. Individuality involves differentiating oneself from other people, from institutions, and from authority, but as Erikson has shown, it also requires integrating oneself with others, with ideals, and with social institutions.[8]

Communality is the tendency to affiliate with others, to identify oneself with human groups, organizations, and causes. Through communal experience, humans form attachments with one another and establish a sense of belonging to one or more groups. Communal bonds are strengthened partly because groups differentiate themselves from one another and, thus, communality often involves alienation from other groups.

By construing the reduction of alienation as equivalent to promoting integration, individuality, and communality, we have drawn upon and simplified a rich tradition of scholarship. These needs reflect aspects of Seeman's analysis of alienation;[9] they incorporate Katz and Kahn's summary of the vast literature on intrinsic motivation;[10] they are consistent with Oliver's review of biosocial needs, which emphasizes a balance between stable, small group life and individual choice;[11] they are recognizable in the sociological work of Marx, Durkheim, Tonnies, and Weber and in political philosophy from Plato to Rousseau. Much of human history can be interpreted as a struggle to achieve some balance between individuality and communality.[12]

School efforts to increase student involvement may focus at the organizational level (creating a small house system), the program level (changing course requirements), or the staff level (human relations training for teachers). Change at one level may have only minimal impact unless accompanied by change at other levels. One might introduce change at the organizational level by reducing the size of the high school to enhance personal relationships, but students may remain detached from schoolwork, because of outmoded course content at the program level. Even with exciting course material, students may remain apathetic because of uninspiring staff. This study focuses mainly on organizational features of schooling, realizing that a comprehensive study of student alienation should also deal with program and staff levels.

Organizational theory and the literature on the social psychology of organizations suggest six general issues relevant to reducing student alienation: the basis of membership, the nature of organizational goals, organizational size, decision-making structure, members' roles, and the nature of work. My review of the literature on these six issues leads me to propose the following guidelines: voluntary choice, clear and consistent goals, small size, participation, extended and cooperative roles, and integrated work.

## VOLUNTARY CHOICE

Organizations vary in their purposes, in whom they claim to serve, and in the basis for members' involvement.[13] Etzioni distinguished among *coercive, remunerative,* and *normative* organizational sanctions and showed the alienating nature of coercive institutions.[14] Schools use all three types of sanctions. Attendance is coerced by law, supposedly remunerated by increased earning power, and normatively valued as an ideal. It may be argued that coercive activities can be benevolent and responsive to individuality and communality, but realistically the coercer's interests may differ from and prevail over those of the coerced. Remunerative sanctions can stimulate passionate involvement, but within an individually competitive economy they tend to alienate people from one another. Normative sanctions, or involvement based on moral motivations, seem to be the least alienating. These emerge most readily in voluntary organizations, where membership, because it is based on intrinsic commitments, is more likely to result in engagement in the organization's activities.

Voluntary normative involvement enhances the potential for individuality and individual integration with organizational activity, but it need not lead to communality in a client-serving institution like the school. On the other hand, if schools were organized like mutual benefit groups in which individuals with shared values create an organization to serve collective as well as individual needs, then more potential for communality would exist.[15]

Student alienation, then, is reduced if students and their parents voluntarily develop and attend schools whose educational purposes they share. Parochial and private schools, and some public schools, do operate in this fashion. There may be legitimate concern about other effects of voluntary choice (racial segregation, economic discrimination), but it does promote personal integration, individuality, and communality in school life.

## CLEAR AND CONSISTENT GOALS

Most complex organizations have ambiguous and conflicting goals.[16] Weick argued that people often join an organization not to pursue common goals, but to pursue diverse goals through a common means.[17] Public schools reflect this diversity and perform a variety of functions—socialization, custody-control, certification, and selection—that sometimes conflict with instruction, which is presumably their most important function.[18] For example, socializing students to accept dominant cultural values can conflict with instruction designed to teach critical analysis of the values themselves. When schools are pressured to teach a multitude of competencies—from reading to driving and physical fitness—it is difficult to arrive at a set of clear priorities, especially when the school is obligated to serve diverse constituents such as college preparatory and vocationally oriented students. Professional controversy continues on how to teach effectively, and the nature of teaching itself is said to defy tight coordination toward centrally agreed upon goals.[19] Conflict and ambiguity also result from discrepancies between professed ideals and actual institutional practice; students may graduate having learned almost nothing, inept teachers may receive high salaries, and some students experience consistent discrimination.

The school's endorsement of diverse, ambiguous goals might be defended as promoting individuality, allowing enough options so that each individual's tastes are satisfied, without imposing monolithic dogma. While individuality does require choice, this should be exercised through continuous pursuit of a reasonably well-defined and integrated set of challenges, not through a randomly assembled collection of options and contradictory experiences. Sharper goal definition is also required for communal identity, for if all students pursue different educational missions, nothing binds them to one another except temporary use of a common facility. Although comprehensive high schools face enormous obstacles in achieving greater goal clarity and consistency, these seem to be required for individuality, communality, and integration.

Rutter et al. found that the most effective schools in terms of achievement, attendance, students' participation in school beyond the required time, and low levels of delinquency were those with a high degree of consensus on goals and enforcement of rules—that is, where there was little ambiguity as to the school's expectations.[20] While that study did not focus on student alienation as defined here, such findings seem consistent with our conclusions. The call for greater clarity and consistency in school goals is not an endorsement of dogmatic, socially homogeneous schools that violate individuality. Rather, the challenge is to build clear, internally consistent goals which are compatible with the values of the school's clientele but which also respond to individual diversity.

## SMALL SIZE

School size is a significant variable because it has an important effect on goals, participation, and roles. Schools should be large enough to offer the variety of resources needed to pursue individual and communal goals, but small enough to facilitate affiliative bonds among members. There has been no systematic empirical research on the relation of school size to student alienation, and Schneider summarized many unanswered questions on the subject of school size.[21] Research on student participation in school activities,[22] on vandalism and delinquency,[23] and on interaction and affiliation among adolescents[24] favors secondary schools of about 500–1200 students. We will use this range to define "small" high schools. Small size alone, like any of the other suggested guidelines, is not sufficient to promote integration, individuality, and communality. A large school can allow for individual privacy and can inspire passionate collective loyalty; a small school can suppress individual choice. However, the opportunity that small schools provide for sustained contact among all members is a significant safeguard against alienation. The larger the school, the more difficult it is to achieve clear, consensual goals, to promote student participation in school management, and to create positive personal relations among students and staff.

## PARTICIPATION

Schools should maximize opportunities for students to contribute to school policy and management. By definition, participatory organizations allow individuals to express their interests and individuality, and they increase the likelihood that collective decisions take the interests of all into account.[25] In contrast, highly centralized, hierarchical organizations accentuate distinctions between governors and governed, increase the risk that individuality will be violated and the interests of the governed suppressed, and promote fragmentation rather than integration.[26]

To advocate student participation in school policy and management is not to delegate unilateral power to students or to relinquish professional staff authority. Taxpayers, parents, and especially staff, deserve a significant voice in governance. Nor does student participation call for all students to have formal input into all school decisions. Rather than adopting only political or legal models, it is possible to design less formal mechanisms for participation. Increasing the amount of sustained time that students spend with individual teachers and broadening the ways in which they relate, for example, is likely to offer greater student input and to increase faculty responsiveness.

Hirschman provided a novel conception of the ways in which workers, consumers, and clients may affect organizations.[27] They may exercise "voice" formally by participant representation in decision-making bodies, as well as informally if leaders continuously seek input and show by their actions that the concerns have been taken seriously. When clients lack the power to choose organizational leaders or to control an organization's resources, voice is ineffective without the ultimate economic power to exit, and thereby deprive the organization of the ability to function. In organizations such as prisons or schools where clients have no opportunity to exit, badly deteriorating organizations can remain in operation.

To promote integration, individuality, and communality in schools, students must have voice backed by the power of exit—to move to another school, for example. Too easy an exit, however, can have an alienating outcome—students might change from one school to another without developing stable affiliation with any group. Hirschman noted that if organizations are to be renewed, they must retain a critical mass of loyal followers who help to reform the organization rather than deserting it. Such commitment to school can be stimulated to the extent that students have a significant voice in school affairs, contribute their time and effort to managing and maintaining school functions, and spend a significant period of time in one school.

## EXTENDED AND COOPERATIVE ROLES

If students are to perceive integration between their interests and their life in school, they must trust their teachers.[28] In the comprehensive high school many aspects of the teachers' role undermine student trust: compulsory assignment of students to teachers, large classes, the conflict between teachers' role as helpers versus judgmental certifiers of student competence, the teacher's ultimate responsibility to school superiors rather than to students, and, most importantly, teachers' transient relationships with students for the sole purpose of teaching a single subject. This limited, specialized relationship creates barriers to understanding one another as individuals and to developing affiliative bonds. Of course, individuals can occasionally overcome the constraints of conventional student-teacher relationships, which produces a limited number of mutually rewarding student-teacher relationships in most comprehensive schools.

Trusting relationships are more likely to develop if students spend sustained time with teachers on an individual basis or in small groups, and if they engage together in a range of activities such as recreation, counseling, dining, housekeeping, or even the study of more than one subject. Extension of the student-teacher relationship beyond the typical meeting in a large group for fifty minutes a day to learn a single subject will give students and teachers a more complete understanding of one another. Extended contact generates a greater sense of communality, mutual caring and responsibility, than conventional transient and fragmented roles. Recent studies on crime, vandalism, and disruption in schools recommend that teachers have contact with fewer students each day and spend greater amounts of continuous time with them so that interpersonal sensitivities and bonds can develop.[29] Wehlage, Stone, and Kleibard found that schools with low dropout rates tended to have extended, rather than limited, role relationships.[30]

Sources of student alienation exist not only in relationships with adults, but also in relations with one another. Generally, instruction is organized to discourage cooperative work among students, and dialogue among students in class is more often punished than rewarded. Group projects are also discouraged because of difficulty in evaluating individual student achievement. Classes are scheduled with no regard for strengthening peer relations, and in some cases deliberately to separate potentially disruptive friends. This preoccupation with individual achievement neglects the importance of cooperative work in building personal competence and is a stark violation of student needs for community. As Cusick and others have shown, students maintain a strong peer culture, but this affiliation is based largely on accentuating a common alienation from school.[31] More constructive forms of communality could be promoted if students were expected to listen to, counsel, and lend support to one another, and if they were to function in groups to accomplish academic goals, provide recreation, offer community service, and care for the school.[32] Extracurricular activities and some vocational programs offer opportunities for cooperative roles that should be expanded to the instructional program and to other aspects of school life.

Generally, student relations with other adults in the school—counselor, custodian, cafeteria worker, administrator, reading specialist—occur only within the narrow domain for which each adult is responsible. Such role specialization threatens integration because individuals express only a small part of themselves in these relationships, and no one except the principal is expected to care about the school as a whole. Students are further alienated by being cast in the role of people who take from all of these adults, but who are not generally expected to contribute to the life of the school. Schools can alter this by creating opportunities for participation in governance, and expecting student assistance in such tasks as tutoring, media work, office work, meal preparation, fund-raising, and plant maintenace.[33] Cooperative work with a broader range of peers and adults will increase the potential for an integrated experience in school, and student contributions to other individuals and to the group should increase a sense of communality.

## INTEGRATED WORK

Most research on alienation addresses the nature of the adult workplace, and does not consider students' work in schools. Although high school students differ in important ways from adult workers, the characteristics of nonalienating work suggest criteria which can be reasonably applied to students' work. Using dimensions of alienation derived from Marx and others, Blauner identified six criteria for meaningful work.[34] Two reflect concern for individuality: the product is uniquely developed by the worker rather than produced in identical form by others; and the worker has some control over the pace at which work is performed and some freedom of physical movement during working hours. One criterion emphasizes communality: the work stimulates social integration and collective identity, either to the employing organization or with peer organizations such as unions, or with primary work groups that lend personal support. Three criteria represent a concern for integration: the worker completes a large part of the product rather than a small part; the worker is responsible for several phases of the production process;[35] and the work is congruent with the worker's commitments beyond the workplace.

These criteria suggest ways to improve the quality of work students do to advance their competence in various subjects. For example, many school subjects can be taught in ways that emphasize unique products and research rather than standard answers from all students. Authors as diverse as Young,[36] Bernstein,[37] Willis,[38] and Ogbu[39] have shown how schoolwork that is incongruent with a student's cultural commitments can assault self-esteem.

A different perspective was offered by Oliver, who argued that work must respond both to primal and modern aspects of human nature.[40] Primal tendencies include the need to experience a direct relationship between work and physical survival, to work with simple tools, cared for and controlled by the worker, and to integrate work itself with human personality. In contrast, modern tendencies emphasize elimination of physical toil connected to survival, the use of complex technology, the training of abstract competencies which separate work from personality. From this perspective, schoolwork responds excessively to the modern side of human nature, failing to integrate primal needs. Students find much schoolwork mystifying because they must rely on the authority of teachers to certify levels of student proficiency. In contrast, some forms of work, such as building trades or wilderness survival, provide concrete, self-evident indications of success or failure. School work that incorporates more activities directly related to human survival, involving concrete signs of success and failure, and that highlights unique contributions of individual students, would help to increase students' sense of integration.

Together, these guidelines for reducing student alienation support creation of small school units with clear, limited goals, voluntarily chosen by students and parents who participate in school governance. Students and staff should engage in extended roles that include cooperative endeavors and contributions to the school's operation, and student work should allow for continuous development of products, flexible individual pacing, and support of both primal and modern work.

The guidelines are not proposed to solve all problems of schools. The suggested organizational changes alone are not even sufficient to reduce alienation; program content and staff performance must also promote individuality, communality, and integration. These guidelines neither prescribe teaching methods to assure the actual development of student competence, nor do they guarantee to reduce students' alienation beyond the school. Policy aimed only at designing nonalienating schools would need safeguards against the lack of opportunity for some students to pursue preferred educational goals because of discrimination or unequal financial resources. While the guidelines are incomplete, they do offer a way of conceptualizing school organization to promote individuality, communality, and integration.

## EFFORTS AT REFORM

To what extent have attempts to improve secondary schools responded to the suggested guidelines? The efforts summarized below represent a variety of reforms. The list alone, however, does not describe alternative forms within each category. We should note that many reforms are used in combination with others; for example, most specialized schools also provide career education.

### School Units

Several innovations depart from the model of a comprehensive high school that tries to serve all educational needs for large numbers of students. Instead, smaller units with general or special programs, or large specialized units, have been tried.

*Schools within schools.* Smaller units within the comprehensive school keep students together for much of their coursework and advising, usually with active participation in governance.[41] Curriculum may be either specialized or general.

*Specialized schools.* Schools provide instruction in particular fields such as the performing arts, social service, and the health professions. Many of these are "magnet" schools.[42]

*Alternative schools.* Of the many kinds of alternative schools,[43] most have 50–400 students enrolled in a general program, place major emphasis on student autonomy in selection of coursework, and provide extensive opportunities for student and staff participation in governance.

## School Processes and Practices

*House system.* Students meet for advising, certain extracurricular activities, and socializing in a small unit within the comprehensive high school. When coupled with an academic program in the house, this system qualifies as a school within a school.

*Personalized advising.* Students are assigned to one faculty member, who serves as a guide and source of support throughout their high school experience.

*Flexible scheduling.* Students are given more control over their time through free periods, off-campus privileges, and variations in the amount of time devoted to different activities.

*Individualized programming.* Programs include continuous diagnosis, planning, and feedback to design learning activities appropriate to individual goals, abilities, and interests. Students work individually with teachers to establish learning objectives and methods.

*Promoting pro-social conduct.* A number of specific practices[44] stimulate cooperative concern and interaction among students and staff. Some of these are: student tutoring, hall guards, service clubs, maintaining and decorating the school, fundraising, and recognition of excellence in these activities.

*Participation in governance.* Students participate in school governance through conferences, committees, councils, courts, and other formal and informal mechanisms.

## Program Emphases

Many reforms try to make the formal curriculum more useful and significant. Most discussion has centered on the following four movements.

*The basics.* Instruction concentrates on fundamental skills in language, mathematics, and sometimes science and social studies.

*Career-vocational education.* Curriculum is designed for direct application to adult working roles, and focuses on technical training, work habits, and career choices.

*Challenge education.* Programs are based on the belief that youth require a dramatic transition to adulthood that can be achieved only by testing themselves and taking risks in such areas, for example, as physical adventure, service to others, and aesthetic creation.[45]

*Community-based learning.* Efforts to reduce the isolation of students from adult roles and institutions in the community include field studies, on-the-job experience, community service, and political participation.

Table 8.1 summarizes the extent to which each reform effort promotes ( + ), violates ( − ), either promotes or violates depending on how it is implemented (?), or has no apparent relationship to the various guidelines (/). For example, schools within schools, alternative schools, and house systems were judged likely to promote small size. However, students may be assigned either voluntarily or involuntarily to schools within schools (?) and the educational goals for such schools may be either clear or ambiguous (?).

Considering the ratings as a whole, the good news is that none of the reforms seems likely to contradict any of the guidelines, and that each reform seems likely to promote at least one of the guidelines. The bad news is that no single reform is likely to be consistent with more than three guidelines, and that almost half of the cells are filled with (?), which means that the reforms, while they have the potential to fill many of the guidelines, also have the potential to violate them, depending upon how the reforms are implemented. Of the thirteen reform efforts, about half positively address student choice and goal clarity, but no more than a few necessarily address the other four guidelines. This inventory shows that most of the salient reform efforts in secondary education are two-edged swords, capable either of reducing or exacerbating student alienation in school, if they affect it at all. Although several of the reforms are congruent with some of our guidelines, and many could be implemented congruently, no one of them is explicitly comprehensive. Moreover, a search through the literature, as well as consultation with national authorities, revealed not a single comprehensive public high school that met most of the guidelines.[46] This apparent absence of exemplary schools may be due in part to a lack of information, for various reports indicate that some schools are less

Table 8.1

Ratings of Extent to Which Reforms Implement Guidelines for Reducing Alienation

| REFORMS: | voluntary choice | clear-consistent educational goals | small size | partici-pation | extended and cooperative roles | integrated work | TOTALS + | TOTALS ? | TOTALS / |
|---|---|---|---|---|---|---|---|---|---|
| | | | | | | | + | ? | / |
| Schools Within Schools | ? | ? | + | ? | ? | ? | 1 | 5 | 0 |
| Specialized Schools | + | + | ? | ? | ? | ? | 2 | 4 | 0 |
| Alternative Schools | + | ? | + | + | ? | ? | 3 | 3 | 0 |
| House System | ? | ? | + | ? | ? | / | 1 | 4 | 1 |
| Personalized Advising | + | / | / | ? | ? | ? | 1 | 3 | 2 |
| Flexible Scheduling | + | ? | / | / | ? | / | 1 | 2 | 3 |
| Individualized Programming | ? | + | / | + | ? | ? | 2 | 3 | 1 |
| Pro-Social Conduct | / | + | / | ? | + | / | 2 | 1 | 3 |
| Participation in Governance | + | ? | / | + | ? | / | 2 | 2 | 2 |
| The Basics | ? | + | / | / | ? | ? | 1 | 3 | 2 |
| Career-Vocational Education | ? | + | / | / | ? | + | 2 | 2 | 2 |
| Challenge Education | + | ? | / | / | ? | + | 2 | 2 | 2 |
| Community Based Learning | + | + | / | / | ? | ? | 2 | 2 | 2 |
| TOTAL: + | 7 | 6 | 3 | 3 | 1 | 2 | 22 | | |
| ? | 5 | 6 | 1 | 5 | 12 | 7 | | 36 | |
| / | 1 | 1 | 9 | 5 | 0 | 4 | | | 20 |

GUIDELINES

KEY:
+ Reform likely to result in practice that promotes the guideline.
− Reform likely to result in practice that contradicts the guideline.
? Reform could be implemented in ways that promote or contradict the guideline.
/ Reform largely irrelevant to the guideline, no basis for assessing potential promotion or contradiction.

alienating than others.[47] There is good reason to believe, however, that only rarely would any school meet most of the guidelines.

Analyses of implementation of innovation,[48] the politics of schooling,[49] and organizational dynamics[50] indicate that school policies emerge largely in response to specific concerns and focus in a piecemeal way on limited aspects of school life: crime and vandalism, moral and values education, integration and racism, competence testing, teenage pregnancy, or youth unemployment. The preoccupation with such topics tends to deflect attention from a more general interest in reducing alienation in students' total experience. Specialization in roles also fragments approaches to school improvement: administrators tend to focus on organizational arrangements, leaving issues of program content to curriculum specialists and teachers; curriculum developers focus on program content with little attention to organizational content or to staff development; teacher educators often limit their attention to staff interaction with students and pedagogical techniques, with scarce attention to integration of content or to organizational structure. As a result, few efforts at school improvement examine student life comprehensively.[51]

Four dominant perspectives on educational reform illustrate the failure to attend to the totality of students' experience. The *conventional role* perspective attempts to develop competencies and attitudes necessary for successful performance in the familiar adult roles of worker, family member, and citizen. Expressed in a liberal format, this orientation emphasizes placing students in positions of responsibility that require independent thought and action in careers and community activities. In conservative proposals the same perspective stresses teaching students to submit to authority, and to learn basic literacy and discipline before undertaking autonomous roles in the adult community. Both liberal and conservative variants of conventional role ideology may emphasize prosocial behavior: caring for others, respect for property, and obedience to laws. This perspective is analogous to Kohlberg and Mayer's ideology of cultural transmission;[52] it minimizes notions of transcendent individual fulfillment and social reconstruction as primary goals of education.

In contrast, the *developmental* perspective focuses on individual growth along dimensions that include, but transcend, respect for conventional roles. It assumes that attainment of competence and values depends not only upon the interaction of biologically grounded stages or structures of thought and feeling with the environment. From this developmental point of view, the task of education is to stimulate a dialectical process between individuals and their environment to promote growth in such developmental dimensions as cognitive complexity, moral reasoning, and ego integration. This involves trying on conventional roles, with no commitment to accept them unless the individual chooses. Based largely on the work of Dewey, Erikson, and Piaget, this perspective is articulated by Kohlberg and Mayer and represented in models of schooling advocated by Mosher[53] and Conrad and Hedin.[54]

The perspective of *cultural emancipation* is concerned with formal education's contribution to exploitation and domination. While structural emancipationists may operate from either a Marxist framework or a liberal democratic philosophy, both variants are centrally concerned with schooling's contribution to social justice. By studying how the organization of knowledge and processes of schooling favor certain social interests and reinforce social stratification, the structural emancipation perspective focuses on how reforms that may appear beneficial from any of the three other perspectives may actually block progress toward equality and individual emancipation. This perspective, anchored in the work of Marx and Habermas, is represented in Young, Bowles and Gintis, Whitty and Young, and Apple.[55]

Finally, the central concern of the *professional technological* perspective is to clearly specify instructional objectives, and to create instructional materials, pedagogical techniques, and organizational processes for achieving these objectives, regardless of the content or philosophy underlying the school program. This perspective usually claims ideological neutrality, holding that training for any purpose can be instituted efficiently and professionally rather than sloppily with great waste of human resources. The perspective is represented in national curriculum development efforts, the competency-based education movement, and individually guided education.

Arguments over reform priorities often develop from disagreements among these perspectives. None of them, however, is sufficiently comprehensive to reduce alienation in students' total school experience. The developmental and conventional role perspectives tend to focus on limited program goals such as experiences in inquiry, moral reasoning, peer counseling, employment, and punishment for vandalism. Although these may be worthwhile, concern with gaining specific experiences that promote either developmental growth or adaptation to existing roles deflects attention from the issue of improving the quality of life in school as a whole. Some specific programs grounded in these perspectives do address student life beyond the classroom; for example, the just community school, or the prosocial behavior orientation, but neither of the general perspectives calls attention to alienation in the total experience of school.

Paradoxically, the structural emancipation perspective is philosophically tied to a concern for alienation, but its advocates offer few suggestions on how to build less alienating schools. Instead, they may propose a curriculum that raises student-staff consciousness about the nature of hegemony; or they argue that because the school is embedded in a larger social structure of alienated relations, school alienation cannot be reduced without fundamental social change. Rather than offering substantive proposals for school reform, this perspective views school improvement as part of a general political struggle of oppressed people to gain empowerment. This perspective seems reluctant to offer general guidelines for better schools, perhaps because of the belief that solutions must arise from a dialectic process involving participants rather than from analyses by elites.

The professional technological perspective is so rooted in specialization as the solution to human problems and so insistent upon value-neutrality, that the quality of life in school rarely becomes an important issue. Instead, issues are construed in the narrow sense of how to increase reading scores or how to prevent violence in the school, and solutions are sought through consultations with specialized experts rather than those interested in reducing alienation in general.

The failure of each reform perspective to address student alienation probably reflects general public reluctance to recognize alienation as a significant cause of specific problems in modern schools. Despite controversy on the academic effectiveness of schooling, and evidence of increasing vandalism, homicide, and suicide among adolescents, general public confidence in the public schools remains relatively high.[56] If most students make it through high school—the national average dropout rate is about 25 percent—if many find opportunities for employment or higher education, and if schools continue to function in a reasonably orderly fashion so that buses run, lunch is served, and grades are submitted, there is apparently no urgent necessity to reexamine the total pattern of relations toward work and among people within schools.

Although the guidelines suggested in this paper could reduce alienation through promoting individuality, communality, and integration, and although such a reduction in alienation could dramatically improve the quality of our schools, because of values in the society at large, the politics of educational interest groups, and reasonably high levels of satisfaction with the schools by dominant groups, most reforms will probably continue to avoid comprehensive responses to the problem of alienation. Certainly it is possible to learn in extremely alienating environments: slaves, prison inmates, and bureaucrats have educated themselves in organizations perhaps more aversive than schools. The human ability to cope may be the major deterrent to improving school life.

## NOTES

1. G. Lichtheim, "Alienation," *International Encyclopedia of the Social Sciences*, Vol. 1 (New York: MacMillan, 1968); B. Ollman, *Alienation: Marx's Conception of Man in Capitalist Society*, 2d ed. (London: Cambridge University Press, 1971); R. Schacht, *Alienation* (New York: Doubleday, 1970).

2. M. Seeman, "Alienation Studies," *Annual Review of Sociology*, Vol. 1, (Palo Alto, CA: Annual Reviews, 1975).

3. S. Long, "Urban Adolescents and the Political System: Dimensions of Disaffection," *Theory and Research in Social Education,* 8 (1980), 31–45.

4. S. Abramowitz and E. Tenenbaum, *High School '77: A Survey of Public Secondary School Principals* (Washington, D.C.: National Institute of Education, 1978); M.R. Asner and J. Broschart, eds., *Violent Schools—Safe Schools: The Safe School Study Report to the Congress*, Vol. 1 (Washington, D.C.: National Institute of Education, 1978); B. F. Brown, ed., *The Reform of Secondary Education: A Report to the Public and the Profession* (New York: McGraw- Hill, 1973); Carnegie Council on Policy Studies in Higher Education, *Giving Youth a Better Chance: Options for Education, Work and Service* (San Francisco: Jossey-Bass, 1979); J.S. Coleman, *Youth: Transition to Adulthood*, Report of the President's Science Advisory Committee (Chicago University of Chicago Press, 1974); National Panel on High School and Adolescent Education, *The Education of Adolescents* (Washington, D.C.: U.S. Government Printing Office, 1976); R.E. Stake and J.A. Easley, *Case Studies in Science Education* (Washington, D.C.: National Science Foundation, 1978).

5. R.A. Nisbet, *The Sociological Tradition* (New York: Basic Books, 1966); R.A. Nisbet, *The Social Bond: An Introduction to the Study of Society* (New York: Knopf, 1970).

6. D. Erickson, "Should All the Nation's Schools Compete for Clients and Support?" *Phi Delta Kappan,* 61 (1979), 14–17.; M. Rutter et al., *Fifteen Thousand Hours: Secondary Schools and Their Effects on Children* (Cambridge: Harvard University Press, 1979); G. Wehlage, C. Stone, and H.M. Kliebard, *Dropouts and Schools: Case Studies of the Dilemmas Educators Face* (Madison: University of Wisconsin, 1980); E.A. Wynne, *Looking at Schools: Good, Bad, and Indifferent* (Lexington, Mass.: Heath, 1980).

7. Ollman, *Alienation*; E.H. Erickson, "Identity and the Life Cycle," *Psychological Issues*, Vol. 1 (1 Mono. No.1, 1959).

8. E.H. Erickson, *Childhood and Society* (New York: Norton, 1960).

9. M. Seeman, "Alienation and Engagement," in *The Human Meaning of Social Change*, ed. A. Campbell and P.E. Converse (New York: Russell Sage, 1972).

10. D. Katz and R.L. Kahn, *The Social Psychology of Organizations*, 2d ed. (New York: Wiley, 1978).

11. D.W. Oliver, *Education and Community: A Radical Critique of Innovative Schooling* (Berkeley: McCutchan, 1976).

12. R.A. Nisbet, *Community and Power* (New York: Oxford University Press, 1962).

13. See taxonomies proposed by R.G. Corwin, "Models of Educational Organization," in *Review of Research in Education*, ed. F.N. Kerlinger and J.B. Carroll, Vol. 2 (Itasca, Ill.: Peacock, 1974); H. P. Dachler and B. Wilpert, "Conceptual Dimensions and Boundaries of Participation in Organizations: A Critical Evaluation," *Administrative Science Quarterly*, 23 (1978), 1–39; J.G. March, ed., *Handbook of Organizations* (Chicago: Rand McNally, 1965).

14. A. Etzioni, *A Comparative Analysis of Complex Organizations* (New York: Free Press, 1961).

15. P.M. Blau and W.R. Scott, *Formal Organizations* (San Francisco: Chandler, 1962).

16. Corwin, "Models of Educational Organization"; March, *Handbook*; J.G. March and J.P. Olsen, *Ambiguity and Choice in Organizations* (Bergen: Universitets Forlaget, 1976).

17. K.E. Weick, *The Social Psychology of Organizing* (Reading, Mass.: Addison-Wesley, 1979).

18. J.E. Coons and S.D. Sugarman, *Education by Choice: The Case for Family Control* (Berkeley: University of California Press, 1978); W. Spady, "The Authority System of the School and Student Unrest: A Theoretical Exploration," in *The Seventy-Third Yearbook of the National Society for the Study of Education* (Part 2), ed. C.W. Gordon, (Chicago: University of Chicago Press, 1974).

19. M.W. Meyer and Associates, eds., *Environments and Organizations* (San Francisco: Jossey-Bass, 1978); J.W. Meyer and B. Rowan, "The Structure of Educational Organizations," in *Environments and Organizations*, ed. M.W. Meyer and Associates; K. Weick, "Educational Organizations as Loosely Coupled Systems," *Administrative Science Quarterly*, 21 (1976), 1–19.

20. Rutter et al., *Fifteen Thousand Hours*.

21. B. Schneider, *America's Small Schools* (Las Cruces, N.M.: ERIC Clearinghouse on Rural Education and Small Schools, 1980).

22. R. Barker and P. Gump, *Big School, Small School: High School Size and Student Behavior* (Stanford: Stanford University Press, 1964).

23. J. Gargarino, "The Human Ecology of School Crime: A Case for Small Schools," in *School Crime and Disruption: Prevention Models*, ed. E. Wenk and N.

Harlow (Washington, D.C.: National Institute of Education, 1978); G.D. Gottfredson and D. Daiger, *Disruption in Six Hundred Schools (Rep. 289)* (Baltimore, Md.: Johns Hopkins University, Center for Social Organization of Schools, 1979).

24. J. Garbarino, "Some Thoughts on School Size and Its Effects on Adolescent Development," *Journal of Youth and Adolescence* 9, No. 1 (1980), 19–31.

25. M. Aiken and J. Hage, "Organizational Alienation: A Comparative Analysis," *American Sociological Review,* 31 (1966), 497–507; P. Blumberg, *Industrial Democracy: The Sociology of Participation* (London: Constable, 1968); Katz and Kahn, *The Social Psychology of Organizations*; L. Kohlberg, "High School Democracy in Educating for a Just Society," in *Moral Education: First Generation of Research and Development,* ed. R. L. Mosher (New York: Praeger, 1980); W.K. Hoy, R. Blazovsky, and W. Newland, "Organizational Structure and Alienation from Work" (Paper presented at the American Educational Research Association, Boston, April 1980).

26. F.M. Newmann, "Political Participation: An Analysis Review and Proposal," in *Political Education in Flux*, ed. J. Gillespie and D. Heater (London: Sage, 1981); C. Pateman, *Participation and Democratic Theory* (New York: Cambridge University Press, 1970).

27. A.O. Hirschman, *Voice and Loyalty: Responses to Decline in Firms, Organizations, and States* (Cambridge: Harvard University Press, 1970).

28. C. Bidwell, "The School as a Formal Organization," in *Handbook of Organizations*, ed J. March (Chicago: Rand McNally, 1965); C. Bidwell, "Students and Schools: Some Observations on Client Trust in Client- Serving Institutions," in *Organizations and Clients*, ed. W.R. Rosengren and M. Lefton (Columbus, Ohio: Merrill, 1970).

29. Gottfredson and Daiger, *Disruption.*

30. Wehlage, Stone, and Kliebard, *Dropouts and Schools.*

31. P.A. Cusick, *Inside High School: The Student's World* (New York: Holt, Rinehart and Winston, 1973).

32. Literature dealing with peer teaching and peer counseling (N.A. Sprinthall, "Learning Psychology by Doing Psychology: A High School Curriculum in the Psychology of Counseling," in *Adolescents' Development and Education*, ed. R.L. Mosher [Berkeley: McCutchan, 1979]), student accomplishments in group-based service and research (D. Conrad and D. Hedin, "Citizenship Education Through Participation," in *Education for Responsible Citizenship*, ed. B.F. Brown [New York: McGraw-Hill, 1977]), specific pedagogy to stimulate more cooperative learning in the classroom (D.W. Johnson and R.T. Johnson, *Learning Together and Alone: Cooperation, Competition, and Individualization* [Englewood Cliffs, N.J.: Prentice-Hall, 1975]), and ways of promoting school spirit (Wynne, *Looking at Schools*) suggests a number of ways in which students' work in school might be altered to promote less alienating relations.

33. See Wynne, *Looking at Schools*, for other suggestions.

34. R. Blauner, *Alienation and Freedom: The Factory Worker and His Industry* (Chicago University of Chicago Press, 1964).

35. H. Braverman, *Labor and Monopoly Capital* (New York: Monthly Review Press, 1974).

36. M.F. Young, ed., *Knowledge and Control: New Directions for the Sociology of Education* (London: Collier-Macmillan, 1971).

37. B. Bernstein, *Class, Codes and Control: Toward a Theory of Educational Transmissions*, Vol. 3 (London: Routledge and Kegan Paul, 1975).

38. P.E. Willis, *Learning to Labour* (Lexington, Mass.: Heath, 1977).

39. J.U. Ogbu, *Minority Education and Caste: The American System in Cross-cultural Perspective* (New York: Academic Press, 1978).

40. Oliver, *Education and Community*.

41. R.L. Mosher, "A Democratic High School: Damn It, Your Feet Are Always in the Water," in *Adolescents' Development and Education*, ed. R. L. Mosher (Berkeley: McCutchan, 1979); National Association of Secondary School Principals, "Schools within Schools," *Practitioner*, 3 (1976), 1–12.

42. D.U. Levine and R.J. Havighurst, eds., *The Future of Big-City Schools: Desegregation Policies and Magnet Alternatives* (Berkeley: McCutchan, 1977).

43. A. Glatthorn, *Alternatives in Education: Schools and Programs* (New York: Dodd, Mead, 1975).

44. See Wynne, *Looking at Schools*.

45. M. Gibbons, *The New Secondary Education: A Phi Delta Kappa Force Report* (Bloomington, Ind: Phi Delta Kappa, 1976).

46. Examples of literature consulted include D. Rogers, *An Inventory of Educational Improvement Efforts in the New York City Public Schools* (New York: Teachers College Press, 1977): Levine and Havighurst, *The Future of Big-City Schools;* Abramowitz and Tenenbaum, *High School '77;* Far West Laboratory for Educational Research and Development, *Educational Programs That Work,* 5th ed. (San Francisco: Author, 1978); J.S. Park, ed., *Education in Action: 50 Ideas That Work* (Washington, D.C.: U.S. Government Printing Office, 1978); T. Burns, *The Urban High School Reform Initiative: Final Report* (Washington, D.C.: U.S. Office of Education, 1979); Carnegie Council, *Giving Youth a Better Chance;* H.J. Klausmeier, *Profiles of Selected Innovating Secondary Schools* (Madison: Wisconsin Research and Development Center for Individualized Schooling, 1979); and Wynne, *Looking at Schools*.

47. Carnegie Council, *Giving Youth a Better Chance;* Wehlage, Stone, and Kliebard, *Dropouts and Schools;* and Wynne, *Looking at Schools*.

48. P. Berman and W. McLaughlin, *Federal Programs Supporting Educational Change: Implementing and Sustaining Innovations*, Vol. 8 (Santa Monica, Calif.: Rand Corporation, 1978).

49. F.M. Wirt, ed., *The Policy of the School* (Lexington, Mass.: Heath, 1975).

50. Meyer and Associates, *Environments and Organizations*.

51. Much attention has been given to a school climate emphasizing openness, trust, participation in goal setting, and problem solving, but apparently neglecting the alienating nature of underlying structures, role definition, or conceptions of work: see E.L. McDill and L.C. Rigsby, *Structure and Process in Secondary Schools: The Academic Impact of Educational Climates* (Baltimore Md.: Johns Hopkins University Press, 1973); R.A. Schmuck and P.A. Schmuck, *A Humanistic Psychology of Education: Making the School Everybody's House* (Palo Alto, Calif.: National Press, 1974); and R.A. Schmuck et al., *The Second Handbook of Organizational Development in Schools* (Palo Alto Calif.: Mayfield, 1977).

52. L. Kohlberg and R. Mayer, "Development as the Aim of Big-City Schools: Desegregation Policies and Magnet Alternatives," *Harvard Educational Review,* 42 (1972), 449–496.

53. Ibid; R.L. Mosher, *Adolescents' Development and Education* (Berkeley: McCutchan, 1979).

54. Conrad and Hedin, "Citizenship Education."

55. Young, *Knowledge and Control;* S. Bowles and H. Gintis, *Schooling in Capitalist America: Education Reform and the Contradictions of Economic Life* (New York: Basic Books, 1976); G. Whitty and M. young, *Explorations in the Politics of School Knowledge* (Driffield, England: Nafferton Books, 1976); M.W. Apple, *Ideology and Curriculum* (London: Routledge and Kegan Paul, 1979).

56. G.H. Gallup, "The 12th Annual Gallup Poll of the Public's Attitudes Toward the Public Schools," *Phi Delta Kappan,* 62 (1980), 33–48.

# Part III

# *Critical Perspectives:*
# *A Look at the Larger Context*

Chapter 9

# The Individual in Collective Adaptation: A Framework for Focusing on Academic Underperformance and Dropping Out Among Involuntary Minorities

The concept of being "at risk" is becoming as popular as the concept of "cultural deprivation" was in the 1960s, and both concepts are applied largely to minority youth. I will suggest in this chapter, by offering an alternative framework, that the concept "at risk" in its various current definitions neither goes far enough in helping us understand the school adjustment and academic performance problems of what I call involuntary minority youth, nor in how to deal with those problems. It is my basic point that the reasons for school dropouts among involuntary minorities are complex and cannot be understood by reference to the "dropout issue" as it is currently conceptualized. I will, therefore, offer an alternative way of understanding the "problem" of low academic performance which tends to characterize a relatively high proportion of involuntary minority youth, thereby contributing to the high dropout rates within this population.

My specific purpose here is twofold. One is to suggest a conceptual framework for studying *variability* in minority school performance. I will call this framework *a cultural model of schooling* or *a folk model of schooling*. My second objective is to show how this framework can be applied to the study of differences in the school responses of minorities at the group or collective level *and* at the individual or subgroup level: that is, in addition to answering the question of why some minority groups are more successful than others, I will also address the question of why, in a given minority group, some individuals are more academically successful than others. In the case of variability among individuals or subgroups I will focus on minority groups that are relatively unsuccessful in school, using black American students to illustrate my point.

## EVIDENCE OF VARIABILITY IN SCHOOL PERFORMANCE

### *Group-Level Variability*

In my comparative research of minority education within the United States and elsewhere, I have come to the conclusion that some minority groups do relatively well in school even though they initially may face language and cultural barriers, and even though as adults they may face barriers in opportunity structure which prevent them from getting employment, wages, and other benefits commensurate with their education. Other minorities who face similar problems do less well in school. Within the United States many local studies provide plenty of evidence for this variability in minority school performance. These studies include my own research in Stockton, California, where I compared the school performance of blacks, Mexican Americans, Chinese, Japanese, Filipinos, and whites; Gibson's study of Punjabi Indians, Mexican Americans, and whites in Valleyside, California; Suarez-Orozco's study of various Hispanic groups in the Mission District of San Francisco; Matute-Bianchi's study of Japanese, Mexican Americans, and Mexicanos in Watsonville, California; and Valverde's study of school dropout among Mexican Americans and Mexicanos in a southwestern city.[1] In all these cases, the minorities who are doing better are immigrants.

My conclusion that immigrant minorities do better in school than nonimmigrants even though the former do not share the language and culture of the dominant group and even though, like the nonimmigrants, they face barriers in adult opportunity structure, is reinforced by two cross-cultural observations. One is that in some instances the minority groups who are doing well in school are the ones more different from the dominant group in culture and language. For example, as already noted, some studies suggest that students from Mexico appear to be more successful in the public schools than native-born Chicanos.[2] In Britain the more different East Asians do better than West Indians.[3]

The second reinforcing observation is that a minority group which does poorly in school in its country of origin or where it has an involuntary status appears to do much better when its members emigrate to another country, where its culture and language are even more different from the language and culture of the dominant group of the host society. A good example of this is the case of the Japanese Buraku outcaste. In Japan itself, Buraku students continue to do poorly in school when compared with the dominant Ippan students. But in the United States the Buraku do as well as other Japanese Americans.[4] A similar contrast exists for Koreans in Japan, where they have an involuntary minority status, and in the United States, where they are voluntary immigrants.[5]

## Variability at the Individual Level

Within a given minority group some students are more academically successful than others; thus there is also variability at the individual level. In the less academically successful minority groups the variability in the school performance of individuals is not easily explained in terms of conventional variables of social-class factors, ability differences, or cultural and language differences. Let me illustrate what I mean by briefly describing two unique features of black students' school performance that first led me to become interested in individual adaptive responses to schooling within the group.

One of the two unique features is that social class variables do not seem to be strongly correlated with academic achievement among blacks, as they do among whites and among voluntary minorities, such as Asians. A good example of this weak correlation can be found in the California Assessment Program test scores for 1987. Both at grade eight and grade twelve the relationship between black students' test scores and parents' education was not particularly positive. For example, black students whose parents had completed only some college consistently outperformed black students whose parents were college graduates.[6] In a study of black and Chicano students at the University of California at Los Angeles, Oliver, Rodriquez, and Mickelson found that social-class background was weakly related to the academic performance of black students, with only mother's education and high school grades having significant effects.[7] Another reason for examining individual strategies is that among black students ability is not always related to academic achievement. For example, in a recent study of thirty-three eleventh graders in a high school in Washington, D.C., Fordham found that both students who were doing well academically and students who were not doing well academically had similar scores in standardized tests of ability.[8]

## VARIABILITY IN SCHOOL PERFORMANCE AND CONVENTIONAL THEORIES

There have been several attempts to account for the relative school success of the immigrants; there have also been several other attempts to explain why the nonimmigrants are less successful in school. From my perspective none of these theories provides a satisfactory explanation of the variability described above. For example, the genetic inferiority or deficiency proposed by Jensen to account for the lower school performance of black Americans cannot explain the relative failure of the Japanese Buraku outcasts in Japanese schools and their relative success in American schools.[9] Nor can the cultural and language conflict theory proposed by educational anthropologists and socialinguists explain why some minorities but not others are able to cross cultural and language boundaries and do relatively well in school.[10]

One reason why current theories cannot account for the variability in minority school performance is that they ignore the minorities' own notion of schooling in the context of their social reality: that is, they fail to take into account the minorities' perceptions and interpretations of schooling and how such perceptions and interpretations affect their responses to schooling. Instead, social scientists have tried to explain the school behavior of the minorities using their own, white middle-class perceptions and interpretations of either their own social reality or the social reality of the minorities as they—the white middle class— perceive it.

One argument of this paper is that minority groups who are doing relatively well in school are not distinguished from other groups by the fact that they possess superior genes for school success; inhabit a home or cultural environment which allows children to develop the white middle-class type of cognitive, linguistic, or social emotional attributes which enhance school success; attend schools that are not inferior or segregated; or as adults face no barriers in opportunity structure. Rather, what seems to distinguish the two types of minorities is that they possess different types of cultural models or different understandings of the workings of American society and their place in that working order. These different understandings lead them to respond differently to schooling (which is a means of preparing children to participate as adults in society).

I will suggest that the concept of *cultural model* is useful in explaining the variability in the school performance of minorities because it permits the inclusion of the minorities' own perceptions and interpretations of schooling in the context of their social reality and how the perceptions and interpretations influence their behaviors. A cultural model is basically a people's understanding of their universe, physical, social, economic, and so on, as well as their understanding of their behavior in that universe. The cultural model of a given population guides their interpretations of events and elements within their universe; it also serves to guide their expectations and actions in that universe or environment. Furthermore, the cultural model underlies their folk theories or folk explanations of recurrent circumstances, events, and situations in various domains of life. It is used by members of the population to organize their knowledge about such recurrent events and situations and to guide their actions in such situations and toward such events. A folk model is developed from collective historical experiences of a given population; and the cultural model so constructed is sustained or modified by subsequent collective events or experiences in that universe. The cultural model has both instrumental and expressive dimensions, as I will show later.

Some students of the cultural model focus on its cognitive organization—how cultural knowledge or people's understanding of their universe is organized inside their heads and the relation of that organization to behaviors or actions. Partly because this school of thought relies so much on "talk" for data, some find problematic the relation of the cognitive organization of knowledge or cultural model and behavior, the relation of thought to action. My focus is different. It is on the nature of the cultural model as it can be learned or constructed from what members of a population *say* (that is, their "talk") and from what they actually *do* (that is, their behavior or actions), rather than on how cultural knowledge is organized inside their heads. As I use the concept, the cultural model is similar to what Bohannan calls "the folk system," which he says is built up through perceived experiences and the interpretations of these experiences by the people themselves.[11]

In a plural society like the United States, different segments of the society, such as the dominant whites and racial and ethnic minorities, tend to have their own cultural models—their respective understanding of how the United States society or any particular domain of it "works" and their place in that working order. The cultural model of the dominant group, like that of a given minority group, is neither right nor wrong; it is neither better nor worse than other cultural models. As Bohannan puts it in his study of the justice system of the Tiv in colonial Nigeria, "The folk systems [or cultural models] are never right nor wrong." They simply "exist" to guide behaviors and interpretations.[12]

In the field of education in the United States, the cultural model of the white middle class coexists with those of black Americans and other minorities. And the cultural model of each group provides its members with the framework for interpreting educational situations and events and guides their behaviors or responses to such situations and events. My comparative research leads me to suggest that the cultural model of each group is to some degree implicated in the relative academic success or failure of its members. My comparative study also leads me to conclude that although the theories I referred to earlier which purport to explain the school performance of minority-group children may be self-consistent and satisfactory to their proponents, they do not necessarily reflect the realities they attempt to explain because they do not include the cultural models of the minorities and the implications of the cultural models for the behaviors of the minorities in the schooling context.[13]

## MINORITY STATUS AND CULTURAL MODELS

Why and how do the cultural models of minorities who are academically more successful differ from the cultural models of the minorities who are less academically successful? There appear to be two principal reasons why the cultural models are different. One has to do with the initial terms by which the minorities were incorporated into American society; the other has to do with both the interpretations of the initial terms of their incorporation and their interpretations and responses to subsequent treatment by white Americans.

## Initial Terms of Incorporation

By most accounts the minorities who are doing better in school are immigrants. Immigrants are people who have moved more or less *voluntarily* to the United States because they believed that this move would lead to more economic well-being, better overall opportunities, or greater political freedom. These expectations continue to influence the way they perceive and respond to their treatment by white Americans and by the institutions controlled by the whites. The Chinese in Stockton, California, and the Punjabi Indians in Valleyside, California, are representative examples.[14]

In contrast, nonimmigrant minorities, whom I will designate as *involuntary minorities*, are people who initially were brought into the United States society through slavery, conquest, or colonization. They usually resent the loss of their former freedom; they perceive the social, political, and economic barriers against them as a part of their underserved oppression. American Indians, black Americans, Mexican Americans in the Southwest, and native Hawaiians are United States examples. Similar minorities exist in Japan, namely, the Buraku and Japan's Koreans, and in New Zealand, namely, the Maoris.

## Response to Subsequent Treatment

Both the immigrants and the involuntary minorities experience prejudice and discrimination at the hands of white Americans. Both may be relegated to menial jobs, confronted with social and political barriers, or given inferior education; and both may face intellectual and cultural derogation and exclusion from true assimilation into the mainstream of American life. Confronted with these *collective problems*, the immigrants tend to interpret them differently compared with the involuntary minorities. The immigrants tend to interpret the economic, political, and social barriers against them as more or less temporary problems, as problems they will overcome or can overcome with the passage of time, hard work, and more education. The immigrants often compare their situation in the United States with that of their former self or of their peers "back home." When they make such comparisons they often find much evidence that they have more and better opportunities in the United States for themselves or for their children. Because of this positive dual frame of reference, the immigrants think that even if they are allowed only marginal jobs they are better off in the United States than they would be in their homeland. Furthermore, they may interpret their exclusion from better jobs as a result of their status as "foreigners," or because they do not speak the language well, or because they were not educated in the United States. As a result, immigrants tend to share the folk theory of getting ahead that is characteristic of the white middle class and tend to behave accordingly, sometimes even in the face of barriers to opportunities. They do not necessarily bring such a theory from their homeland; they often accept the white middle-class theory when they arrive in the United States.[15]

Involuntary minorities interpret the same barriers differently. Because they do not have a "homeland" situation to compare with the situation in the United States, they do not interpret their menial jobs and low wages as "better." Neither do they see their situation as temporary. Quite to the contrary, they tend to interpret the discrimination against them as more or less permanent and institutionalized. Although they "wish" they could get ahead through education and ability like white Americans, they know they "can't." They have usually come to realize or believe that it requires more than education, and more than individual effort and hard work, to overcome the barriers. Consequently, they develop a folk theory of getting ahead which differs from that of white Americans. And their folk theory tends to stress collective effort as providing the best chances for overcoming the barriers to get ahead.

Not only do the two types of minorities differ in their responses to instrumental barriers; they also differ in their cultural systems and responses to cultural differences. Immigrant minorities are characterized by a *primary cultural system*.[16] The differences between the primary cultural system and the cultural system of the dominant group of mainstream white Americans existed *before* the immigrants came to the United States. Thus, Punjabi Indians in Valleyside, California, spoke Punjabi, practiced the Sikh, Hindu, or Moslem religion, had arranged marriages, and had males who wore turbans before they came to the United States, where they continue these beliefs and practices to some extent. These cultural beliefs and practices sometimes cause difficulties for the Punjabi at school and in their relationship with mainstream society in general. The Punjabis interpret some of the cultural differences and language differences as *barriers they have to overcome* in order to achieve the goals of their emigration. And they *try* to overcome them by learning selectively the language and cultural features of the mainstream, without interpreting their behavior as giving up their own culture and language identity. The immigrants' behavior and their interpretation of that behavior—learning the English language—are analogous to the behavior and interpretation of the behavior by Americans who do not yet speak French but desire to go to Paris for a vacation. The would-be vacationers know full well that they would enjoy their vacation more if they spoke and understood French. They therefore embark upon learning French. In doing so the Americans do not interpret their action as detrimental to their English language or American identity. They see themselves as simply acquiring an additional language that would enable them to achieve a specific purpose.

Involuntary minorities, on the other hand, tend to be characterized by a *secondary cultural system* in which the cultural differences between the minorities and the mainstream arise *after* the former have become involuntary minorities. In other words, involuntary minorities tend to develop certain beliefs and practices, including particular ways of speaking or communicating, as *coping mechanisms* under subordination. These beliefs and practices may be a new creation on the part of the minorities or their interpretations of old beliefs and practices. On the whole, the beliefs and practices constitute a new cultural frame of reference or ideal way of believing and acting that identifies one as a bona fide member of the minority group. The minorities perceive their way as not merely different from that of their white "oppressors," but as more or less oppositional to it. The cultural and language differences emerging under this condition also serve as boundary-maintaining mechanisms between the minorities and the dominant group. For these reasons, involuntary minorities do not interpret the cultural and language differences as barriers to be overcome; rather, they interpret them as *symbols of identity.* Their cultural frame of reference gives them both a sense of collective or social identity and a sense of self-worth.

With regard to social identity, the immigrants bring with them a sense of who they are which they had before they emigrated. They perceive their social identity as different rather than oppositional vis-à-vis the social identity of white Americans. And they seem to retain this social identity at least during the first generation, even though they are learning the English language and other aspects of American mainstream culture.

Involuntary minorities, on the other hand, develop a new sense of peoplehood or social identity *after* their involuntary incorporation as well as because of their interpretation of subsequent treatment, including the denial of equal opportunity and true admission into mainstream society; in some cases, involuntary minorities also develop oppositional identity because of forced integration into mainstream society.[17] Involuntary minorities also develop an oppositional identity because they perceive and experience treatment by white Americans as collective and enduring. They usually come to believe that they cannot expect to be treated like whites regardless of their individual differences in ability, training, or education, regardless of differences in place of origin or residence, and regardless of differences in economic status or physical appearance.[18] Furthermore, the minorities know that they cannot easily escape from their birth-ascribed membership in a subordinate and disparaged group by "passing" or by returning to "a homeland".[19] Under this circumstance, involuntary minorities do not see their social identity as merely different from that of white Americans or their "oppressors"; rather, they see their collective identity as more or less oppositional to the collective identity of the whites. The oppositional social identity combines with the oppositional or ambivalent cultural frame of reference to make cross-cultural learning or "crossing cultural boundaries" more difficult for involuntary minorities: for them, to behave in a manner defined as falling within the white American cultural frame of reference appears threatening to their own minority identity and security. Consequently, those who try to behave "like whites" risk peer pressures to refrain from doing so and may be subjected to not only peer criticism but also isolation; they may also experience "affective dissonance".[20]

One other element in the cultural model to be considered is the degree of trust for white Americans and the societal institutions controlled by whites. The two types of minorities may face similar problems in their relationship with white Americans and the institutions, but they have different interpretations of the problems which lead to different degrees of trust. It seems that the immigrants tend to acquiesce more and to rationalize the prejudice and discrimination against them by saying, for example, that they are strangers in a foreign land and have no choice but to tolerate prejudice and discrimination.[21] In their relationship with the schools the immigrants tend to rationalize their accommodation by saying that they came to the United States to give their children the opportunity to get an American education. Furthermore, the immigrants frequently find their relationship with the public schools to be "better" than their relationship with the schools in their home countries. They speak favorably of the fact that in the United States their children are given free textbooks and other supplies.[22]

Involuntary minorities find no justification for the prejudice and discrimination against them in school and society other than the fact that they are minorities. A deep distrust runs through the relationship between white Americans and involuntary minorities and between the public schools and the minorities. In the case of black Americans, there are many historical episodes that have left them with the feeling that white people and the institutions they control cannot be trusted.[23] The public schools, particularly in the inner city, are generally not trusted to provide black children with the "right education." This distrust comes partly from perceptions of past and current discrimination which blacks view as more or less institutionalized and permanent. The discriminatory treatment and prejudice have, of course, been documented throughout the United States and throughout the history of black Americans and black education.[24]

In sum, the cultural models of immigrant or voluntary minorities and the cultural models of involuntary minorities differ in the following key elements: the cultural frame of reference for comparing present status, the folk theory of getting ahead, the collective identity, the cultural frame of reference for judging appropriate behavior, and the extent to which one might trust white people and the institutions they control. I will now show how each of these elements might differentially influence the school orientations and performance of immigrant and involuntary minorities.

## CULTURAL MODELS AND MINORITY SCHOOLING

The contents of the cultural models of the minorities—status mobility frame, folk theory of getting ahead in the United States, survival strategies, trust, identity, and cultural frame of reference—enter into the schooling process by influencing the educational attitudes and strategies of the minorities. The nature of the contents of the immigrants' cultural model leads them to adopt attitudes and strategies more conducive to school success than is the case of the involuntary minorities. The immigrants' dual-status mobility frame and their folk theory of getting ahead stress the importance of school success through the adoption of appropriate academic attitudes and hard work. As already noted, the immigrants tend to believe that they have more and better opportunities to succeed in the United States than in their countries of origin and that, indeed, they may have come to the United States

precisely to give their children an "American education" so that they
can get ahead in the United States or "back home," if they choose to
return to their country of origin. Thus, immigrant parents stress education and take steps to ensure that their children behave in a manner
conducive to school success. For their part, the children, whether they
are Chinese, Central and South American Latinos, Koreans, or Punjabis, appear to share their parents' attitudes toward "American education," take their school work seriously, work hard, and persevere.[25]

The nonoppositional social identity and nonoppositional cultural
frame of reference of the immigrants facilitate their ability to cross
cultural and language boundaries in the school context. They enable
the immigrants to distinguish what they have to learn in order to
achieve the goals of their emigration, such as the English language and
the standard practices of the schools and the workplace, *from* other aspects of mainstream culture which may threaten their minority language, culture, and identity. As noted previously, the immigrants perceive and interpret the language and cultural features necessary for
school success—the language and cultural differences they encounter
in school—as *barriers to be overcome* in order to achieve their long-range
goals of future employment, economic well-being, and other benefits.
Therefore, the immigrants do not go to school expecting the schools to
teach them in their native language and culture. Rather, they expect
and are willing to learn the English language and the standard practices of the school. This is not to say that immigrant children do not experience language and cultural difficulties; but they and their parents
and community perceive the language and cultural conflicts as problems they have to overcome with appropriate programs from the
schools.

Finally, the immigrants' acquiescing and somewhat trusting relationship with the teachers and other school personnel also promotes
school success. Their relative trust and acquiescence stem from three
factors. One is that the immigrants consider the schools in the United
States to be better than the schools of their homelands: their comparative frame of reference is the school they left behind, not the school in
the white suburbs in the United States. Another reason is that the immigrants think that they are treated better by the public school personnel than by the school personnel of their homeland.[26] Finally, as noted
previously, even where the immigrants experience prejudice and discrimination, which they certainly resent, they tend to rationalize such
treatments so as not to discourage themselves from striving for school
success.[27] The overall impression one gains from ethnographic studies

is that immigrant minority parents teach their children to trust school officials, to accept, internalize, and follow school rules and standard practices for academic success, and that the children more or less do so.

In their dual-status mobility frame, involuntary minorities compare themselves unfavorably with the white middle class; and when they do they often think that they are worse off than they should be even when they have similar education and ability. Thus, in their comparison, involuntary minorities find the usefulness of education to be uncertain for their advancement. Their folk theory of getting ahead emphasizes the importance of education, but this verbal endorsement is not usually accompanied by appropriate necessary effort. This is due, in part, to the fact that historically involuntary minorities were not given the same chance to get the kinds of jobs and wages available to whites who had comparable education. Eventually the minorities came to see the treatment as a part of the institutionalized discrimination against them, which is not entirely eliminated by merely getting an education.[28] One result is that the minorities did not develop "effort optimism" toward academic work: that is, they did not develop a strong tradition of cultural know-how, hard work, and perseverance toward academic tasks. Moreover, involuntary minority parents appear to teach their children contradictory things about getting ahead through schooling. This was brought home to me while doing ethnographic research among blacks and Mexican Americans in Stockton, California. On the one hand, the parents tell their children to get a good education and verbally encourage them to do well in school. But, on the other hand, the actual texture of the parents' lives in terms of low-level jobs, underemployment, and unemployment also comes through strongly, reproducing a second kind of message powerful enough to undo their exhortations. For, unavoidably, involuntary minority parents discuss their problems with the system, as well as the similar problems of relatives, friends, and neighbors, in the presence of their children. The result is that involuntary minority children are increasingly disillusioned about their ability to succeed in adult life through the mainstream strategy of schooling.

The folk theory of getting ahead stresses means other than schooling, namely, survival strategies within and outside the mainstream, discussed earlier. The survival strategies affect schooling in a number of ways. One is that they tend to generate attitudes and behaviors that are not conducive to good classroom teaching and learning. When survival strategies, such as collective struggle among blacks, succeed in increasing the pool of jobs and other resources for the minority community, they may encourage minority youths to work hard in school. But such success can also lead the youths to blame "the system" and to rationalize their lack of serious efforts at school work. Clientship or Uncle Tomming is dysfunctional for minority youths because it does not create good role models for school success through hard work. Clientship also teaches minority children manipulative knowledge skills, and attitudes used by their parents in dealing with white people and white institutions. As the children become familiar with other survival strategies, like hustling and pimping or drug dealing, their attitudes toward school are adversely affected. For example, in the norms that support some of these strategies, the work ethic is reversed by the insistence that one should make it without working, especially without "doing the white man's thing." Moreover, for students who are into hustling, social interactions in the classroom are seen as opportunities for exploitation, that is, opportunities to gain prestige by putting the other person or persons down. This may lead to class disruptions and suspensions.[29]

Another problem is that the survival strategies may become serious competitors with schooling as ways of getting ahead, leading young people to channel their time and efforts into nonacademic activities. This is particularly true as involuntary minority children get older and become more aware of how some adults in their communities "make it" without mainstream school credentials and employment.[30] For example, there is some evidence that many young black Americans view sports and entertainment, rather than education, as the way to get ahead; and their perceptions are reinforced by the realities they observe in the community and society as large and by the media. Blacks are overrepresented in the lucrative sports like baseball, basketball, and football. The average annual salary in the National Basketball Association is over $300,000, and in the National Football League it is over $90,000. Many of the superstars who earn between $1 million and $2 million a year are black, and some of these people have had little education. Although the number of such athletes are few, the media make these athletes and entertainers more visible to black youngsters than they make black lawyers, doctors, engineers, and scientists.[31] There is some preliminary evidence, too, to suggest that black parents encourage their children's athletic activities in the belief that such activities will lead to careers in professional sports.[32]

Under the circumstances being described, involuntary minority children, like their parents, verbally express high interest in doing well in school and in obtaining good credentials for future employment in mainstream economy. But they do not necessarily match their wishes and aspirations with effort, even though they know that to do well in school they have to work harder. Black and Mexican American students in Stockton, California, whom I studied, for example, quite correctly explained that Chinese, Japanese, and white students in their school were more academically successful than they were because the former expended more time and effort in their school work both at school and at home. The lack of serious academic attitudes and efforts appears to increase as involuntary minority students get older and apparently become aware of the reality that as members of a subordinate minority group they have limited future opportunities for getting good jobs even with good education. Simultaneously, they increasingly divert their time and efforts away from school work into nonacademic activities.

Involuntary minorities differ in their interpretation of the language and cultural differences they encounter in school. I have previously noted that they interpret the language and cultural differences as markers of a group or social identity to be maintained. This is due to their oppositional or ambivalent identity and cultural frame of reference. They appear not to make a clear distinction between what they have to learn to enhance their school success, such as standard English and other aspects of the school curriculum and standard practices, *from* white American, or their "oppressors'," cultural frame of reference, the learning of which they perceive to be detrimental to their minority language, culture, and identity. The *equation* of standard English, the curriculum, and the standard practices of the school with white culture and identity often results in conscious or unconscious opposition or ambivalence toward learning these things. Those who adopt the attitudes and behaviors conducive to school success are accused by their peers of "acting white" or, in the case of black students, of being "Uncle Toms."[33] They are accused of being disloyal to the cause of their group and risk being isolated from their peers. Furthermore, as DeVos has noted, even in the absence of peer pressures, involuntary minority students may not adopt serious academic attitudes or persevere in academic tasks partly because the individuals have usually internalized the group's interpretations of such attitudes and behaviors and partly because they are uncertain that they would be accepted by whites if they succeeded in learning to act white and then lost their group support.[34] This state of affairs results in "affective dissonance" for involuntary minority children and students. The dilemma of the involuntary minority student, as Petroni has noted, is that he or she has to choose between academic success and maintaining a minority identity and cultural frame of reference, a choice that does not arise for the immigrant minority student.[35] Consequently, involuntary minority students who want to succeed academically have to adopt strategies that shield them from peer criticisms and ostracism.[36] One strategy that works is to engage in other activities that peers define as appropriate for minority students. This, for black students, would include athletic and other team-oriented activities defined as "black." Team-oriented activities are important for Black male students.[37] Another strategy is to camouflage success by assuming the role of a comedian or jester.[38] By acting foolishly the jester is able to cope with the pressures of school achievement and peers who do not endorse his or her striving for academic success. Some students who want to succeed academically engage the protection of "bullies" in exchange for helping the latter with homework. On the whole, black students who are academically successful are careful to avoid bragging about their academic achievement.[39]

Involuntary minorities' distrust of white Americans and the schools the latter control also adds to the lower academic success problem. Involuntary minorities distrust the public schools more than the immigrants do because the former do not have the dual frame of reference that allows the immigrants to compare the public schools with the schools they knew "back home." Therefore, involuntary minorities evaluate their inferior and/or segregated schools more negatively. Since they do not trust the public schools and white people who control them, involuntary minorities are usually skeptical about whether the schools can educate their children well or not. This skepticism of parents and other adult members of the minority community is communicated to the minority youth through family and community discussions as well as through public debates over minority education in general or debates over particular issues, such as school desegregation. Another factor discouraging academic effort is that involuntary minorities—parents and students—tend to question school rules of behavior and standard practices rather than accept and follow them as the immigrants appear to do. Indeed, involuntary minorities not infrequently interpret the school rules and standard practices as an imposition of a white cultural frame of reference which does not necessarily meet their "real educational needs."

My ethnographic research in Stockton provided several examples of instances in which blacks and Mexican Americans expressed skepticism about what they were learning in school and related tasks. One occasion involved an incident at a public meeting after a riot in a predominantly minority high school. The question here was the "relevance" of a high school history textbook, *The Land of the Free*, to the experiences of various minority groups in the state of California. Another concerned the value of a preschool curriculum stressing social development rather than academic learning. Still another was the real purpose of job placement tests, especially in the civil service. The minorities in this case believed that such tests, whether given at school or elsewhere, whether given by white Americans or their minority representatives, are designed to keep minorities down.

The problems associated with the distrustful relationship become more complicated because of the tendency of the schools to approach the education of involuntary minorities defensively. I have suggested that under this circumstance involuntary minority parents will have difficulty in successfully teaching their children to accept and follow school rules of behavior and standard practices that lead to academic success, and that involuntary minority children, particularly the older ones, will have difficulty accepting and following the school rules of behavior and standard practices.[40] During my ethnographic interviews with black and Mexican American youths, in fact, they admitted that they do not always listen to their parents' advice concerning their school behaviors.[41]

## INDIVIDUAL STRATEGIES IN COLLECTIVE ADAPTATION

In the foregoing pages I have argued that immigrant minorities are relatively more academically successful than the nonimmigrants or involuntary minorities because their more or less voluntary minority status generates a cultural model which enhances attitudes and behaviors conducive to school success. This does not mean that all immigrant minorities are successful and all nonimmigrants are unsuccessful in their academic striving. What I have described is more or less the dominant trend in the academic adaptation of each type of minority. Within each pattern of adaptation there are variations in the strategies that individuals adopt. Some of the strategies lead to greater school success; some do not. I will use the case of black Americans to illustrate the variation in individual strategies within each type of minority.

In the early part of this chapter I discussed two unique features of black American school performance. One is that social-class variables do not appear to have the same strong positive relationship for black school performance that they have for white school performance. The other is that ability also does not appear to have the same kind of positive relationship with black school performance that it does with white. I also noted that these were among the reasons why I became interested in examining the schooling strategies of individual black and minority students. What then are the schooling or academic strategies used by black students which may account for differences in the school performance of students from similar social-class backgrounds and students with similar abilities?

The initial interest was, however, to determine why the relationship between social-class variables and the academic performance of blacks was weak and why the relationship between ability and academic achievement of black students was also weak. A preliminary review of some ethnographic studies of black school experience suggested that part of the answer lies in the kinds of academic or schooling strategies used by black students as a result of their cultural model. What I report here is no more than a preliminary finding from an exploratory study of a small number of ethnographic research studies on the black school experience and a small number of black autobiographies in which the authors describe their school experiences. What this preliminary study shows is that among black youth there are recognizable strategies that individuals striving for school success use to shield themselves from peer criticisms, isolation, and affective dissonance, and in other ways to enhance their school success. Some of the strategies are more conducive to school success than others. I will now describe the adaptive types among the youth and their strategies.

*ASSIMILATORS* are the youths who choose to disassociate themselves from or to repudiate the black identity and cultural frame of reference in favor of the white cultural frame of reference, a position which amounts to a kind of cultural passing. They may choose to maintain "a raceless identity."[42] There are youths who have come to prefer white norms and values that are in conflict with those of black Americans, especially their black peers. For these youths it appears that one cannot remain a good member of the black community or peer group and be successful in school or mainstream institutions. Therefore, they reason that in order to succeed they must repudiate or abandon their black peers, their black identity and cultural frame of reference. They are usually successful in school but at the price of peer criticism and isolation.

*EMISSARIES* are black youths who play down black identity and cultural frame of reference in order to succeed in school and mainstream institutions by mainstream criteria but without rejecting black identity and culture. As a school counselor in Stockton, California, explained it to me, their motto is "Do your Black Thing but know the Whiteman's Thing." The emissaries approach school learning or participation in mainstream institutions with a belief that their success by mainstream criteria would contribute to the advancement of the black race or black people. (This was explained to me by the black youths I studied in Stockton, California, who said that they were trying to succeed in school because of their race, that is, to advance their race.) These youths may even deny that race is important in determining school success. They deliberately choose to follow school rules of behavior and standard practices of the classroom. They remain marginal to black peer group solidarity: that is, they do not become encapsulated in black peer activities or interests. As they get older, they tend to make their career plans on the basis of their individual interests and abilities with little or no reference to the fact that they are black. For some, school success generally leads to a spectator role with regard to civil rights activities because they think that they can best make their contribution to the cause of their race by their individual success in mainstream institutions and by mainstream criteria. This often conscious decision enables the emissaries to handle many contradictions inherent in their situation, namely, the necessity to follow the rules and standard practices established by white Americans while being keenly ware of their membership in a disparaged racial minority.[43]

*ALTERNATORS* are the youth who more or less adopt the "immigrants' model" of schooling, namely, the model of accommodation without assimilation. These students do not reject the black identity and cultural of reference but elect to play by the rules of the system. They tend to adopt definite strategies to cope with the conflicting demands of peer groups and those of the school. The specific secondary strategies adopted by the alternators shield them from peer criticisms. These strategies include getting involved in what their peers define as "black activities" or acting as class clowns.

*The REAFFILIATED* are those black students who might have repudiated the black cultural frame of reference and identity until they were confronted with "an unacceptable" experience with white people, the school personnel, or white students which they interpreted as due to "race." They then become more involved in "black activities" and with their black peers, but may still continue to do well in school.

*IVY-LEAGUERS* are described by Ellis and Newman as black youths who emulate middle-class behaviors, belong to social clubs or fraternities in college, abide by school laws and routines, and dress well by middle-class standards.[44] Ivy-leaguers tend to be churchgoers, and are well liked by their families and the authorities. They are generally considered good students.

*The REGULARS,* according to Perkins, are black youths who are accepted members of the street culture but do not subscribe to all of its norms.[45] These youths know how to get along well with everyone without compromising their own values. They can interact with their peers without being encapsulated. They are not fully committed to street or peer culture. Their values resemble those of the middle class. At school they are good students who conform to most conventional rules. They maintain close family ties and rarely belong to gangs. The survival skills of the Regulars include knowing the street culture in coping with ghetto life, engaging in relatively safe activities, knowing how to handle "trouble" successfully, and ensuring that trouble does not recur.[46] Their school success lies in their ability to camouflage.

*The AMBIVALENTS* are those students who are caught between the need or desire to be with their black peers and the desire to achieve by the criteria of the school or mainstream. They do not successfully resolve this conflict. As a result, their academic performance tends to be quite erratic.[47]

*The ENCAPSULATED* are those black youths who not only equate school learning with "acting white" but make no attempt to "act white" or get around it in order to succeed in school. They reject schooling because it is "acting white." They simply do not try to learn and to conform to school rules of behavior and standard practices, since these are defined as being within the white American cultural frame of reference. The encapsulated generally do not do well in school.[48]

## 'AT-RISK MINORITY YOUTHS':
## A CONCEPT IN SEARCH OF A DEFINITION

I would have liked to go into a more in-depth discussion of the concept of "at-risk" as applied to involuntary minority youths in the light of the conceptual framework I have presented. But there is neither space nor time to do so in this chapter. I will conclude, however, by repeating a point I stated earlier: At the moment the definition and explanation of the school adjustment and academic performance problems of the minorities are based on a white middle-class cultural model, not the cultural model of the minorities which influence the latter's school orientations and behaviors. However, such definitions and explanations are incomplete until they incorporate the minorities' own notion of schooling which influences their school behavior. And until such an incorporation is made, social policies or remedial problems based on the definitions and explanations such as those embedded in the dropout literature are not likely to be particularly effective.

## NOTES

1. John U. Ogbu, *The Next Generation: An Ethnography of Education in an Urban Neighborhood* (New York: Academic Press, 1974); M. A. Gibson, *Accommodation Without Assimilation: Punjabi Sikh Immigrants in an American High School and Community* (Ithaca N.Y.: Cornell University Press, 1988); M. M. Suarez-Orozco, *In Pursuit of a Dream: New Hispanic Immigrants in American Schools* (Stanford: Stanford University Press, forthcoming); M. E. Matute-Bianchi, "Ethnic Identities and Patterns of School Success and Failure among Mexican-Descent and Japanese-American Students in a California High School: An Ethnographic Analysis," *American Journal of Education,* 95, No. 1 (1986): 233–255; S. A. Valverde, "A Comparative Study of Hispanic High School Dropouts and Graduates: Why Do Some Leave School Early and Some Finish?" *Education in Urban Society,* 19, No. 3 (1987): 320–329.

2. R. M. Fernandez and F. Nielsen, *Bilingualism and Hispanic Scholastic Achievement: Some Baseline Results* (Department of Sociology, University of Arizona, unpublished manuscript); M. E. Matute-Bianchi, "Ethnic Identities"; Valverde, "Comparative Study"; K. A. Woodlard, *Ethnicity in Education: Some Problems of Language and Identity in Spain and the United States* (Department of Anthropology, University of California, Berkeley, unpublished manuscript).

3. John U. Ogbu, *Minority Education and Caste: The American System in Cross-Cultural Perspective* (New York: Academic Press, 1978).

4. George A. DeVos, *Socialization for Achievement: Essays on the Cultural Psychology of the Japanese* (Berkeley: University of California Press, 1973); H. Ito, "Japan's Outcastes in the United States," in *Japan's Invisible Race: Caste in Culture and Personality,* ed. G. A. DeVos and H. Wagatsuma (Berkeley: University of California Press, 1967) 200–221; N. K. Shimahara, *Mobility and Education of the Buraku: The Case of a Japanese Minority* (Paper presented at the Annual Meeting of the American Anthropological Association, November 1983).

5. G. A. DeVos, *Ethnic Persistence and Role Degradation: An Illustration from Japan* (Paper prepared for the American Soviet Symposium on Contemporary Ethnic Processes in the USA and the USSR, New Orleans, LA, April 14–16, 1984); Y. Lee, *Koreans in Japan and the United States* (Department of Anthropology, Northwestern University, unpublished manuscript); T. Rohlen, in G. DeVos, *Koreans in Japan: Ethnic Conflict and Accomodation* (Berkeley: University of California Press, 1981).

6. K. Haycock and Navarro, *Unfinished Business: Report from the Achievement Council* (Oakland, Calif.: The Achievement Council, 1988, unpublished manuscript).

7. M. L. Oliver, C. Rodriguez, and R. A. Mickelson, "Brown and Black in White: the Social Adjustment and Academic Performance of Chicano and Black Students in a Predominantly White University," *The Urban Review*, 17, No. 2 (1985): 3–24.

8. S. Fordham and J. U. Ogbu, "Black Students' School Success: Coping with the Burden of 'Acting White,'" *The Urban Review*, 18, No. 3 (1986): 176–206.

9. A. R. Jensen, "How Much Can We Boost IQ and Scholastic Achievement?" *Harvard Educational Review*, 39 (1969): 1–123.

10. F. Erickson and J. Mohatt, "Cultural Organization of Participant Structure in Two Classrooms of Indian Students," in *Doing the Ethnography of Schooling: Educational Anthropology in Action*, ed. G. D. Spindler (New York: Holt, 1982): 132–175; S. U. Philips, "Commentary: Access to Power and Maintenance of Ethnic Identity as Goals of Multi-Cultural Education," *Anthropology and Education Quarterly*, 7, No. 4 (1976): 30–32; S. U. Philips, *The Invisible Culture: Communication in Classroom and Community on the Warm Springs Indian Reservation* (New York: Longman, 1983).

11. P. Bohannan, *Justice and Judgement among the Tiv* (London: Oxford University Press, 1957), 4; Ogbu, *The Next Generation*.

12. Bohannan, *Justice and Judgment*, 5.

13. Ogbu, *The Next Generation*.

14. Gibson, *Accommodation Without Assimilation*; Ogbu, *The Next Generation*.

15. Suarez-Orozco, *In Pursuit of a Dream*.

16. John U. Ogbu, "Cultural Discontinuities and Schooling," *Anthropology and Education Quarterly*, 13, No. 4 (1982): 290–307.

17. G. P. Castile and G. Kushner (eds.), *Persistent Peoples: Cultural Enclaves in Perspective* (Tucson: University of Arizona Press, 1981); G. A. DeVos, "Essential Elements of Caste: Psychological Determination in Structural Theory," in *Japan's Invisible Race: Caste in Culture and Personality*, ed. G. A. DeVos and H. Wagatsuma (Berkeley: University of California Press, 1967): 332–384; DeVos, "Ethnic Persistence"; E. H. Spicer, "The Process of Cultural Enclavement in

Middle America," *36th Congress of International de Americanistas*, Seville, 3 (1966): 267–279; DeVos, "Ethnic Persistence"; E. H. Spicer, "Persistent Cultural Systems: A Comparative Study of Identity Systems that Can Adapt to Contrasting Environments," *Science,* 174 (1971): 795–800.

18. V. Green, "Blacks in the United States: The Creation of an Enclaving People?" in *Persistent Peoples: Cultural Enclaves in Perspective*, 69–77.

19. DeVos, "Essential Elements of Caste"; John U. Ogbu, *Understanding Community Forces Affecting Minority Students' Academic Achievement* (Oakland, Calif.; The Achievement Council, 1984, unpublished manuscript).

20. DeVos, *Ethnic Persistence*.

21. Gibson, *Accommodation Without Assimilation*.

22. Suarez-Orozco, *In Pursuit of a Dream*.

23. John U. Ogbu, "Variability in Minority School Performance: A Problem in Search of an Explanation," *Anthropology and Education Quarterly,* 18, No. 4 (1987): 312–334.

24. H. M. Bond, *The Education of the Negro in the American Social Order* (New York: Octagon, 1966); R. Kluger, *Simple Justice* (New York: Vintage Books, 1977); John U. Ogbu, *Minority Education and Caste*; M. Weinberg, *A Chance to Learn: A History of Race and Education in the United States* (New York: Cambridge University Press, 1977).

25. M. A. Gibson, "The School Performance of Immigrant Minorities: A Comparative View," *Anthropology and Education Quarterly,* 18, No. 4 (1987): 262–275; Eun-Young Kim, *Folk Theory and Cultural Model Among Korean Immigrants in the U.S.: Explanation for Immigrants' Economic Life and Children's Education/Schooling* (Department of Anthropology: University of California, Berkeley, Special Project, 1987, unpublished manuscript); M. M. Suarez-Orozco, "Becoming Somebody: Central American Immigrants in U.S. Inner-City Schools," *Anthropology and Education Quarterly,* 18, No. 4 (1987): 287–299; C. Ong, *The Educational Attainment of the Chinese in America* (Department of Anthropology, University of California, Berkeley, Special Project, 1976, unpublished manuscript).

26. Suarez-Orozco, "Becoming Somebody"; Suarez- Orozco, *In Pursuit of a Dream*.

27. Gibson, *Accommodation Without Assimilation*.

28. Ogbu, "Cultural Discontinuities and Schooling."

29. John U. Ogbu, "Origins of Human Competence: A Cultural-Ecological Perspective," *Child Development,* 52 (1981): 423–429; John U. Ogbu, "A Cultural Ecology of Competence Among Inner-City Blacks," in *Beginnings: Social and Affective Development of Black Children*, ed. M. B. Spencer et al. (Hillsdale, N.J.: Lawrence Erlbaum Associates, 1985); Ogbu, "Variability in Minority School Performance."

30. A. Bouie, *Student Perceptions of Behavior and Misbehavior in the School Setting: An Exploratory Study and Discussion* (San Francisco: Far West Labora-

204     *John U. Ogbu*

tory for Educational Research and Development, 1981); Ogbu, *The Next Generation*.

31. M. L. Wong, *Education Versus Sports* (University of California, Berkeley, Special Project, 1987, unpublished manuscript).

32. Ibid.

33. Fordham and Ogbu, "Black Students' School Success"; F. A. Petroni, "'Uncle Toms': White Stereotypes in the Black Movement," *Human Organization* 29, No. 4 (1970): 260–266; M. Semons, *The Salience of Ethnicity at a Multiethnic Urban High School* (University of California, Berkeley, Graduate School of Education, 1987, unpublished doctoral dissertation).

34. DeVos, "Essential Elements of Caste."

35. Petroni, "'Uncle Toms.'"

36. John U. Ogbu, "Diversity and Equity in Public Education: Community Forces and Minority School Adjustment and Performance," in *Policies For America's Public Schools: Teachers, Equity, and Indicators*, ed. R. Haskins and D. MacRae (Norwood, N.J.: ABLEX, 1988): 127–170.

37. S. Fordham, *Black Student School Success as Related to Fictive Kinship* (Final Report to the National Institute of Education, Washington, D.C., 1985).

38. Ibid; Ogbu, "A Cultural Ecology."

39. Fordham and Ogbu, "Black Students' School Success."

40. Ogbu, "Diversity and Equity."

41. Ogbu, *The Next Generation*; Ogbu, *Understanding Community Forces*; Ogbu, "Variability in Minority School Performance"; Ogbu, "Diversity and Equity."

42. S. Fordham, "Racelessness as a Factor in Black Students' School Success: A Pragmatic Strategy or Pyrrhic Victory?" *Harvard Educational Review*, 58, No. 1 (1988): 54–84.

43. R. L. Haynes, *Minority Strategies for Success* (Department of Anthropology, University of California, Berkeley, Special Project, 1985, unpublished manuscript); Fordham, *Black Student School Success*.

44. H. D. Ellis and S. N. Newman, "Gowsher, Ivy- Leaguer, Hustler, Conservative, Mackman, and Continental: A Funcational Analysis of Six Ghetto Roles," in *The Culture of Poverty: A Critique*, ed. E. B. Leacock (New York: Simon and Schuster): 293–314, 304.

45. E. Perkins, *Home is a Dirty Street* (Chicago: Third World Press, 1975): 41.

46. Ibid., 42.

47. J. Mitchell, "Reflections of a Black Social Scientist: Some Struggles, Some Doubts, Some Hopes," *Harvard Educational Review*, 52, No. 1 (1982): 27–44.

48. Fordham and Ogbu, "Black Students' School Success."

Chapter 10

# *American Realities: Poverty, Economy, and Education*

## INTRODUCTION

It is almost impossible to pick up an issue of the most popular journals in education, to read our daily newspapers, or to listen to the statements made by federal, state, and local education officials without being confronted with the problem of dropouts. For many officials, especially those who are worried about our economic future, the claims seem to look like the following: if students didn't drop out there would be almost no unemployment and poverty in our inner cities; there would be better-paying and more fulfilling jobs awaiting them; the country as a whole would recover its economic productivity and competitiveness; and, finally, the norms and skills the students would learn in school would prepare them to be productive and responsible citizens in the rosy economic future that would result. First solve the dropout problem in schools and we will go a long way in solving the social and economic problems in local communities. So goes much of the accepted litany. Thus, fix the educational system and we have fixed just about everything else.

Yet, so much space is devoted to dropouts, and so many of the criticisms of our educational system are based on them, that we may be in danger of losing the ability to locate the issue in a more critical appraisal of its larger political and economic context. Although placing the spotlight on school dropouts is not totally a form of "educational hype," the insistent focus on it as largely (and often only) an educational problem—one that can be solved by small increments in funding, relatively minor changes in educational policies and practices, or limited programs of business and school "cooperation"—can ultimately lead us to misrecognize the depth of the issue. It can also make it nearly impossible for us to generate policies in the larger social arena that will make it possible for all of the hard work educators and others are putting in to actually succeed.

My aim here is to have us take much more seriously than we have been apt to the fact that focusing on the issue of dropouts as primarily an educational problem, and thus one that has primarily an educational solution, is *not* part of the solution but is itself part of the problem. The assumption that we will find long-term answers to the dropout dilemma and to the realities of poverty and unemployment by keeping our attention within the school is largely wrong. Lasting answers will require a much more searching set of economic questions and a considerably more extensive restructuring of our social commitments. Further, they will need to be accompanied by the democratization of our accepted way of distributing and controlling jobs, benefits, education, and power. Until we take this larger economic and social context as seriously as it deserves, we shall simply be unable to adequately respond to the needs of youth in this country. In order to more fully understand this, we shall need to examine what this context actually looks like.


## AMERICAN REALITIES

Behind the rhetoric of economic recovery is another reality. This is a reality of crisis, of an economy that increases the gap between rich and poor, black and brown and white. It is driven by a set of policies in which the real lives of millions of people count less than "competitiveness," "efficiency," and above all profit maximization. We live in a time when economic concentration is reflected in our economic, political, and cultural lives. Although this may help the affluent, many commentators have raised serious doubts about its effects on those who have historically been less well served by our political and economic structures.

Carnoy, Shearer, and Rumberger put it in this way: "Adam Smith notwithstanding, profit maximization by large, economically powerful, private corporations has not maximized the public good." The investment and employment decisions that business has made have in large part generated "dislocation, discrimination, declining real wages, high unemployment, pollution, poor transportation systems, and run down crime-ridden cities."[1] These are not costed out when the corporate sector makes these decisions, but these social costs *are* borne by the public. The effects on communities, on the health and welfare of the bulk of the population, and on our cultural lives and education have been enormous.[2]

For those educators interested in working on a set of policies and practices that would have more democratic outcomes than these, one of the first steps is to gain a more adequate picture of the reality of this crisis. To do this, it is essential that we focus directly on the economy. Other national leaders, educators, and industrialists have, of course, urged us to do the same thing. In report after report, we are told that we must make clearer linkages between schooling and the economy. The reason there is unemployment, poor motivation, a lack of competitiveness, and so forth is that schools aren't teaching work skills and the "basics" and are not as closely connected to economic priorities as they should be. Schools become inefficient and lead nowhere. Students drop out. And the cycle continues.

As I have argued elsewhere, the conservative and neoconservative position that stands behind these calls for redefining the goals of the educational system into those primarily of industry and the Right simply acts to export the crisis in the economy onto the schools.[3] Here I want to go further, to look more directly at what the current and future economy seems to have in store for us. No serious discussion of dropouts can go on unless we situate it in the context of what is happening outside the school. In a relatively brief chapter, it will not be possible to deal with all aspects of our economy. What I shall do here is select certain aspects that tend to highlight the current and future prospects of the paid labor market. I shall pay particular attention to the structures of poverty in the United States and to the emerging trends in job loss and job creation in the economy. In the process, I want to focus on some of the class, race, and gender dynamics that have played such a major role in structuring the opportunities for youth employment. Finally, I want to relate some of the experiences that many youth have on the job, experiences that should make us question our notions of success.

In a series of previous studies, I have drawn a picture of the structure of inequalities in American society. Let me briefly summarize these findings.[4] It is estimated that in 1985 a poor family was at least 5 percent less well off than in 1981, whereas a middle-class family was 14 percent better off. A rich family showed a 30 percent gain in its already large advantage. These figures, even if taken by themselves, indicate a marked redistribution of income and benefits from the poor to the rich.[5] They are made even more significant by the fact that the middle class itself may actually be shrinking as the numbers at the extremes grow. We have more and more a "double peaked" economic distribution as the numbers of well-to-do and poor increase.

These inequalities—though growing—have been around for quite some time. In the United States, the bottom 20 percent of the population receives a smaller percentage of total after-tax income than the comparable group in Japan, Sweden, Australia, Norway, the Netherlands, France, West Germany, and a number of other nations. This gap is not being reduced at all within the United States. In fact, in the past three decades, the gap between the bottom 20 percent of U.S. families and the top 5 percent has nearly doubled. The percentage of families that received less than half of the median national income actually increased between 1950 to 1977. If we again take the early 1950s as our starting point, in 1951 the top 20 percent of the population received 41.6 percent of the gross national income and the bottom percentile received only 5 percent. When we look at more current figures, in 1981 for instance, the bottom 20 percent still received the very same 5 percent, but the top 20 percent had "captured a 41.9 percent share."[6] Although these changes do not seem overwhelming, the amount of money this entails is vast and is certainly indicative of a trend favoring the top 20 percent.

Yet this is not all. One out of every seven Americans lives in poverty, as does one out of every five children under the age of six. And both of these groups seem to be growing, as I shall indicate later. More than one-quarter of all Hispanics and more than one-third of all Afro-Americans live below the poverty line. "In 1981, even before the major Reagan cuts, more than 40 percent of families living below the poverty line received no food stamps, medicaid, housing subsidies, or low price school lunches." Even the government has estimated that the diet of those living at the official poverty level is so deficient "that it is suitable only for 'temporary or emergency use.'"[7]

The poverty rate is basically an indicator of the state of the economy.[8] The effects of the deteriorating economic conditions of the last decade are clearly visible in the fact that from 1978 to 1983 "pre-transfer poverty" (that is, the poverty rate before government assistance is computed in) rose from 20.2 percent to 24.2 percent.[9] In the same period, even when we factor in all transfer payments, the poverty rate climbed from approximately 11 percent to well over 15 percent. Much of this effect was the result of the decline in the value of the transfers poor people received.[10] Put simply, although the poverty rate did show a real decline from 1959 to 1969 and showed some modest reduction until 1978, it has turned up sharply in the 1980s.[11] Rather than getting better, for those on the bottom it is getting much worse. This may be accepted by many Americans because of the Right's increasing ability to create a more selfish society, one in which our sense of the common good has begun to whither.[12]

Gary Burtless paints a less than sanguine picture of this situation.

> In view of American's deep seated beliefs, there are scant grounds for optimism that the lot of this nation's poor will soon be radically improved. The steep rise in social welfare spending between 1960 and 1980 substantially raised the well-being of many poor families, and these improvements ought not be lightly dismissed. But much of the increased spending was concentrated on the lucky poor insured by our social insurance programs—the aged, the infirm, and the insured unemployed . . . In the recent past, government initiative to reduce poverty has come to a halt and may even have been reversed.[13]

Gender, race, and age inequalities, as well, are so pervasive as to be almost painful to recount. Women working full-time outside the home earn less than two-thirds of what men working full-time earn. Black women working full-time earn only 53 percent and Hispanic women only 40 percent of what men earn. In 1980, one in three women working full-time outside the home earned less than $7,000 a year. In the same year, women with college degrees averaged only 56.5 percent of the income men with high school diplomas earned. In 1981, nearly 53 percent of the families headed by black women and over 27 percent of those headed by white women were officially poor, and more recent data indicate a worsening of this situation. If we consider the elderly poor, 72 percent are women, and, in 1980, of the elderly black women living alone, 82 percent were near or below poverty.[14]

Black and brown men earn 80 percent of the income of white men with comparable levels of education and of similar age. "More than 60 percent of black men and 50 percent of all Hispanic men are clustered in low-paying job classifications."[15] Access to comparable jobs is just about blocked and seems to be worsening given current economic conditions and policies.

Finally, examining unemployment makes the picture of this part of our economy even more graphic. Some econometric measures indicate that the unequal cumulative impact of unemployment on minorities and women actually doubled between 1951 and 1981. The data on unemployment rates tell a similar story. Though current figures are lower than the nearly 21 percent for blacks and 9.7 percent for whites in 1982, the differential has not lessened. For white teenagers, the unemployment rate was approximately 25 percent; for black youth it was a staggering 50 percent, and even higher in many urban areas. For these and other reasons, "the income gap between white and black families has actually widened . . . since 1970, as black median income dropped from 66 percent to 65 percent of white median income."[16]

## THE CURRENT STRUCTURING OF PAID EMPLOYMENT

The issue of unemployment is of considerable importance here and needs further discussion, especially its relation to the racial and sexual divisions in American society that I just described. Certain trends are truly disturbing.

The historical changes are striking. Although the labor force participation of white men declined from 82 percent in 1940 to 76 percent in 1980 (in large part because of a drop in participation by white men over the age of fifty-five), for black men the story is dramatically different. In 1940, 84 percent were in the paid labor force. By 1980, only 67 percent participated in the labor force. The figures become even more graphic if we increase the time span. In 1930, 80 percent of all black men were employed; in 1983 this had fallen to 56 percent. This, of course, has connections to the transformation of agricultural labor in the United States. The decline was particularly steep for blacks aged twenty-four or younger.[17]

Though bad enough, this does not tell the entire story. When one combines the joblessness with the high rates of mortality among black men, and includes the rate of incarceration (the United States seems to have decided to deal with poverty by jailing a large percentage of people of color, many of whose crimes are directly related to the economic and housing conditions and the patterns of racial segregation they experience), the proportion of black men in anything near stable employment is even lower than the current labor force or unemployment statistics indicate.[18] This has had a dramatic impact on family structure and on the sense of a future among black youth.

The Center for the Study of Social Policy has projected that if current economic trends continue, by the end of this century we may witness 70 percent of all black families headed by single women and less than 30 percent of all black men engaged in paid work.[19] This condition is best stated by Ellwood and Summers in their discussion of the employment possibilities of black youth: "By every conceivable measure the labor market situation for young blacks is bad and getting worse." They go on to say, "The magnitude of the problem cannot be overstated: in 1980, before the recession exerted a major effect, only one out-of-school black youth in three had any job."[20] Today's figures are no better. Of all out-of-school youth of color living in nonfarm areas, only 35 percent were engaged in paid work. This is vastly lower than the figure for similar white youths, 62 percent of whom have paid work.[21]

Once people of color are indeed hired, however, their rates of advancement continue to be slower. They are also considerably more vulnerable to job loss during periods of economic retrenchment. The supposedly booming "new" service economy has not changed this situation in any appreciable way. The paid employment patterns show the usual positions: the secondary labor market dominated by low-paying jobs with little or no benefits, little job security, and non-unionized states. And many of these jobs are less than full-time.[22]

This picture highlights an important point. Unemployment rates are differentiated by what kind of paid job one has had. In all Western countries, manual and "unskilled" workers suffer much greater unemployment than workers with professional and nonmanual occupations. Sex and race play a major part here, as do the international division of labor and what is called "capital flight," where companies shift their plants from country to country seeking cheaper and ununionized workers in the Third World. Women's paid work is also concentrated in the secondary labor market in the same way as minority paid employment. In fact, in all Western industrialized nations the unemployment rate is lower for men than women. And these differences may actually be understated, since "the discouraged worker effect" tends to have a greater impact on women, especially in times of economic decline.[23]

One last and increasingly significant element in this situation needs to be noted, especially since it bears heavily on the issue of dropouts. Since 1973, a particular feature of unemployment has been growing. This is the disproportionate effect of unemployment on potential young workers. In the United States, the youth unemployment rate in 1984 was 13.3 percent, whereas the rate for all workers was 7.4 percent. In the United Kingdom, nearly 22 percent of youth were unemployed compared with 13 percent for all workers. This picture presents a major ideological as well as economic problem. For a substantial portion of the new generation of youth what is being offered is a future with no long-term prospect of earning one's living outside of meager welfare benefits. "Neither diligence and discipline, nor mass consumption, are likely to rise out of that experience."[24] The concentration of unemployment among the young has not been seen in other previous economic crises. Its social consequences will undoubtedly be with us for years to come.[25]

Thus, it is clear that the burden of unemployment falls unequally across age, race, and sex groups. Persons of color, women, and the young are the most affected.[26] *Since fully 70 percent of working-class positions in the United States are now held by women, people of color, and youth*, and since these groups dominate the lowest paid and least autonomous positions in the economy,[27] the ways in which our economy creates divisions in employment and unemployment and its concomitant generation and exacerbation of social tensions should give us pause.

These unemployment statistics are very deceptive, however. The measured unemployment rate does not capture the severity of the problem. It does not reflect alterations in the *duration* of joblessness. Thus, some surveys in Western capitalist nations have documented that the average length of unemployment rose from seven weeks in 1970 to over forty-five weeks in 1984. "Over one-half of those who were unemployed in 1984 had been without jobs for more than six months compared with fewer than 7 percent in 1970." Thus, most often these statistics on unemployment refer to people who are still unemployed and "relate only to their current period of unemployment."[28]

Just as significantly, the usual measures of unemployment do not register what has been called the "hidden unemployed," those people who have become so discouraged that they no longer actively seek paid work given the constant negative experiences of finding little or nothing. It is not unusual to find that there are nearly as many individuals in this category as in the official unemployment statistics.[29] When the ability to only find part-time work is added in to this, we would have to come close to doubling the official rates at a minimum if we were to have an accurate picture of what is really going on.

Yet, even this does not tell all of the story. As I noted, the differential rates and kind of employment available between men and women and between whites and people of color make it clear that the sexual and racial divisions of labor structure the experiences of groups of people in markedly different ways.

Finally, simply having paid work does not tell us what changes have occurred in the *kinds* of work people do. For instance, it is a qualitatively different kind of job to work as a janitor making minimum wage when one worked before in a steel mill for $15.00 an hour. Yes, one is employed. But the jobs available, the rate of pay, the social relations on the job, the autonomy, the respect, and so on are radically different. The lowering of the official unemployment rate may hide what is really going on in truly significant ways.

## THE FUTURE ECONOMY

The previous section gave an indication of how the economy and the paid labor market now looks if we *reposition* ourselves and look at it not from the top down but from the bottom up, from the perspective of women, people of color, and youth. (It is important to state that these groups are not, of course, mutually exclusive.) Given this present structure, what does the future hold in store in terms of the paid labor market for youth who will make decisions about their schooling?

We need, of course, to be very careful about generalizing too readily from the economic data I shall review in this section. I am reminded of two rather biting lines about economists: "If all economists were laid end to end, they would still not reach a conclusion" and "An economist is an expert who will know tomorrow why the things he predicted yesterday didn't happen today."[30] Even with these cautions, however, there are certain tendencies that can be seen. Among the most important for discussions about dropouts are the long-term trends in job loss and job creation.

In the manufacturing sector, approximately 3 million new jobs are expected to be added by 1990. However, from 1990 to 1995 this sector is likely to see a major decline in its rate of growth, falling to about 1.3 million. Technological changes and pressures to increase productivity while limiting employment and lowering wages will limit job expansion. It is in the service sector that most new positions will be found.

This sector broadly includes transportation, communications, public utilities, trade, finance, real estate, and other services. It is projected to account for fully 75 percent of all new jobs created between 1982 and 1985.[31]

It is these so-called other services that will continue to grow the fastest in the next one and one-half decades. Medical care, business services, "professional" services, hotel services, and "personal" services will encompass one out of every three new jobs, and manufacturing will produce only one out of every six.[32]

The Bureau of Labor Statistics develops projections for 1,500 individual occupations. The top ten are shown in Table 10.1[33] and are projected to account for one-fourth of the total employment change in the United states for the period of 1982–1995. One notices that the top five occupations—custodians, cashiers, secretaries, office clericals, and salesclerks—in general do not require high levels of education.[34]

The ten occupations with the fastest growth rates during the period are most often linked to the emerging technological restructuring of parts of our economy or with medical services. Table 10.2 documents these trends.[35] By and large, the occupations represented in these data require a good deal of skill and training and do signify the growing emergence of a technically sophisticated sector of the paid labor market. Yet, with this said, it is of great importance that we examine this latter table carefully. For although the fastest growth rates occur in these occupations, *taken together they constitute less than 4 percent of the total em-*

Table 10.1
Ten Occupations with Largest Absolute Job Growth in the United States

| Occupation | Change in Total Employment (in Thousands) | Percent Change | Percent of Total Job Growth |
|---|---|---|---|
| Building Custodians | 779 | 27.5 | 3.0 |
| Cashiers | 744 | 47.4 | 2.9 |
| Secretaries | 719 | 29.5 | 2.8 |
| General Clerks, office | 696 | 29.6 | 2.7 |
| Salesclerks | 685 | 23.5 | 2.7 |
| Nurses, registered | 642 | 48.9 | 2.5 |
| Waiters and waitresses | 562 | 33.8 | 2.2 |
| Teachers, kindergarten and elementary | 511 | 37.4 | 2.0 |
| Truckdrivers | 425 | 26.5 | 1.7 |
| Nursing aide and orderlies | 423 | 34.8 | 1.7 |

Table 10.2
Ten Fastest Growing Occupations in the United States

| Occupation | Change in Total Employment (in Thousands) | Percent Growth | Percent of Total Job Growth |
|---|---|---|---|
| Computer service technicians | 53 | 97 | 0.21 |
| Legal assistants | 43 | 94 | 0.17 |
| Computer systems analysts | 217 | 85 | 0.85 |
| Computer programmers | 205 | 77 | 0.80 |
| Computer operators | 160 | 76 | 0.62 |
| Office machine repairers | 40 | 72 | 0.16 |
| Physical therapy assistants | 26 | 68 | 0.09 |
| Electrical engineers | 209 | 65 | 0.82 |
| Civil engineering technicians | 23 | 64 | 0.09 |
| Peripheral electronic data processing equipment operators | 31 | 64 | 0.12 |

*ployment growth in the entire nation.*[36] Thus, the comparison leads to a less sanguine understanding of where the bulk of the paid employment will be. Even with the rapidity of growth in high-tech-related jobs, the kinds of work that will be increasingly available to a large portion of the American population will not be highly skilled, technically elegant positions. Just the opposite will be the case. The labor market will instead be increasingly dominated by low-paid, repetitive work in the retail trade and service sectors. This is made strikingly clear by one fact. There will be more janitorial jobs created—approximately 779,000—by 1995 than all of the new computer service technicians, programmers, systems analysts, and computer operators *combined.*[37]

Yet it is not only job creation and job loss in the lower-paying areas of the service sector of the economy that will be of concern. The middle class will itself begin to fell the impact of these processes. One knowledgeable economist puts it this way.

> Just as employers have an economic incentive to fragment jobs into component parts in order to reduce labor costs, they also have an economic incentive to automate jobs that pay the highest wages. Thus expert systems and other sophisticated technologies are more likely to eliminate more skilled, high-salaried jobs than less-skilled, low-salary ones. The increased use of these devices will create new jobs in industries where they are manufactured and new jobs related to their use and maintenance. But recent employment projections for the U.S. suggest that few new jobs will be created in these areas.[38]

As I have argued elsewhere, and as others have maintained as well, even those high-tech occupations that have previously required considerable skill—computer programming offers a good example—are increasingly being subject to deskilling, less autonomy, and lower pay. This may be related to the "feminization" of many of these jobs, as well as to the tendency to mechanize and standardize them.[39] Unfortunately, given the power of patriarchal assumptions and relations in our society, the paid and unpaid labor of women have historically been subject to significant pressures of rationalization, proletarianization, loss of autonomy and control, and lowered respect.[40] Thus, other occupations that have traditionally been seen as largely "women's jobs" will be affected by the technological restructuring that is occurring. Clerical work, banking services, telecommunications, and so forth will all see the effects of these processes of deskilling.[41]

Yet no discussion of what is happening to "women's work" is complete unless we seriously face an issue of critical import in any analysis of the economy. We need to remember that young women face the prospects of a *dual* labor market. They are trained for the paid labor market outside the home and for unpaid labor within the home. Too often, discussions of dropouts, youth employment and unemployment, and of the economic structures surrounding the school focus totally on paid work. This is a serious deficiency and vitiates much of the power of these analyses since they cannot adequately deal with the realities which young women face every day, not only in making decisions about schooling and paid work, but in structuring the experiences of so much of their lives. These analyses, hence, tend to be all too often based on a lack of understanding of the importance, both in terms of identity and in terms of the economy, of the labor of caring that women do. Their logic may tacitly reflect patriarchal assumptions. Although I cannot go into detail here about this subject, it is essential that we begin to more fully understand not only the effects of the political economy of capitalism on the lives and futures of youth but the political economy of patriarchal relations as well.[42]

## EXPERIENCING PAID WORK

Given what I have shown here about what the future holds in store, it should be clear that for a large portion of youth—especially those who are poor or working class, many young women, and persons of color—certain kinds of paid jobs will be all that they will find. These jobs will tend to be concentrated even more in the secondary labor market. They will be characterized by low pay, poor working conditions by and large, few benefits, and an unskilled or deskilled labor process.[43] One might want to question why they would rush to jobs like these in the first place or why they would see a relationship between schooling and the supposedly marvelous future of paid and unpaid work.

This issue is made more poignant in the comments—which are repeated time and again by others in similar circumstances—of young men and women who have been able to find a path to a first paid job in the secondary sector. The deskilled nature of the paid jobs available can be seen in a quote from a young woman who after only three days on a clerical job already felt the burden of how her future work would be: "It was very boring and I [spent all] three days [doing] photocopying. It's not right, that they make one person do the same job all the time. I should've been switched round with some of the others. I wouldn't want to do that for a job all the time."[44] Another student put it even more graphically in describing a low-paid building maintenance job in which he was finally placed: "I was treated like slave labor. I hated it and left after a day. They were . . . telling me to do this and not doing it themselves, so I told 'em to fuck off and went home in the afternoon and didn't go back again."[45] One final quote may illuminate the reality of these jobs: "I was cooking in kitchens and it was boring. You couldn't talk to the others much because they (machines) were organized in separate sections and you cooked in one section or another. It was stupid really. They didn't have to work it like that. They just did."[46]

What is interesting about these perceptions is that each of these individuals looked forward to leaving school and finally getting paid work.[47] Yet the experience of the job was so boring and often so demeaning that it was clear that the dream of finally becoming autonomous and getting the economic rewards associated with a paid job were shattered by the reality of the workplace itself. In all these comments, one is reminded of John Masefield's lines:

> To get the whole world out of bed,
> and washed, and dressed, and warmed, and fed,
> to work, and back to bed again,
> Believe me, Saul, costs worlds of pain.[48]

The future world of paid and unpaid work that so many of our students will face, the structures of inequality, and the realities of poverty that they will experience and that are growing should make us pay much

closer attention to whether we can solve our educational problems
without dealing with the root causes of our dilemmas. This is a point I
want to highlight in my concluding section.

## PLACING THE BLAME WHERE IT BELONGS

To attack the schools for the decline of "excellence" and for the
economic crisis is easy. But to deal with the processes that actually
cause this decline is much harder. As I hinted at the end of the prior
section, without dealing with the social causes of dropouts and the
larger issue of educational differentiation in general, without taking
seriously the historic dominance of structures of class, race, and gender
stratification that are so fundamental a part of American society inside
and outside the school, we simply will fail.[49]

We must resist the urge to place the blame on the educational system for the problems of our economic decline, for our lack of economic
competitiveness, for unemployment, and so on. If we take two para-
digm cases of industries that have declined over the past years—steel
and automobile—these declines may be due much more to managerial
failure and conscious decisions to deindustrialize than to things such
as skill shortages. "These examples might lead to reforming business
schools or investment practices" or to national economic policies that
are considerably more democratic both in planning and outcomes, but
one thing they do not provide is any consistent justification for blaming
the school for the economic disarray we face.[50]

What are the reasons that educational restructuring is given so
much importance in dealing with unemployment and underemployment? One reason is the government's need for legitimacy. It must *be
seen* to be doing something about these problems.[51] Reforming education is not only widely acceptable and relatively unthreatening, but just
as crucially, "its success or failure will not be obvious in the short-term."
Second is what is partly a Social Darwinist principle which distances
the economy as a major cause of its own troubles. "The assertion that
unemployment is due to the lack of skills of the labor force helps sustain a belief in the basic virtues of the economic system. If *only* the individual had studied harder, or was willing to take lower wages, the inequalities in society arising with unemployment could be eliminated!"[52]

Even though the American public "may find it reassuring to believe
that poor children will enjoy the same economic prospects as everyone
else if only they learn to read and do their sums, this reassuring belief is
wrong." In fact, when one examines the instances where students from

different economic backgrounds do equally as well on such measures as widely used standardized tests, this supposed equality of achievement only reduced the difference in the earnings they made as adults by one-third. The issue then may not revolve as much around school achievement as it does in the socioeconomic relations and structures that organize the society.[53]

It is quite possible, in fact, that the narrowing of school achievement differences between the poor and the nonpoor will make very little difference on poverty or inequality. We may have a situation in which credential inflation creates what is known as a queuing system in which advantaged groups maintain their own positions. The level of educational achievement and the credential thay may once have qualified someone for a specific type of employment is "discounted." The credential needed for the job is raised and the previous required achievement level is only useful to open the door to a lesser-paying job.[54] The issue of dropping out needs to be considered in this light.

We will need to face the fact that economic disparities that are "based on race, sex and family headship are extremely difficult to reduce." Though it is essential that we do focus on those areas of our educational system that need to be restructured, securing answers to the problem of dropouts will require more than short-term interventions such as limited training programs, counseling, and placement services. It requires long-term changes in the structure of labor markets, "in the provision of transitional income, employment, and in kind support." It involves expanding educational opportunities and large-scale and continued funding for such educational programs. Finally, and perhaps most importantly, it requires a growing economy that has meaningful jobs at the end on one's school experience.[55]

Whether this can be accomplished given our current economic assumptions and given the conservative restoration is questionable. But there are sets of progressive economic and social policies that have been articulated that could be more than a little helpful in moving us toward a more democratically controlled economy, polity, and educational system. In particular, the work of Nove, Carnoy, Shearer and Rumberger, Raskin, and Bastian deserve much greater attention from educators concerned with the relationship between education and the economy.[56]

One transitional goal should be to add one more inalienable right to every American: the right to a decent job.[57] This would, of course, require both that we work toward a fundamental restructuring of our economic priorities and that we challenge the Social Darwinist assumptions that stand behind so much of our economic system. (You know—He got poor or unemployed the old fashioned way. He earned it.) The poor and the under-and unemployed didn't "earn it." The shattering of their hopes and dreams, the disintegration of their families, communities, and educational institutions, the despair and struggles, are a "gift" from our economy. This is one time a gift should be sent back, unopened.

As I have documented in this chapter, by confining our analysis of dropouts to the internal qualities of our educational system we will miss the economic realities that surround the school and provide the present and future context in which our youth will function. It would not be an overstatement to say that our kind of economy—with its growing inequalities, its structuring of what are more and more alienating, deskilled, and meaningless jobs, its emphasis on profit no matter what the social cost—"naturally" *produces* the conditions that lead to dropping out. The phenomenon of the dropout is not an odd aberration that randomly arises in our school system. It is structurally generated, created out of the real and unequal relations of economic, political, and cultural resources and power that organize this society. Solutions to it will require that we no longer hide ourselves from this reality. The first step is looking at our economy honestly and recognizing how the class, race, and gender relations that structure it operate.

What should guide us in dealing with these dilemmas is the political principle of *the common good, not simply profit. This principle asserts that "no inhuman act should be used as a short cut to a better day" and that any program in education, in politics, in health and welfare, in the economy, or elsewhere must be evaluated "against the likelihood that it will result in linking equity, sharing, personal dignity, security, freedom and caring."*[58] *Current economic and social policies fall well short of this. The result is untold misery for millions of people and a future that is more than a little bleak for many of the youth of this nation. Perhaps we could begin by asking ourselves a question that has a long history in the tradition of democratic movements in the United States. Whose side are you on?*

## NOTES

An earlier version of this paper was first presented to the Friday Seminar at the University of Wisconsin, Madison. I would like to thank the members of the seminar for their many helpful comments. Lois Weis also offered her usual perceptive suggestions on an earlier draft.

1. Martin Carnoy, Derek Shearer, and Russell Rumberger, *A New Social Contract* (New York: Harper and Row, 1983), p. 61.

2. For further discussion of this, see Michael W. Apple, *Teachers and Texts: A Political Economy of Class and Gender Relation in Education* (New York: Routledge and Kegan Paul, 1986) and Michael W. Apple, *Education and Power* (New York: Routledge and Kegan Paul, 1982).

3. Apple, *Teachers and Texts.* I have written extensively on the importance of a "relational" and nonreductive approach to the connections between education and the larger society, and have warned us not to be overly economistic in our analyses. However, we need to be reminded that even with these arguments, economic dynamics are among the most powerful forces in capitalism. For further discussion of this nonreductive program, see Apple, *Education and Power.*

4. These data are taken from a more extensive discussion in Apple, *Teachers and Texts.*

5. Carnoy, Shearer, and Rumberger, *A New Social Contract,* pp. 22–23.

6. Joshua Cohen and Joel Rogers, *On Democracy: Toward A Transformation of American Society* (New York: Penguin Books, 1983), p. 30.

7. Ibid. p. 31. The official poverty income level and rate fluctuate, of course, and are manipulated for political purposes.

8. David T. Ellwood and Lawrence H. Summers, "Poverty in America," in Sheldon H. Danziger and Daniel Weinberg, eds., *Fighting Poverty: What Works and What Doesn't* (Cambridge: Harvard University Press, 1986), p. 82.

9. Sheldon H. Danziger, Robert H. Haveman, and Robert D. Plotnick, "Antipoverty Policy: Effects on the Poor and the Nonpoor," in Danziger and Weinberg, eds., *Fighting Poverty,* p. 64.

10. Ibid., p. 69

11. Ellwood and Summers, "Poverty in America," p. 81.

12. See Michael W. Apple, "The Redefiniton of Equality in the Conservative Restoration," in Walter Secada, ed., *The Meaning of Equity in Education* (Philadelphia: Falmer Press, 1988).

13. Gary Burtless, "Public Spending for the Poor: Trends, Prospects, and Economic Limits," in Danzinger and Weinberg, eds., *Fighting Poverty, p. 48.*

14. Cohen and Rogers, *On Democracy,* pp. 31–32.

15. Ibid., p. 32.

16. Ibid.

17. William Julius Wilson and Kathryn M. Neckerman, "Poverty and Family Structure," in Danzinger and Weinberg, eds., *Fighting Poverty,* p. 252.

18. Ibid., p. 253.

19. Ibid., p. 259.

20. Ellwood and Summers, "Poverty in America," p. 99.

21. Ibid., p. 101.

22. Charles V. Hamilton and Dona C. Hamilton, "Social Policies, Civil Rights, and Poverty," in Danzinger and Weinberg, eds., *Fighting Poverty,* p. 307.

23. Francis Green and Bob Sutcliffe, *The Profit System: The Economics of Capitalism* (New York: Penguin Books, 1987), p. 321.

24. Ibid., pp. 321–322.

25. Paul Willis makes the provocative claim that high rates of youth unemployment will have ideological consequences. Since young men and women will not have paychecks, yet will still "hang out" in malls and shopping centers, they will consume products only with their eyes. This may subvert the basis of capitalism's wage accord with young laborers. The connection between consumption and the wage will be severed. The effect on patriarchal relations within working-class households will also be immense. See Paul Willis, "Youth Unemployment: Thinking the Unthinkable," unpublished paper, Wolverhampton, England, Wolverhampton Polytechnic, n.d.

26. Rebecca M. Blank and Alan S. Blinder, "Macroeconomics, Income Distribution, and Poverty," in Danzinger and Weinberg, eds. *Fighting Poverty*, p. 191.

27. Erik Olin Wright et al., "The American Class Structure," *American Sociological Review*, 47 (December 1982), 709–726.

28. Ronald Kutscher, "The Impact of Technology on Employment in the United States," in Gerald Burke and Russell Rumberger, eds., *The Future Impact of Technology on Work and Education* (Philadelphia: Falmer Press, 1987), p. 57.

29. Ibid. I have remained at the statistical level here, but it is important to keep reminding ourselves of the enormous social and emotional costs of being unemployed. No set of statistics can ever fully encompass the reality of these costs and of the lost lives they signify.

30. Donald N. McCloskey, *The Rhetoric of Economics* (Madison: The University of Wisconsin Press, 1985), p. xix.

31. Kutscher, "The Impact of Technology on Employment in the United States," p. 45.

32. Taken from ibid.

33. Ibid., p. 47.

34. Taken from ibid., p. 46. Many of these emerging jobs will be done by women and will be part-time, as well. This will not only lead to lower pay but to a situation in which companies will not have to pay benefits. Thus, the economic implications are found not only at the level of salary and working conditions, but at the level of support for health care, retirement, and so forth. The ultimate public cost may be immense.

35. Ibid., p. 48.

36. Ibid.

37. Russell Rumberger, "The Potential Impact of Technology on the Skill Requirements of Future Jobs," in Burke and Rumberger, eds., *The Future Impact of Technology on Work and Education*, p. 90.

38. Ibid.

39. See Apple, *Teachers and Texts*, and W. Norton Grubb, "Responding to the Constancy of Change: New Technologies and Future Demands on U.S. Education," in Burke and Rumberger, eds., *The Future Impact of Technology on Work and Education*, p. 122.

40. Apple, *Teachers and Texts*, especially Chapters 2 and 3.

41. Of course, women have organized and will continue to do so to counter

these threats and will often be successful in mediating and altering them. See Alice Kessler Harris, *Out To Work: A History of Wage-Earning Women in the United States* (New York: Oxford University Press, 1982).

42. See Michele Barrett, *Women's Oppression Today* (London: New Left Books, 1980). An excellent treatment of what young women experience in their paid and unpaid labor can be found in Christine Griffin, *Typical Girls* (London: Routledge and Kegan Paul, 1985). The issue of unpaid labor is linked to the wider question of identity. We may need a redefinition of work that is not tied into the capitalist economy, one in which the "labor of caring" that is often done by women is much more highly valued.

43. Chris Shilling, "Work Experience as a Contradictory Practice," *British Journal of Sociology of Education,* 8 (December, 1987) p. 22.

44. Ibid., p. 9.

45. Ibid.

46. Ibid., p. 14.

47. Ibid.

48. Quoted in Lilian Rubin, *Worlds of Pain* (New York: Basic Books, 1976), p. 14.

49. Grubb, "Responding to the Constancy of Change," p. 130.

50. Ibid., p. 120.

51. Gerald Burke, "Reforming the Structure and Finance of Education in Australia," in Burke and Rumberger, eds., *The Future Impact of Technology on Work and Education*, p. 180. On the government's need to maintain legitimacy, especially in times of crisis, see Apple, *Education and Power*.

52. Burke, "Reforming the Structure," pp. 180–181.

53. Christopher Jencks, "Comment," in Danziger and Weinberg, eds., *Fighting Poverty*, pp. 176–177.

54. Nathan Glazer, "Education and Training Programs and Poverty," in Danziger and Weinberg, eds., *Fighting Poverty*, p. 154.

55. Danziger, Haveman, and Plotnick, "Antipoverty Policy," p. 75.

56. Especially useful here are Alec Nove, *The Economics of Feasible Socialism* (Boston: George Allen and Unwin, 1983); Carnoy, Shearer, and Rumberger, *A New Social Contract*; Martin Carnoy and Derek Shearer, *Economic Democracy* (White Plains, N.Y.: M.E. Sharpe, 1980); and Marcus Raskin, *The Common Good* (New York: Routledge and Kegan Paul, 1986). For an interesting set of policies on education, see Ann Bastian, Norm Fruchter, Marilyn Gittell, Colin Greer, and Kenneth Haskins, *Choosing Democracy: The Case for Democratic Schooling* (Philadelphia: Temple University Press, 1986).

57. Hamilton and Hamilton, "Social Policies, Civil Rights, and Poverty," p. 311. As I noted in note 42, however, this requires a serious questioning of what *counts* as a job. Most definitons privilege male definitions and give less attention to the work involving caring and connectedness that women usually do. Thus, we may need to alter our very definitons of labor and support the labor of caring in a greater fashion both ideologically and economically.

58. Raskin, *The Common Good*, p. 8.

# Contributors

Michael W. Apple is Professor of Curriculum and Instruction and Educational Policy Studies at the University of Wisconsin, Madison.

Alan J. DeYoung is Associate Professor of Educational Policy Studies at the University of Kentucky.

Eleanor Farrar is Associate Professor of the Department of Educational Organization, Administration and Policy, State University of New York at Buffalo.

Michelle Fine is Associate Professor of Psychology in Education at the University of Pennsylvania.

Robert L. Hampel is Associate Professor of Education at the University of Delaware.

Walt Haney is Associate Professor and Senior Research Associate at the Center for the Study of Testing, Evaluation and Policy, Boston College.

Karen Huffman is Curriculum Coordinator in Braxton County High School, Sutton, West Virginia.

Amelia E. Kreitzer is a Research Associate at the Center for the Study of Testing, Evaluation and Policy, Boston College.

George F. Madaus is Professor of Education and Director of the Center for the Study of Testing, Evaluation and Policy, Boston College.

Fred M. Newmann is Professor of Curriculum and Instruction and Director of the Center for Effective Secondary Schools, University of Wisconsin at Madison.

John U. Ogbu is Professor of Anthropology at the University of California–Berkeley.

Hugh G. Petrie is Dean of the Graduate School of Education, State University of New York at Buffalo.

R. Patrick Solomon is with the Board of Education, City of Etobicoke, Ontario, Canada.

Charles Payne is Associate Professor in the Department of African American Studies, Northwestern University.

Mary Ellen Turner is a Dropout Consultant in Braxton County High School, Sutton, West Virginia.

Lois Weis is Professor of Sociology of Education and Associate Dean of the Graduate School of Education, State University of New York at Buffalo.

Gary G. Wehlage is Professor and Associate Director of the National Center on Effective Secondary Schools, University of Wisconsin, Madison.

Nancie Zane is with the Faculty of Education at the University of Pennsylvania.

# Index

Abortion, 98
Abuse, sexual. *See* Sexual abuse
Academic achievement, 14
  and black peer pressure, 83, 85
  of voluntary minorities, 195
  tests, 72, 131
  variable, among minorities, 182–83
Academic engagement, 10, 11
  and black academic development, 90
  and black sports subculture, 84
Academic failure, 13, 17
  and athletic aspiration, 86
Academic progress
  and teacher–student relations, 126
  female, 48
  remedial, 121
Academic schedules, 14
Accountability in education, 114, 131, 136, 144
Achievement tests, 72. *See also* Standards, Statewide school exit exams
Administrators, school. *See* School administrators
Adolescent Yellow Pages, 45
Adults
  and school dropouts, 69
  and student relations, 164
  caring, 16
Advocacy within schools, 46
Afro-Caribbean students. *See* West Indian Students

Age inequalities, 209–10
Agricultural price supports, 57
Alcohol use. *See* Drinking, teenage
Alienation, 153
  among students, 163
  and school size, 161
  and school transfer, 162
  and student peer culture, 164
  as personal psychological phenomenon, 155
  as result of social forces, 157
  between students and teachers, 155, 163
  historical applications, 154
  reduction in schools, 156–57
Alternative schools. *See* Schools, High schools
Anorexia, 97, 107
Appalachian Regional Commission, 62, 69
Appalachian schools. *See* Rural education issues
Asian-American students, 182–84, 187
  and language/culture acquisition, 192
  Chinese, 182, 187, 192, 195
  Filipino, 182
  Hawaiian, 187
  Japanese, 182, 183, 184, 195
  Korean, 183, 192
  Punjabi Indian, 182, 187, 188, 192
Athletes. *See* Black students, Jocks, Media, Sports

230 *Index*